THE WORD
in their Voices

A CATHOLIC PILGRIM'S JOURNEY
THROUGH SCRIPTURE AND POETRY

AUGUSTINE JEYARAJ

PARTRIDGE

Copyright © 2025 by Jeyaraj Prema Raj.

Library of Congress Control Number: 2025913041
ISBN: Hardcover   978-1-5437-8431-2
             Softcover   978-1-5437-8430-5
             eBook   978-1-5437-8432-9

All rights reserved. No part of this book may be used or reproduced by any means, graphic, electronic, or mechanical, including photocopying, recording, taping or by any information storage retrieval system without the written permission of the author except in the case of brief quotations embodied in critical articles and reviews.

This book is a work of non-fiction. Unless otherwise noted, the author and the publisher make no explicit guarantees as to the accuracy of the information contained in this book and in some cases, names of people and places have been altered to protect their privacy.

Because of the dynamic nature of the Internet, any web addresses or links contained in this book may have changed since publication and may no longer be valid. The views expressed in this work are solely those of the author and do not necessarily reflect the views of the publisher, and the publisher hereby disclaims any responsibility for them.

Holy Bible, New International Version®, NIV® Copyright ©1973, 1978, 1984, 2011 by Biblica, Inc.® Used by permission. All rights reserved worldwide.

ESV—English Standard Version Scripture quotations are from the ESV® Bible (The Holy Bible, English Standard Version®), copyright © 2001 by Crossway, a publishing ministry of Good News Publishers. Used by permission. All rights reserved.

Print information available on the last page.

To order additional copies of this book, contact
Toll Free +65 3165 7531 (Singapore)
Toll Free +60 3 3099 4412 (Malaysia)
orders.singapore@partridgepublishing.com

www.partridgepublishing.com/singapore

Contents

Dedication ix
Foreword xi
Introduction xiii
Acknowledgments xvii

THE TWO POPES

The Two Popes 1
    Before I Go: A Pope's Benediction 5
    'Before I Go: A Pope's Benediction' (The Shepherd's Farewell) ... 7
    Pope Leo XIV: Answering a Call 12
    Annotation of 'Pope Leo XIV: Answering a Call' 15

ORDO ARMORIS

Commentary on Ordo Amoris (Order of Love)
(in the voice of St. Augustine) 27
Ordo Amoris 31
Annotation 35

GOOD FRIDAY–EASTER SUNDAY: A MEDITATION

Good Friday–Easter Sunday: A Meditation 45
    Introduction to 'I Am the Cross' 47
    I Am the Cross 48
    Annotation Of The Poem 51
    Mary: A Reflection on Michelangelo's Pieta 54
    Introduction to the Poem 55
    Mary: Reflection on Michelangelo's Pietà 59
    Mary: Annotation on Michelangelo's Pietà 61

GOOD FRIDAY BIBLE STUDY

Introduction to the Good Friday Bible Study............ 69
Good Friday Bible Study: Seven Reflections 72
Introduction to Judas 94
Judas... 100
Annotation 105

FROM LAW TO LIFE : SIN, CONVERSION AND THE FLAME OF THE SPIRIT

From Law to Life : Sin, Conversion and the Flame of the Spirit 115
Introduction to 'The Power of Sin Is the Law' 117
The Power of Sin Is the Law 121
Annotations : The Power of Sin is the Law 124
Reflection Questions.. 133
Paul.. 135
Paul: A Life Overturned 137
Annotations: Paul: A Life Overturned 141
Reflection Questions for "Paul"........................... 149

HOLY SPIRIT

Introduction to Holy Spirit 153
The Holy Spirit – The Breath of God made life.... 156
Full Annotation of Holy Spirit 160
Note to the Reader 168
Reflection Questions for The Holy Spirit: The Breath of God Made Life 170

MARTYRDOM FOR CHRIST: STILL VERY MUCH ALIVE

Introduction to the Seven Reflections and Poem of St Stephen 175
St Stephen: The First Martyr................................ 177
Annotations: St Stephen...................................... 179
Martyrs: The Church is very much alive in the present 184

WRITINGS: REFLECTIVE MEDITATIONS

Introduction to 'When Evil Hides Behind a Smile'................221
    When Evil Hides behind a smile 222
    Annotated Version: When evil hides behind a smile 225
    Introduction to 'The Unknown Saint' 230
    The Unknown Saint 232
    Annotated Version of 'The Unknown Saint 234

RUTH

Introduction 243
    Ruth (From Farewell to Fulfilment) 245
    Annotations and Explanations for the Poem....................... 248
    Textual Criticisms 260
    Exegesis vs Eisegesis.. 263

HEBREW

Why We Need to Appreciate Hebrew 277
    Jesus Forgives the Adulteress 279
    Annotation: 'Jesus Forgives the Adulteress' 285
    The Sacred Name of God: The Importance of Hebrew in
    Understanding Scripture 299
    John 21:9-11. The symbolism of 153 fish caught. 301

Conclusion 307
    Jesus, Do I Know You 309
    Annotation: Jesus do I know you..311
Bibliography of Patristic and Theological Sources.........................315
Patristic and Theological Quotations by Source............................317
Theological Quotations from St. Bonaventure by Poem/Theme ...321
Bibliography of Papal Encyclicals and Apostolic Documents.........323

Dedication

To my beloved children—
Joshua, Lai Lin, Rebecca, and Aaron—
your lives are my greatest joy,
and your questions (even in heated debates), laughter, and love
have inspired many of these words.

To my wife, Justina,
whose steadfast love is a light in my life,
and whose quiet strength has eased many burdens—
My **eshet chayil** (אֵשֶׁת חַיִל), the woman of valor in my life.
"Many women do noble things, but you surpass them all."
— *Proverbs 31:29*

Thank you for walking beside me, always.

And to Father Ambrose Vaz,
spiritual guide, mentor, and faithful friend—
thank you for believing in me, even when I doubted myself.
Your unwavering support has helped bring this book to life.

Foreword

It is one thing to know the Word of God; it is another to live it – and to help others do the same. That is what Dr. Augustine Jeyaraj Prema Raj has done so beautifully in *The Word in Their Voices: A Catholic Pilgrim's Journey Through Scripture and Poetry*.

I have known Dr Prema as a man of deep integrity, someone whose life has been marked by a rare combination of professional excellence and profound spiritual depth. As a liver specialist, his vocation has been one of healing, often in situations that require precision, patience, and compassion. In this Book, what stands out is Dr Prema's sense of mission that the Catholic faith has to be understood and articulated and his hope that this Book will be able to equip us in our mission as disciples of Jesus.

This book reflects both the scholar and the pilgrim in him. It is well researched, rich with theological and scriptural insight, yet never detached or abstract. On the contrary, every reflection is grounded in scholarly insight and personal faith experience. It helps us to know that we too can apply these principles in our lives.

Dr Prema offers us not just interpretation but *companionship*. His style of writing is very easy to read, thus making this Book remarkably accessible. The poetry throughout, resonates with our own struggles and longings. The reflection questions and practical examples are clear and easily relatable to real life, encouraging us not only to read but to *respond!*

In my opinion, what makes *The Word in Their Voices* so valuable is that it does what spiritual writings should do – it draws us closer into the Word of God, and then gently turns us outward, back into our own lives, to live that Word with greater intention and faith.

I am thankful that Dr Prema wrote this Book and offering it to all of us who are on this journey.

Fr Ambrose Vaz, SSL.

Introduction

The Word in Their Voices: A Catholic Pilgrim's
Journey through Scripture and Poetry

If you have bought this book, I welcome you. I'm glad, and I'm grateful—for your trust in opening these pages and in seeking, with me, the living Word of God.

I write not as a scholar or theologian but as a fellow pilgrim, walking the same road that you are. I do not claim expertise. What I offer is the fruit of years spent studying the Scriptures, listening to the Church, and searching for God with a heart that longs to understand. Since coming to the Catholic faith in 2003, I have been nourished by the writings of the early Church Fathers, the great Doctors of the Church such as St. Augustine and St. Thomas Aquinas, and most recently, by the light that comes from understanding Hebrew Scripture in its original depth and beauty. What began as a flickering light within me has, over time, become a small flame—a flame that I now strive to nurture into a torch.

My baptismal name is Augustine, chosen in honour of the great saint whose *Confessions* shaped much of my inner life. Like him, I wandered and struggled to order my loves. Like him, I found rest only in Christ. I have devoted my life to medicine and healing, and now, I wish to dedicate the rest of it to sharing the good news, as a witness, a poet, and a Catholic seeking to walk ever closer with Christ.

In our times, we are witnessing an onslaught of misinterpretations and distortions of Catholic teaching—both within and outside the Church. It is no longer enough to leave the defence of truth solely to the Pope, the cardinals, or the clergy. We, the lay faithful—each individual member of the Body of Christ—must take a stand. But we can only do so effectively if we understand the beauty of what we believe and why we believe it. We must be able to articulate the faith cogently, clearly, and confidently, rooted in scripture, tradition, and the enduring wisdom of the Church. I hope this book, in some small way, helps to equip and encourage you in this mission.

This book is a testimony to that journey. It is not a manual or a theology textbook, but a Batik of poetic reflections , meditations and scriptural insights, layered like dye on wax upon a fabric of faith. It is a loving invitation to you, my fellow pilgrim, to enter the world of the Bible, not as a distant observer but as a participant in its unfolding drama. The stories of Mary, Judas, St. Stephen, and the Cross are not frozen in time—they echo through our own lives. In reading them anew, I hope you may find yourself renewed.

The structure of this book follows a simple yet deliberate pattern: each poem is preceded by a short introduction and followed by annotations that unpack its meaning and biblical context. Because the poems are written in the first person, I have provided background notes to help the reader enter more fully into the voice of each figure. Where necessary, I've also explained Hebrew words and scriptural nuances to make the reflections more accessible to all readers, regardless of prior familiarity with the Bible or Church tradition. Many of the papal encyclicals referenced throughout—such as *Evangelii Gaudium*, *Lumen Gentium*, *Redemptoris Missio*, and others—are freely available on the Vatican's official website for those who wish to go deeper.

Each poem is accompanied by detailed annotations and scriptural reflections, designed to guide you deeper into the Word. I've included insights from Hebrew, theological tradition, and the teachings of the Church Fathers—particularly St. Augustine, St. Francis of Assisi, and Ignatian spirituality—to open a path of meditation that is both intellectual and personal.

This is a form of Bible study through poetry—what I call **Lectio Poetica**—a spiritual fusion of *Lectio Divina* and poetic voice. It draws the reader not just to understand Scripture but to enter it. The poems may be read as stand-alone meditations or within the broader context of the book's journey: from Genesis to the Gospels, from exile to redemption, from sin to sanctity.

Just after the section on the two Popes, you will find a reflection poem titled 'Ordo Amoris', written in the voice of St. Augustine. This was my most challenging poem to pen. To reflect Augustine faithfully meant immersing myself not only in his language but in the deep tensions he wrestled with—between sin and grace, love and disordered love, time and eternity. Understanding Augustine may seem daunting at first, but at its heart, his writing explores the most basic doctrines and the most pressing controversies—both in his day and in ours. I have pointed the way to his great treatises and tried to explain them simply, so that more Catholics can appreciate these beautiful works passed down to us through the centuries. For me, Augustine is more than a saint or theologian—he is a lens through which to explore the Holy Scriptures. His voice is not a relic of the past but a living guide, helping us wrestle with God's Word in the present. Augustine speaks across time through the pages of his books. I hope I have been able to capture even a small part of that voice.

Following the section on the martyrs, I have also included two poems—'When Evil Hides Behind a Smile' and 'The Unknown Saint'. These stand apart from the biblical character narratives and are closer in spirit to the *Ketuvim* (Writings) of Hebrew Scripture. They are reflective meditations, not spoken by scriptural figures, but born out of the moral and spiritual landscape we navigate today. One addresses the subtle deceptions of evil when it disguises itself in noble intentions; the other is a tribute to hidden sanctity and humble love. Both explore the challenges Catholics face in discerning truth, goodness, and holiness in a world of confusion. They are offered as contemplations on the nature of evil and saintliness and how both shape the formation of conscience and the calling to holiness.

I included the story of *Ruth*, which rightfully belongs in the writings as it is a story of loyalty, love, and divine providence. A Moabite widow, Ruth chooses to follow her mother-in-law Naomi back to Bethlehem, uttering the immortal words, *'Where you go, I will go . . . your God will be my God'*. In doing so, she steps into salvation history not only as a woman of great fidelity but as the great-grandmother of David, and thus part of the lineage of Christ.

This poem gives voice to Ruth as she reflects on her journey from foreigner to family, from stranger to beloved. Her story reminds us that God's grace often moves through unexpected people and quiet acts of love. Ruth's courage, her humility, and her trust in God's providence shine as an example for all who seek to walk faithfully, even in uncertainty. I have used Ruth to explain and examine the differences between Christian and Judaic arrangement of the Old Testament scripture. I leave all conclusions to you, the reader.

Alongside these theological reflections, I have also explored the value of understanding Hebrew when reflecting on the scriptures. To truly hear the Word as it was first heard, we must place ourselves in the mindset of those who lived two or three thousand years ago. Their cultures, traditions, languages, and ways of understanding the world were different from ours. This brings us to an important principle in Bible study: *exegesis and hermeneutics*. *Exegesis* seeks to uncover what the text meant in its original context; *hermeneutics* considers what the text means for us today. There are two aspects of hermeneutics—*low-context* and *high-context*. A *low-context* reading occurs when there is a great distance in time and culture between the writer and the reader. A *high-context* reading assumes closeness in time, tradition, and worldview. For us modern readers, **approaching scripture is largely a low-context endeavour**—which is why we must work intentionally to bridge that gap. This book is my attempt to do just that.

The book begins with 'The Two Popes' and concludes with the meditation 'Jesus, Do I Know You?'—a prayerful reminder that all our reading, study, and theological reflection are of little value if they do not lead us into a living relationship with Christ. Christ, for me, is my friend. I hope He is—or becomes—yours.

Let us walk together, onward—toward the One who is our origin and our end.

Truth is not an abstract concept in these pages—it is a Person, a Shepherd, a Cross, a Love that never fails.

And as Augustine reminds us:

"*Truth conquers, and the victory of truth is love.*" (Sermon 358,1)

Acknowledgments

I would like to express my heartfelt thanks to all those with whom I have journeyed in the Catholic faith. Your encouragement, insights, and companionship have been a constant source of strength and inspiration. In particular, I am grateful to my RTE group, the Road to Emmaus group, and my Friday Bible study group for the fellowship and formation and friendship you've provided.

To Lee Mei Lin, thank you for giving so much of your time, and for your valuable advice and guidance.

To my wife, Justina, for your careful proofreading, your love, and for making me a better writer—and to Father Ambrose Vaz: your support, mentorship, and steadfast faith in me have been instrumental in the shaping of this book.

A very special thanks to the team at Partridge for believing in me and for your enduring encouragement. To Jon Goden, Julius Artwell, Jerry Gabrielle and Emman Villaran—thank you for patiently walking me through the entire publication process. Your guidance and steadfast support helped bring this book to life.

כִּי עִמְּךָ מְקוֹר חַיִּים בְּאוֹרְךָ נִרְאֶה אוֹר
Ki imkha mekor ḥayyim, be'orkha nir'eh or

For with You is the fountain of life; in Your light we see light
— Psalm 36:9

THE TWO POPES

The Two Popes

Introduction to 'The Two Popes: A Legacy of Evangelization'

The transition from Pope Francis to Pope Leo XIV marks the end of one era and the beginning of another, yet both Pontiffs remain deeply rooted in the Church's ongoing mission of evangelization. This mission, firmly established by the Second Vatican Council, is not a sudden shift but a continuous journey that began long before, tracing its roots to the visionary papacies of Pope Leo XIII, Pope Paul VI, and Pope John Paul II.

From Pope Leo XIII's encyclical *Rerum Novarum*, which laid the groundwork for social teaching, to Pope Paul VI's *Evangelii Nuntiandi*, which emphasized the Church's missionary nature, the focus has remained on reaching out to the world with the love of Christ. This path was reaffirmed in the documents of Vatican II, particularly *Lumen Gentium* and *Ad Gentes*, which call the Church to be both a sign and instrument of intimate union with God and of the unity of the whole human race. Later, Pope John Paul II's *Redemptoris Missio* reignited the missionary zeal, calling for a new evangelization that engages contemporary culture while upholding the timeless truth of the Gospel.

Pope Francis, following this trajectory, emphasized the need for a Church that goes out to the peripheries, living the joy of the Gospel as articulated in *Evangelii Gaudium*. His papacy championed the mission of the Church as one of Communion, Commission, and Conversion—a transformative journey where faith is not merely professed but lived out in acts of service and love. In Pope Leo XIV, we see a dynamic continuation of this spirit, as he embraces the legacy of *Evangelii*

Gaudium with renewed fervour, guiding the Church to live out its mission with passion and commitment.

Pope Leo XIV continues this legacy, embodying the spirit of Pope Francis while bringing his unique focus and pastoral zeal. While marking a new era, his leadership is not a break but a continuation, affirming that the Church's mission of evangelization remains steadfast and unbroken. His commitment to *Evangelii Gaudium* reflects his desire to engage the world with the joy and hope of the Gospel, not only maintaining the vision of his predecessor but executing it with fresh vigour and dedication.

It is crucial here to make a distinction between *evangelizing* and *proselytizing*. *Evangelizing*, as embraced by the Church, is an invitation—a loving call to encounter Christ and experience His transformative grace. It respects human freedom and approaches others with humility and love. In contrast, *proselytizing* imposes beliefs, often without regard for the personal journey of faith. The Church's mission is to evangelize, not to proselytize—to proclaim rather than impose.

Understanding this distinction helps illuminate the monumental moment in which the Church finds itself—a time of continuity, renewal, and mission. Both Pope Francis and Pope Leo XIV exemplify this spirit, guiding the faithful not only through words but through living testimonies of faith. Yet this mission is not solely the task of the Pope; it is the vocation of every Catholic. We are called to live as witnesses, to be sent forth in Communion, with the Commission to proclaim the Gospel, and with the willingness for Conversion—not only of others but of our own hearts.

In writing these two poems, I aim to explore this profound journey through the voices of two popes—Pope Francis and Pope Leo XIV—whose lives, though separated by generations, reveal a remarkable continuity in the papal vocation. While I adopt their perspectives in poetic form, I fully acknowledge that these are my interpretations, shaped by my reflections on their lives and legacies. In doing so, I seek to capture the gravity of their roles, the human moments that reveal their hearts, and the sacred continuity they represent.

For Pope Francis, 'A Pope's Benediction', I was moved by the poignant moment when he, frail and nearing the end, pushed himself to offer one final blessing to the crowd. In that simple act of love and duty, I saw the heart of a shepherd who, even in weakness, seeks to serve and bless his flock.

For Pope Leo XIV, 'Answering a call' reflects the unprecedented moment of his election as the first American pope—specifically, the first from Peru—that stirred me. His brief yet profound greeting from the balcony—marked by kindness, humility, and the visible tears in his eyes—revealed the weight of his new office and the vulnerability of a man suddenly called to lead. The conclave itself, marked by the participation of the largest number of cardinals in history and lasting only two days, spoke to me of the Holy Spirit at work, guiding the Church to this new shepherd.

'The Conclave Chooses but God Decides'—I wrote this in my Pope Francis poem before the Conclave even started. It is amazing how true this rang for me when I first saw Cardinal Robert Francis Prevost emerge as Pope Leo XIV. Instantaneously, it was so clear to see God's hand at work—that he had chosen.

Furthermore, I found a natural progression in the transition from Pope Francis to Pope Leo XIV. Moving from a Franciscan to an Augustinian pope feels harmonious for the Church, as both spiritual traditions deeply emphasize humility, service, and the pursuit of truth. In Pope Leo's poem, I incorporated Augustinian insights, reflecting on the inner journey of faith, humility, and the longing for God's guidance—a thematic continuity that complements the Franciscan spirit of simplicity and love embodied by Pope Francis.

Pope Leo XIV chose his papal name partly in honour of Pope Leo XIII, whose commitment to social justice and the rights of workers left a profound legacy. As the new pope himself stated in interviews, there were other personal reasons as well, but his choice signifies a deep respect for the social teachings of his predecessor. In referencing Attila the Hun in my poem, I draw a historical parallel to Leo I, who courageously confronted a monumental threat to Rome. In a similar spirit, Pope Leo XIV now faces the modern 'Attilas' of power, greed, relativism, and social injustice that challenge human dignity and moral integrity in all corners of the world.

In these poems, I reflect not only on the individual moments that moved me but also on the larger, enduring reality of the papacy itself: a lineage stretching through the centuries, marked by continuity, responsibility, and the ever-present guidance of the Holy Spirit. The voices of these two popes, each distinct yet unified by their sacred office, remind us that while times may change, the essence of the papal mission remains steadfast.

I have also annotated both poems at the end of each with the specific Bible references that I drew upon. This grounded me in the sacred duty that manifested and manifests respectively in their lives.

Pope Leo XIV faces an unprecedented challenge to the fundamentals of our faith. While he is the leader and gives direction, we the flock are also stewards of the faith and must reflect Christ in our lives to fight this battle ground up. However, I end his poem with his quote from St Augustine. This captures the essence of what his papacy will be about: that first and foremost, he remains a humble Christian.

May these poems allow us to reflect on the Popes, the times we live in, and our own responsibilities in the New Evangelization.

Let us pray for both of them and for strength and courage and love for Pope Leo XIV to lead our Church in these difficult times.

BEFORE I GO: A POPE'S BENEDICTION
(The Shepherd's Farewell)

I look upon my flock
in last moments with undying love
I am their shepherd, and they—the Lord's sheep.
My time here draws near its end
but Heaven's door opens to receive me
One last time, my eyes rest on the joy of my life.

I had turned to the Lord when He called me—
A young man, sure of his path.
As Samuel once replied, so did I:
'Speak, Lord, your servant is listening.'

I listened, and I obeyed with all my being.
I was touched by His peace and love
I see His image in all humanity—
No soul beyond his grace.

The marginalized, the orphan, the widow
The labourer, the downtrodden—
The LGBTQ, the outcast, the forgotten
All with spirits low and troubled—
I love them as my Savior does.

My arms lift to bless them
one last time as they call out to me.
I tear with emotion for I am being called to his arms.
My life flashes before me—from childhood
To my ordination, to the slums of Argentina.

The Word in their Voices

Though many recount the sacrifices I made
I count them not, for love is unconditional.
In the poor and the broken
I beheld the face of the Lord

My heart sings with a joy
Transcending all words,
That the Lord, in His mercy,
Chose me to lead His flock.

After me, the Lord will provide
Another to carry on this work—
To hold the torch when mine is dimmed
The Conclave will choose, but it is God who decides

As Peter was, so am I—
The Rock, not because I am strong
But because I am weak without the Lord.

I have run the race
For the Author and Perfecter of our faith.

Goodbye, beloved. I go now to my room.
May you one day join me
In the many rooms
Of our Lord's eternal palace.

'BEFORE I GO: A POPE'S BENEDICTION' (THE SHEPHERD'S FAREWELL)

The title sets the tone of finality and blessing.

- The phrase *'Before I go'* echoes 2 Timothy 4:6–7 where Paul says, *'I am already being poured out like a drink offering, and the time for my departure is near'*.
- *Benediction* suggests a final blessing, while *'The Shepherd's Farewell'* alludes to the pastoral role of the Pope, akin to Psalm 23 where the Lord is depicted as the shepherd.

Stanza 1: Reflection and Love

I look upon my flock
in last moments with undying love
I am their shepherd, and they—the Lord's sheep.
My time here draws near its end
but Heaven's door opens to receive me
One last time, my eyes rest on the joy of my life.

Themes: Love, pastoral care, acceptance of death.

Biblical Reference:

- 'I am their shepherd, and they—the Lord's sheep' reflects *John 10:11*, 'I am the good shepherd. The good shepherd lays down his life for the sheep.'
- 'Heaven's door opens to receive me' echoes *John 14:2*, 'In my Father's house are many rooms.'

The Word in their Voices

Stanza 2: Calling and Obedience

I had turned to the Lord when He called me—
A young man, sure of his path.
As Samuel once replied, so did I:
'Speak, Lord, your servant is listening.'

Themes: Vocation, divine calling.

Biblical Reference:

- The line 'Speak, Lord, your servant is listening' directly quotes *1 Samuel 3:10* when the young Samuel responds to God's call.

Stanza 3: Divine Encounter

I listened, and I obeyed with all my being.
I was touched by His peace and love
I see his image in all humanity—
No soul beyondHis grace.

Themes: Obedience, inclusivity, divine image.

Biblical Reference:

- 'I see His image in all humanity' alludes to *Genesis 1:27*, 'So God created mankind in his own image.'
- The phrase 'No soul beyond His grace' resonates with *Romans 8:38–39*, 'Neither death nor life . . . will be able to separate us from the love of God.'

Themes: Deeply compassionate, affirming the dignity of every human.

Stanza 4: Inclusivity and Love

The marginalized, the orphan, the widow
The labourer, the downtrodden—
The LGBTQ, the outcast, the forgotten
All with spirits low and troubled—
I love them as my Savior does.

Themes: Mercy, social justice, solidarity.

Biblical Reference:

- 'The orphan and the widow' reflects *James 1:27*, 'Religion that God our Father accepts as pure and faultless is this: to look after orphans and widows . . .'
- Jesus' love for the marginalized, *Matthew 25:40*, 'Whatever you did for one of the least of these brothers and sisters of mine, you did for me.'

Stanza 5: Blessing and Farewell

My arms lift to bless them
one last time as they call out to me.
I tear with emotion for I am being called to His arms.
My life flashes before me—from childhood
To my ordination, to the slums of Argentina.

Themes: Final blessing, life reflection, humility.

Biblical Reference:

- The final blessing mirrors *Numbers 6:24–26*: 'The Lord bless you and keep you . . .'
- The phrase 'I tear with emotion' conveys human vulnerability, capturing a moment of spiritual surrender.

Stanza 6: Love and Sacrifice

Though many recount the sacrifices I made
I count them not, for love is unconditional.
In the poor and the broken
I beheld the face of the Lord

Themes: Selfless love, humility.

Biblical Reference:

- 'I count them not' echoes *Philippians 3:7*, 'But whatever were gains to me I now consider loss for the sake of Christ.'
- 'I beheld the face of the Lord' resonates with *Matthew 25:35–40*, Jesus is found in the poor and marginalized.
- St Francis always represented selfless love and humility.

Stanza 7: Succession and Divine Choice

The Conclave will choose, but it is God who decides

Themes: Papal succession, *divine will*.

Biblical Reference:

- Reflects *Proverbs 16:33*: 'The lot is cast into the lap, but its every decision is from the Lord.'

Stanza 8: Petrine Ministry

As Peter was, so am I—
The rock, not because I am strong,
But because I am weak without the Lord.

Themes: Papal authority, humility.

Biblical Reference:

- *Matthew 16:18:* 'You are Peter, and on this rock, I will build my church.'

Final Stanza: Peaceful Departure

I have run the race,
For the Author and Perfecter of our faith.

Goodbye, beloved. I go now to my room.
May you one day join me
In the many rooms
Of our Lord's eternal palace

Themes: Completion, hope, eternal life.

Biblical Reference:

- *2 Timothy 4:7:* 'I have fought the good fight, I have finished the race, I have kept the faith.'
- *Hebrews 12:2:* 'Fixing our eyes on Jesus, the pioneer and perfecter of faith.'
- *John 14:2:* 'In my Father's house are many rooms.'

The Word in their Voices | 11

Pope Leo XIV: Answering a Call

I came to choose
But I was chosen.
I came to serve the conclave—
Now I serve the whole Church and humanity.
God sees the path ahead and its end—
The conclave chose, but he decided.

I accept this calling
For when He asked,
'Whom shall I send?'
I responded as Isaiah did—
'Here I am, Lord.'

My journey has changed
As I stand in this role, I recall Pope Leo I—
The fearless shepherd who faced Attila the Hun
Defender of the Church, unyielding in faith
A lion in spirit, unshaken by threats.
May I, too, stand as a rock
Guarding my flock with courage and love.

I remember Pope Leo XIII,
His mission and love for the poor in spirit.
I have become 'Servus servorum Dei'—
The servant of the servants of God.
I will listen as Moses did
For His plans will be revealed.

I step out on the balcony—
Tears well, love swelling in my chest
As I set my eyes on the sea of the faithful
My flock, my people, my beloved.

The arms of St. Peter's Basilica embrace them
As the Church must embrace all—
Loving, forgiving, nourishing—
A shelter in the storm, a hospital for the sick

There is a battle to fight—
Against evil, hubris, vanity, and power—
As David did against the giant of old
We shall overcome these Goliaths of destruction.

Armed not with violence,
but with the armour and shield of God
We will use scripture sharper than any sword
And sling love, stronger than any stone.

I look upon the crowds and I remember Peru—
The trials and tribulations I faced in Chiclayo—
Where love, humility, and fellowship conquered
The impossible set before us.

Walk in faith, walk in love, walk together—
For our restless hearts will be stilled in Him.
The path ahead will be difficult
Many will seek to make me stumble.
But I will speak truth to power.

The seraphim will place his coal upon my lips
And the Holy Spirit will rescue me.
I accept God's commission—
He has seen my heart
And deemed me worthy to be the rock.

This is the dawn of a new era—
Pope Francis brought us to this river
And now, like Joshua, I must carry the torch—
To guide the Church across this crossing
To the promise of tomorrow.

I am Pope Leo XIV and
From Leo the Great to Leo the Just
To Francis the merciful—
Their light I carry into this hour
As I gaze upon the multitudes in the crowd
I understand the reality of my task
May I be like Christ, the true Lion of Judah.

I pray silently, 'Lord, give me strength
Vision and courage to prepare me,
Most of all, fill me with your love and kindness'.

'Let my mercy be endless,
My love for my flock unwavering.
May I shepherd them with faith unbreakable,
And serve with love that knows no bounds.'

I raise my hands and bless them,
My parting words to them:
'For you I am a Pope,
with you I am a Christian'
because 'in the One we are One'.

Annotation of 'Pope Leo XIV: Answering a Call'

1. Opening Lines: Divine Choice and Calling

I came to choose
But I was chosen.
I came to serve the conclave—
Now I serve the whole Church and humanity.

Biblical Reference:

- *John 15:16*: 'You did not choose me, but I chose you and appointed you so that you might go and bear fruit . . .'
- *Jeremiah 1:5*: 'Before I formed you in the womb I knew you, before you were born I set you apart . . .'

Augustinian Theme:

- In his *Confessions* (book I, chapter 1), Augustine reflects on how God's grace precedes human action, emphasizing that God calls us even before we recognize it ourselves.
- This line echoes Augustine's understanding that human will is secondary to divine choice, stressing that true vocation is God-initiated.

Explanation:

- These lines illustrate the tension between human intention and divine calling. Although Pope Leo IV willingly participates in the conclave, it is God's will that ultimately appoints him.
- The juxtaposition of *choose* and *chosen* captures the mystery of divine election.

The Word in their Voices | 15

2. Acceptance of the Call: Isaiah's Response

I accept this calling
For when he asked,
'Whom shall I send?'
I responded as Isaiah did—
'Here I am, Lord.'

Biblical Reference:

- *Isaiah 6:8*: "Then I heard the voice of the Lord saying, "Whom shall I send? And who will go for us?" And I said, "Here am I. Send me!"'

Augustinian Theme:

- Augustine saw the Christian's duty as responding to God's call with humility and willingness, much like Isaiah. In his sermons, he emphasizes that accepting God's mission requires surrendering one's own will.
- The line reflects Augustine's idea that true leadership arises from a humble submission to God's prompting.

Explanation:

- The Pope mirrors Isaiah's willingness to serve, acknowledging the divine initiative and showing his readiness to take on the burden of papal duty.
- This portrays the Pope not as self-appointed but as one who humbly answers God's call.

3. Historical Reflection: Pope Leo I

As I stand in this role, I recall Pope Leo I—
The fearless shepherd who faced Attila the Hun,
Defender of the Church, unyielding in faith
A lion in spirit, unshaken by threats.

Historical Context:

- Pope Leo I (Leo the Great) met Attila the Hun in 452 AD and convinced him to spare Rome.
- Leo I's legacy includes both theological clarity (defending Christ's divinity) and courage in crisis.

Augustinian Theme:

- In his writings, Augustine often highlights that spiritual authority lies not in power but in moral courage. Leo I exemplifies this through his pastoral strength and theological integrity.

Explanation:

- The Pope invokes Leo I's legacy to ground his own leadership in a tradition of courage, faith, and resilience.
- The metaphor of being a 'lion in spirit' also connects to Christ as the Lion of Judah (Revelation 5:5), suggesting moral fortitude.

4. Servant Leadership:

I have become 'Servus servorum Dei'—
The servant of the servants of God.

Biblical Reference:

- *Matthew 20:26–28:* 'Whoever wants to become great among you must be your servant . . .'

- *John 13:14:* 'Now that I, your Lord and Teacher, have washed your feet, you also should wash one another's feet.'

Augustinian Theme:

- Augustine often taught that humility is foundational to leadership. In Sermon 340, he says,
  'For you I am a bishop, with you I am a Christian.'
- This phrase emphasizes that Christian authority is rooted in service, not dominance.

Explanation:

- By adopting this title, the Pope identifies himself with the tradition of humility and service. It is a declaration that his leadership is not about commanding but serving.

5. Emotional Connection: Stepping onto the Balcony

I step out on the balcony—
Tears well, love swelling in my chest
As I set my eyes on the sea of the faithful,
My flock, my people, my beloved.

Biblical Reference:

- *John 10:11:* 'I am the good shepherd. The good shepherd lays down his life for the sheep.'

Augustinian Theme:

- Augustine often reflected on the shepherd's role as one of deep emotional commitment and love for the flock, as seen in his sermons on pastoral care.

Explanation:

- These lines convey a pastoral intimacy, where the Pope's love for his people mirrors Christ's love for his followers.
- The image of the sea of the faithful symbolizes the vast and diverse body of the Church, united under the Pope's spiritual care.

6. Church as a Place of Healing:
A shelter in the storm, hospital for the sick.

Biblical Reference:

- *Matthew 9:12:* 'It is not the healthy who need a doctor, but the sick.'
- *Psalm 46:1:* 'God is our refuge and strength, a very present help in trouble.'

Augustinian Theme:

- Augustine often described the Church as a 'hospital for sinners', where people come to find healing and grace.
- He believed that the Church must offer spiritual solace, as seen in his reflection on pastoral care in 'The City of God'.

Explanation:

- The metaphor of the Church as a hospital highlights its mission to heal both physical and spiritual wounds, reflecting Pope Francis' vision of the Church as a 'field hospital'.
- It also underscores the Pope's role as a healer and comforter, not just a leader.

7. Spiritual Warfare: Battling Giants
There is a battle to fight—
Against evil, hubris, vanity, and power—

The Word in their Voices | 19

As David did against the giant of old
We shall overcome these Goliaths of destruction.

Biblical Reference:

- *1 Samuel 17:45–47:* 'David said to the Philistine, "You come against me with sword and spear and javelin, but I come against you in the name of the Lord Almighty . . ."'
- *2 Corinthians 10:4–5:* 'The weapons we fight with are not the weapons of the world. On the contrary, they have divine power to demolish strongholds.'

Augustinian Theme:

- Augustine frequently taught that the true battle of faith is against spiritual forces, not against flesh and blood.
- In *The City of God*, Augustine argued that pride and power are the root of evil, contrasting the City of Man (based on self-love) and the City of God (based on love of God).
- The line 'hubris, vanity, and power' directly reflects Augustine's understanding that moral failings arise from pride and self-exaltation.

Explanation:

- By likening modern challenges to Goliaths, the Pope acknowledges that the real threats to the Church are moral and spiritual rather than physical.
- The reference to David's faith as a weapon signifies that faith and humility are the Pope's tools for confronting contemporary moral evils.

8. Spiritual Armor: Nonviolent Resistance

'*Armed not with violence, but with the armour and shield of God,*
We will use scripture sharper than any sword
And sling love, harder than any stone.'

Biblical Reference:

- *Ephesians 6:11–17*: 'Put on the full armour of God . . . the belt of truth, the breastplate of righteousness . . . the shield of faith . . . the sword of the Spirit, which is the word of God.'
- *Hebrews 4:12* - *'For the word of God is alive and active. Sharper than any double-edged sword . . .'*
- *1 Corinthians 13:13*: 'And now these three remain: faith, hope and love. But the greatest of these is love.'

Augustinian Theme:

- Augustine emphasized that the 'weapons of the Christian' are truth and love, not force or domination.
- In his letters and sermons, he stated that 'love is the fulfilment of the law' (Romans 13:10), emphasizing that spiritual victories come through faith and love, not coercion.

Explanation:

- The Pope's stance of 'nonviolent resistance' echoes the Christian principle of overcoming evil with good (Romans 12:21).
- The phrase 'sling love, harder than any stone' connects David's victory with the idea that true power lies in love and scriptural truth, rather than physical force.

9. God will prepare you

'The seraphim will place His coal upon my lips,
And the Holy Spirit will rescue me.'

Biblical Reference:

- *Isaiah 6:6–8*: Then one of the seraphim flew to me with a burning coal . . . He touched my lips with it and said 'See this coal touched your lips. Now your guilt is removed, and your sins are forgiven'

Explanation:

- God prepares by forgiving your sins and allows his presence to enter you and guide you in your commission. Once you are aligned with God in heart mind and soul everything falls into place.

10. A New Era: Leadership and Hope
This is the dawn of
a new era—
Pope Francis brought us to this river
And now, like Joshua, I must carry the torch—
To guide the Church across this crossing
To the promise of tomorrow.

Biblical Reference:

- *Joshua 3:7–17*: 'The Lord said to Joshua, "Today I will begin to exalt you in the eyes of all Israel . . ."'
- *Isaiah 43:19*: 'See, I am doing a new thing! Now it springs up; do you not perceive it? I am making a way in the wilderness and streams in the wasteland.'
- *Matthew 5:14–16*: 'You are the Light of the world . . . let your shine before others.'

Augustinian Theme:

- Augustine viewed leadership as a journey where the leader is called to move people from sin to grace, much like Joshua leading the Israelites.
- In his Sermon 23, Augustine spoke of crossing the river as a metaphor for moving from a state of sin to a state of grace, paralleling the journey of faith.

Explanation:

- The metaphor of crossing the river signifies transition and renewal, highlighting that Pope Leo IV sees his mission as guiding the Church into a new spiritual era.
- Pope Francis is seen as a precursor, much like Moses, while Pope Leo IV steps into the role of Joshua, leading through faith and resilience.
- The torch metaphor represents being a light to guide others which is fundamental to Christian leadership

11. Clarity, Purpose and Insight
I pray silently, Lord, give me strength,
Vision and courage to prepare me

Biblical Reference:

Proverbs 29:18: 'Where there is no vision, the people perish . . . .'

Explanation:

- With the torch metaphor, the Pope's role is not merely leading but also foreseeing, illuminating the path ahead, and guiding the church into a new spiritual era.

12. Humble Farewell: The Shepherd's Blessing
As I bid farewell to my beloved
I raise my hands and bless them
My parting words to them:
'With you I am a Christian
For you I will be your Shepherd.'

Biblical Reference:

- *Luke 24:50–51*: 'When he had led them out to the vicinity of Bethany, he lifted up his hands and blessed them. While he was blessing them, he left them and was taken up into heaven.'
- *John 10:14*: 'I am the good shepherd; I know my sheep and my sheep know me.'

Augustinian Theme:

- Augustine's famous statement in Sermon 340: 'For you I am a bishop, with you I am a Christian.'
- Augustine believed that the bishop's role is primarily to be a fellow believer who serves, rather than a lord over the faithful.
- The blessing mirrors Augustine's idea that being a shepherd is an act of love and humility, not just an assertion of authority.

Explanation:

- The final blessing serves as an act of pastoral love and unity, reinforcing the Pope's commitment to his flock as both a leader and a fellow Christian.
- The gesture of raising hands not only mirrors Christ's farewell but also symbolizes divine blessing and pastoral protection.
- The Pope's acknowledgment that he shares the same Christian identity as his people echoes Augustine's deep sense of humility and communal faith.
- Being Pope is a duty, but being Christian is a shared identity
- The essence of Papal leadership is rooted in shared faith

ORDO ARMORIS

St. Augustine

COMMENTARY ON ORDO AMORIS *(Order of Love)* (IN THE VOICE OF ST. AUGUSTINE)

> *'You have made us for Yourself, O Lord, and our heart is restless until it rests in You.'*
> —St. Augustine, *Confessions* I.1

This poem is a personal and poetic meditation on *Ordo Amoris (Order of Love)*, Augustine's profound teaching that the disorder of human life arises not from loving the wrong things, but from loving the right things in the wrong order—a journey from inner chaos to divine peace.

I wrote this in Augustine's voice—not to imitate his language, but to echo his confessional journey, his spiritual logic, and his desire to place God once more at the centre of love, purpose, and being. Augustine does not separate theology from the self. His truths are born in his wounds. Likewise, this poem is shaped by my own reflections on the abyss we create when we place our own desires, knowledge, or pride above the divine order.

What first prompted me to revisit *Ordo Amoris* was a sense of unease—alarm, even—at how this once-beautiful concept is being used today to justify personal or ideological agendas. Rather than leading souls into deeper communion, love is sometimes twisted to validate division, control, or self-interest. I realized then that we, as pilgrims walking together in faith, need to reclaim and re-understand what this teaching truly means. We cannot afford to let such a foundational truth be misused or misunderstood.

That is why I have tried, in this poem, to render *Ordo Amoris* in a way that is spiritually rich yet accessible—not for scholars, but for all who seek to live and love rightly. For fellow pilgrims, like Augustine, have searched for peace in worldly wisdom and found it lacking. For all who sense that the heart's deepest longing can only be satisfied by the One who made it.

The structure of this poem follows Augustine's own path: from disorder and inner imprisonment to the whispered invitation of grace, to the reshaping of the soul by Mercy. The inclusion of Monica's intercession, the whispered *tolle lege*, and the moment of divine light entering the 'prison' of the self, all intentionally mirror the turning point in *Confessions*—where divine love finally unravels the knotted loves of the heart.

This poem also serves a larger function in this collection. It is not merely a stand-alone reflection, but the spiritual hinge of the book— the key with which to read all the voices that follow. Before we can truly enter into the lives of those who encountered God in scripture, we must first understand how the soul is reordered by divine love. This poem orients us. It teaches us how to read not only with the mind, but with the heart rightly attuned. *Ordo Amoris* is the quiet architecture behind every faithful life we are about to hear.

At the heart of this poem lies a central tension:
We are made for communion but live in isolation.
We are born with truth, love, and compassion, but trade them for ambition and self-preservation.
We are given grace yet often hunger for control.

When Augustine speaks of *Ordo Amoris* in *De Doctrina Christiana* (Book I), he teaches that every object of love must be properly aligned with God. We are to love things in God, through God, and for God. The soul finds peace not when it suppresses desire, but when desire is rightly ordered—when God is the sun, and all else orbits in His light.

The stanza beginning with '*Ordo Amoris—pure, created for love . . .*' is meant to capture that moment of distortion—when divine truth is twisted by human vanity, when the heart turns in on itself (*incurvatus in se*). Yet this is not the end of the story. What follows is revelation, restoration, and return. The soul cries not to fix itself, but to be remade by Mercy. And in that prayer, a new order begins.

This poem also reflects the mystical geometry of grace:
God is the centre of the wheel, and we are on the rim of the wheel. His grace radiates to us like the spokes of a wheel.
Only when we turn from the centre do we become unstable, disjointed, and lost.
Only in returning to the centre do we become radiant again.

The final lines—'*This is the prize …. Not fleeting gain …. Eternity and rest with God*'—are offered as both a conclusion and an invitation. This is not a moralistic teaching, but a call to realign the soul with its origin. It is about rediscovering what was once freely given, reclaiming the childlike purity that knew how to love without counting.

One word that deserves definition is metanoia. The word *metanoia* comes from the Greek μετάνοια, often translated in English Bibles as 'repentance.' But this translation only captures part of its depth. *Metanoia* literally means a 'change of mind,' but in biblical and theological usage, it implies far more than mental adjustment. It is a radical reorientation of the whole self—mind, heart, and will—away from sin and toward God.

In Augustinian terms, *metanoia* is the moment when the will turns from disordered loves (*amor sui*, 'the love of self') to properly ordered love (*amor Dei*, 'the love of God'). It is not merely sorrow for wrongdoing, but the beginning of conversion—the soul returning from its wandering into the self, back toward its origin and true home in God.

In this poem, I address this as the journey 'walked within—through metanoia' reflecting this interior turning, echoing *Confessions* VIII.12 where Augustine, after years of restless searching, finally surrenders—not by moving geographically, but by turning inward in truth and grace.

May this poem speak to your heart as it has spoken to mine.
May it help reorder what has been scattered.
And may it prepare you, as it prepared Augustine, and me and so many others, to meet again the voices of scripture—voices no longer bound to the past, but alive in the light of rightly ordered love.

ORDO AMORIS
Sancte Augustine, vox tua resonat in corde meo!

*(Order is the order of love
Saint Augustine, your voice resounds in my heart!)*

I created an abyss in my mind—
A void both vast and barren.
This became my silent prison.

My mother's unceasing pleas
To the One I was yet to know.
Were answered in a whisper to me:
Take and read.

Now, with the keys of the evangelion
I unlocked my prison and the light came in

A long journey have I travelled
From the dark recesses of my mind.
A journey not of physical steps
But one walked within—
through metanoia.

The One I had sought all my life
Waited in patience to enter my heart.

As children—pure, untainted—
Truth, love, and compassion
are seeds planted by God.
But as the wheel of time
turns
Worldly wisdom strips away our innocence.

The Word in their Voices | 31

There is the one Way —with the shepherd.
Without Him, we stray into many.
We walk toward ruin
imagining our wandering is wisdom.

We descend into the valley of desires
Where flesh dims the Divine.

And so we forge our cage
Becoming willing prisoners—
In a cell without a key
Thinking it a palace
Thinking this freedom.

Self-love, a flickering candle
Not willing the good of the other.
We are not mountains standing apart
but stones fitted together in one temple
called to communion, not to isolation.

Ordo Amoris—pure, created for love
Now corrupted—
twisted—
turned to serve selfish ends.
This is the curse and hubris
of human vanity:
To place knowledge above divine truth.

God is the centre of the wheel of life
And we, moving upon its perfect rim
Are bathed in the radiance of His grace.
This is the truth of ordered love revealed.
To embrace this is to receive peace—
A gift Divine.

Love rightly ordered shines;
Mirrors the One who is Love—
Loving each wholly without discount
For all are made in His image.

Love cannot be apportioned—
Like a meal to be shared
It is folly to think
God's infinite love be limited:
Its store is a treasury inexhaustible.

Human nature yearns to take—
Divine nature longs to give.
A war within—the mind knows truth
but the heart clings to lesser loves.

And so I cried—
not to fix myself,
but to be remade by Mercy.

O Love that stooped to meet me
To unravel what I had twisted—
Taught my heart to love in order.
This is *Ordo Amoris*.

The love of Christos revealed—
To give and not to count
He is the true centre of the wheel
In Him all love finds its order and rest.
To serve and not to seek reward
To help, not for gain but for grace.

What came naturally as children
we have unlearnt as men and women.
So I seek to teach again—
What once was freely given still remains:
Salvation is found in Christ Alone.

This is the prize we seek:
Not fleeting gain
But peace that surpasses understanding—
in this life
and the next.
Eternity and rest in God.

ANNOTATION

Stanza 1:

I created an abyss in my mind—
A void both vast and barren.
This became my silent prison.

Annotation:
This opening evokes *Confessions* Book I and II, where Augustine reflects on the inner emptiness that sin creates. The 'abyss' mirrors the *tohu wa-bohu* ('formless void') of *Genesis 1:2*—a state of spiritual chaos. The transition from 'created' to 'became' subtly shifts the tone from active rebellion to a realization of consequences. The 'silent prison' echoes both Augustine's inner torment and Ignatian concepts of being 'trapped in disordered attachments.'

Stanza 2:

My mother's unceasing pleas,
To the One I was yet to know,
Were answered in a whisper to me:
Take and read.

Annotation:
A direct allusion to *Confessions* VIII.12, where Monica's prayers are answered when Augustine hears the childlike voice say, *'tolle lege.'* The voice is both gentle and decisive, representing the intersection of divine grace and human readiness. The phrase also recalls the role of *lectio divina*—reading as an act of revelation and response.

The Word in their Voices | 35

Stanza 3:

Now, with the keys of the evangelion,
I unlocked my prison and the light came in.

Annotation:
'Evangelion' (Greek for Gospel) is used here liturgically, hinting at Christ's authority (cf. *Matthew 16:19*) and the freedom found in Scripture. The shift from past to present tense (*Now*) universalizes the moment—it is a continual unlocking available to all. The metaphor of light recalls *John 1:5* and Augustine's moment of intellectual and spiritual illumination.

Stanza 4–5:

A long journey have I travelled
From the dark recesses of my mind.
A journey not of physical steps
But one walked within—
through metanoia.

The One I had sought all my life
Waited in patience to enter my heart.

Annotation:
The structure here parallels *Confessions* Book X and XIII, where the journey is inward, not geographical. '*Metanoia*' (Greek for repentance) conveys a turning of the mind and heart, rooted in both the *Gospels* (*Mark 1:15*) and Ignatian spirituality (discernment and interior movement). The waiting Christ echoes *Revelation 3:20*—'Behold, I stand at the door and knock.'

Stanza 6:

As children—pure, untainted—
Truth, love, and compassion
Are seeds planted by God.
But as the wheel of time
turns
Worldly wisdom strips away our innocence.

Annotation:
An echo of Augustine's concept of *original grace*, later obscured by *concupiscentia*. The 'wheel of time' may allude to both *Ecclesiastes* ('there is a season . . .') and *Bonaventure's Itinerarium Mentis in Deum*. The 'seeds planted by God' evoke the parable of the sower (*Matthew 13*), and their loss reflects *Romans 1:22*.

Stanza 7–8:

There is the one Way—with the Shepherd.
Without Him, we stray into many.
We walk toward ruin
Imagining our wandering is wisdom.
And so we descend into the valley of desires
Where flesh dims the Divine.

Annotation:
A beautiful synthesis of *John 14:6* ('I am the Way') and *Psalm 23* ('the valley of the shadow of death'), now reimagined as the *valley of disordered desires*. This valley is both geographic and spiritual, recalling Augustine's descent into sensuality in *Confessions* Book II. 'Flesh dims the Divine' echoes *Romans 8:7* and *Galatians 5:17*.

Stanza 9–10:

And so we forge our cage
Becoming willing prisoners—
In a cell without a key
Thinking it a palace
Thinking this freedom.

Annotation:
This stanza distils Augustine's central insight from *Confessions*: that sin is a false freedom, a self-chosen bondage (cf. *Romans 6:16*). The paradox of 'willing prisoners' mirrors *City of God* Book XIX's critique of worldly freedom without God. The illusion of the palace evokes the 'far country' of the prodigal son *(Luke 15)*.

Stanza 11:

Self-love, a flickering candle
Not willing the good of the other.
We are not mountains standing apart
But stones fitted together in one temple
Called to communion, not to isolation.

Annotation:
Here, *ordo amoris* is contrasted with *amor sui*—the love of self over love of God and neighbour.'Not willing the good of the other' quotes Aquinas' definition of charity. The 'stones fitted together' alludes to *Ephesians 2:21* and *1 Peter 2:5*. Franciscan theology is echoed in the emphasis on community over individualism.

Stanza 12–13:

Ordo Amoris—pure, created for love
Now corrupted—
twisted—
turned to serve selfish ends.

This is the curse and hubris
of human vanity:
To place knowledge above divine truth.

God is the centre of the wheel of life
And we, moving upon its perfect rim
Are bathed in the radiance of His grace.
This is the truth of ordered love revealed:
To embrace this truth is to receive peace—
A gift Divine.

Annotation:
The core theological statement of the poem. *Ordo Amoris'* comes directly from Augustine's *De Moribus Ecclesiae*—true virtue is rightly ordered love. The 'wheel' metaphor echoes both medieval cosmology and mystical theology: God as unmoved centre (cf. Dante's *Paradiso* XXXIII).'Peace as a gift Divine' echoes *Philippians 4:7* and Augustine's definition of rest as union with God.

Stanza 14–15:

Love rightly ordered shines
Mirrors the One who is Love—
Loving each wholly without discount
For all are made in His image.

Love cannot be apportioned—
Like a meal to be shared
It is folly to think
God's infinite love be limited:
Its store is a treasury inexhaustible.

Annotation:
'God is love' *(1 John 4:8)* is central here. The poem critiques human attempts to ration love, a common failure in both ethics and

The Word in their Voices | 39

relationships. 'Without discount' reinforces *agape*, not transactional love. 'Treasury inexhaustible' echoes *Romans 11:33* and Franciscan imagery of divine abundance (St. Clare's letters speak of the 'fountain of inexhaustible light').

Stanza 16–17:

Human nature yearns to take—
Divine nature longs to give.
A war within—the mind knows truth
But the heart clings to lesser loves.

And so I cried—
Not to fix myself
But to be remade by Mercy.

Annotation:
A stark contrast between fallen *natura* and divine *gratia*. The 'war within' reflects *Romans 7:23* and Augustine's description of conflicted will (*Confessions* VIII). 'Remade by Mercy' alludes to *Titus 3:5* and Ignatius' emphasis on surrendering to grace rather than striving by effort alone.

Stanza 18–19:

O Love that stooped to meet me
To unravel what I had twisted—
Taught my heart to love in order.
This is Ordo Amoris.

The love of Christos revealed—
To give and not to count
He is the true centre of the wheel
In Him all love finds its order and rest.
To serve and not to seek reward
To help, not for gain but for grace.

Annotation:
A mini doxology. 'Stooped to meet me' evokes *Philippians 2 (kenosis)*. The unravelling of twisted love recalls *Confessions* VIII's imagery of sin as knots. 'Christos' is intentionally Greek, reminding us of the incarnate Logos who reorders love. 'To give and not to count' echoes the Ignatian prayer: *'To give and not to count the cost . . .'*

Stanza 20–21:

What came naturally as children
We have unlearnt as men and women.
So I seek to teach again—
What once was freely given still remains:
Salvation is found in Christ alone.

This is the end of the journey we seek:
Not fleeting gain
But peace that surpasses understanding—
in this life
and the next.
Eternity and rest in God.

Annotation:
This closing stanza is the poetic expression of *Confessions* I.1: *'Our hearts are restless until they rest in Thee.'* The journey ends not with worldly attainment but with peace in God (*Philippians 4:7*). 'Eternity and rest in God' captures the final beatific vision (*1 John 3:2*). The tone is Ignatian: the examen of a life reordered by grace.

Concluding Commentary

This poem is the *spiritual hinge* of the collection. Rooted in Augustine's *ordo amoris*, it maps the soul's journey from self-enclosure to divine communion. I have tried to use each line to reflect both personal confession and universal theology, echoing Scripture, patristic wisdom, and the rhythm of conversion. I invite you, the reader, not just to observe a transformation—but to participate in it, through humility, mercy, and the reordering of love in Christ. *Ordo Amoris* is not merely a doctrine—*it is the very shape of salvation.*

GOOD FRIDAY– EASTER SUNDAY: A MEDITATION

The Voices in Scripture

Good Friday–Easter Sunday: A Meditation

Good Friday stands as a profound intersection of sorrow, redemption, and human frailty. It is the day when love and betrayal meet at the foot of the Cross, where suffering is transformed into salvation, and where the weight of humanity's sin converges with the promise of grace.

In this chapter, I seek to explore the multifaceted dimensions of this sacred day through poetry and reflection. We begin with 'I Am the Cross', a poem that personifies the instrument of Crucifixion itself, voicing the paradox of being both the symbol of ultimate sacrifice and the bearer of human suffering. The Cross, weathered and weary, stands as a silent witness to the collision of divinity and mortality.

Following this, we encounter *Mary*, the mother of Jesus, through the lens of poetic reflection. Her grief at the foot of the Cross is a poignant reminder of the human cost of redemption—a mother's love enduring the unimaginable loss of her son. In this poetic meditation, we see Mary not only as the chosen vessel of God's incarnation but as a mother bearing the weight of the world's sin alongside her son.

To deepen our understanding, I include insights from a comprehensive Good Friday Bible study—a structured reflection that journeys through the Passion and victory of Christ. The study comprises seven reflections, each anchored in the following pattern: an Old Testament verse foreshadowing the event, a New Testament verse reflecting its fulfilment, a Psalm for meditation, and thematic reflections that connect Scripture with personal application. From the Fall of humanity to the triumph of the Resurrection, these reflections trace the redemptive arc of history, highlighting key moments such as the suffering of Christ, the final cry of 'It is finished,' and the hope of eternal rest. Through this journey, we are invited to see Good Friday not just as a moment of grief but as a turning point where loss gives way to new life.

Finally, we end with 'Judas', a poem that confronts the darker side of human agency. In the betrayal of Christ, we are challenged to reflect on our own capacity for disloyalty and self-deception. Judas' story forces us to grapple with the tension between divine sovereignty and human choice, reminding us that even in failure, the potential for redemption remains.

Together, these poetic and reflective elements weave a tapestry of Good Friday, inviting us to enter the mystery of the Cross not just as an event, but as an ongoing call to reflect, repent, and find hope.

Introduction to 'I Am the Cross'

The Cross, in its essence, was never intended to be a symbol of hope or salvation. In the brutal hands of the Roman Empire, it was a weapon of terror—a barbaric instrument of public execution designed to inflict maximum suffering and humiliation. The cross, without Christ, is akin to a modern weapon—a gun, a noose, an electric chair—carrying with it the weight of cruelty and death.

Yet through Christ's sacrifice, this ancient apparatus of execution is transformed. The Cross, once a sign of defeat, becomes the emblem of victory. The very wood that bore the curse of death now heralds the promise of eternal life. The power of Christ's saving grace reaches even to the Cross itself, redeeming it from a symbol of pain to a proclamation of hope.

In this poem, I sought to give voice to the Cross—a silent, often overlooked witness to the Passion. The Cross tells its own story of transformation, from a gnarled tree of death to a blossoming branch of hope. It laments the violence it once held yet rejoices in the light of redemption. The Cross, like us, was chosen and repurposed, its darkest moment reshaped by Love into an everlasting symbol of grace.

Importantly, the Cross is portrayed as an unwilling participant in the events of the Crucifixion. It did not choose to become an instrument of death; it simply obeyed, rooted and steadfast, enduring the unspeakable violence enacted upon it. In giving voice to this unwilling bearer of the world's sins, I seek to reflect on how even the most tragic and brutal of realities can be transformed through Christ.

By personifying the Cross, I invite readers to see it not merely as an object but as a participant in the greatest act of love the world has ever known. In this transformation, the Cross itself becomes a disciple—redeemed, repurposed, and now pointing the way to salvation.

The Word in their Voices

I Am the Cross

(Ever present yet unseen—
Ever known yet ignored)

I am the Cross—weathered and weary
Violent echoes haunt my silent wood.
Oh, if I could weep, my tears would rot my wood—
I bear witness, as sight most despised

The dawn brings dusk for men—
Iron nails bind flesh to wood
Blood seeps into my grain
Mingling with sorrow.
Bones linger, breath shudders
Life slips into dream.

The stench of death upon my frame
The destroyer of man I became.
Destinies entwined in dark despair
Their loved ones weeping in anguish—
To whom will our cries avail?

I did not ask, from bark, to be cross.
The gift of free will to me denied.
Silently I stood, an obedient guide
An unwilling witness to their anguished tide.

Then came the day—sky a tempestuous canvas
Mirroring the turmoil at my foot.
The Chosen One ascended my height
His bones unbroken—pure in plight.
Blameless, spotless, without stain—
I felt His sorrow and His pain.

His mother's cry, I still remember—
As if a sword had pierced her soul.
With His final breath, He called His Father.
He promised paradise to the other
Forgiving all—'They know not what they do.'
I sensed the difference in Yeshua.

From His side, blood and water flowed—
Love and mercy, a river loosed.
Freedom from sin—a final gift.
To the Father, His spirit returned.
With despicable mirth, soldiers cast lots for His robe.

A moment's silence—stretched to eternity.
The crowd held its breath
Watching life ebb upon my splintered form.
Then thunder cracked, and the sea did roar
The earth shook; the veil was torn.
The crowd fled—
And I, I felt the light.
All the while, it was I He had borne.

Now, with unveiled sight, His plan made clear—
A ransom paid in grace and tears.
All creation wrapped in His embrace.
A frame once forged for evil's end
Now saved by the Son of Man.

Once a Cross of death—
Now through me they cross from death to life
Lifted from shadow to dawn by grace
Generations will sing of me with awe.
Darkness conquered—by Love and Faith.

Evil chose me from the abyss of night
But Love transformed me to a beacon bright—
Like Bethlehem's star that pierced the sky
I shine forth in Salvation's light.
Redeemed by Him, I—the Cross—now mean Life.

My form a mirror to all who believe
United with every soul, I become one.
Hope, rest, and steadfast love shall pursue us
Now we are his channel—a river of grace.
No soul lies beyond His merciful reach.
Now remains for us the call:
'Here I am—send me,' we cry.

Annotation Of The Poem

The poem is a tapestry of Scripture (which I enjoy), drawing the reader into the ongoing story of redemption and response.

Biblical Allusions and References

I Am the Cross
(Ever present yet unseen—
Ever known yet ignored)

- *Luke 9:23, 14:27*: Jesus calls followers to 'take up their cross daily,' showing the cross is a constant, if often neglected, part of discipleship.
- The 'cross' has been a core Christian symbol for centuries, and many take it for granted—hence 'known, yet ignored.'

1. The Sorrow and Shame of the Cross

The Cross is described as 'despised,' 'weathered and weary,' and marked by 'violent echoes.' These resonances evoke Isaiah 53's suffering servant who is 'despised and rejected,' and the shame and horror attached to crucifixion (Hebrews 12:2). The Cross, instrument of death, represents both historical suffering (of many) and the cosmic scandal of the Messiah's execution.

2. Crucifixion Imagery

Brushstrokes of crucifixion are clear: iron nails binding flesh to wood, blood and water mingling, cries and weeping, the soldiers' cruelty, and the agony of the condemned. These details mirror the Gospel passion narratives—especially John 19 and Luke 23.

- 'His bones unbroken' directly references John 19:36 ('Not one of his bones was broken') and fulfils Psalm 34:20.
- 'From His side, blood and water flowed' echoes John 19:34, linking to Christian sacraments (baptism, communion).

The Word in their Voices | 51

3. Christ's Unique Death and Redemption
The poem distinguishes 'the Chosen One' (Acts 3:14, Matt. 12:18), highlighting Jesus' innocence ('blameless, spotless') and the prophecy of Mary's grief ('a sword will pierce your own soul,' Luke 2:35). His words from the cross ('Father, forgive them . . .', 'You will be with me in paradise') are direct references to Luke 23.

4. Supernatural Signs
Cosmic upheaval—the earth shaking, sky darkening, temple veil tearing—are woven together as signs found in the Gospels (Matt. 27:45, 51). These acts symbolize the breaking of barriers between God and people, the old order passing, and a universal hope dawning.

5. Theological Reversal
The poem sharply turns to a theological reversal:

- The Cross, once the destroyer of man, becomes the passage from death to life (John 5:24).
- A frame forged for evil becomes the greatest sign of grace (Genesis 50:20; Romans 8:28).

6. Resurrection Hope and Salvation
Transformation pervades the conclusion:

- Shadow to dawn echoes resurrection themes (Psalm 30:5, Ephesians 2:5).
- 'Generations will sing of me' evokes the lasting praise and centrality of the Cross in Christian worship and proclamation.

7. New Identity and Mission for Believers
In closing, the poem relates the Cross to every Christian's experience:

- 'A mirror to all who believe' (2 Corinthians 3:18), reflecting how Christ's suffering and victory shape the believer's life.
- 'United with every soul'—echoes the biblical notion of the Church as a single body (1 Corinthians 12:12–13).

- 'Hope, rest, and steadfast love shall pursue us' echoes Psalm 23:6's 'goodness and mercy shall follow me.'
- 'Now we are his channel—a river of grace' links to being vessels of God's love and Spirit (John 7:38, Romans 5:5).
- 'No soul lies beyond His merciful reach' combines Luke 19:10 and Romans 8:38–39.
- The poem ends with a calling ('Here I am, send me', Isaiah 6:8), a reminder that the experience of the Cross commissions believers for service and mission.

Mary: A Reflection on Michelangelo's Pieta

The title directly references Michelangelo's Pietà, a Renaissance sculpture depicting Mary cradling the lifeless body of Jesus. The poem mirrors the emotional intensity and theological depth of this iconic artwork. The word 'Reflection' suggests a deep, personal meditation, not just on the sculpture but on Mary's internal experience of grief and love.

It is important to understand what the Great artist had in mind when he presented this beautiful sculpture to the world It is his reflection of Mary's heart after the 'Crucifixion and death' of Christ. The introduction I give will help you understand my thoughts in penning this poem. I used Mary's voice, and this had an unexpected effect on me.

Introduction to the Poem

'Mary – Reflection on Michelangelo's Pietà' is a contemplative and deeply personal poetic meditation that seeks to portray Mary, the mother of Jesus, not only as a figure of grief and sorrow but as a dynamic, enduring presence of love and intercession. Inspired by Michelangelo's iconic sculpture, the poem moves beyond the traditional static image of Mary as a silent mourner to explore her multifaceted role as mother, disciple, and intercessor

Why I Wrote This Poem

This poem aims to challenge and expand upon the conventional depictions of Mary found in classical, modern, and liturgical poetry. Often, Mary is portrayed merely as a passive symbol of suffering, a figure immobilized by grief at the foot of the cross. While this image conveys the depth of her sorrow, it overlooks the active, resilient faith that characterizes Mary's journey both during and after the crucifixion.

1. Mary as Mother:

- Central to the poem is the portrayal of Mary as a mother whose love transcends death. The lines 'Once I carried you with joy, / I hold you now enveloped in dark despair' reflect the profound transformation of maternal joy into unimaginable pain.
- Rather than dwelling solely on her loss, the poem highlights how Mary's identity as a mother remains unbroken despite the tragedy, emphasizing the continuity of her love.
- Mary's relationship with Jesus, even in death, is portrayed as enduring and nurturing, showing that her maternal bond cannot be shattered by loss.

The Word in their Voices

2. **Mary as Disciple:**

- The poem also reflects on Mary's discipleship, recognizing her not only as Jesus' mother but as one who followed His mission with unwavering faith.
- In the line 'Your place on the altar, / A vision I wrestled with, / Now a reality I cannot bear,' Mary's struggle is evident as she comes to terms with God's will and accepts that Jesus' sacrifice is part of the divine plan.
- This portrayal emphasizes that Mary is not simply a passive recipient of divine events but an active participant in the story of salvation.
- By grappling with the reality of the altar as a place of sacrifice, Mary demonstrates the tension between human love and divine mission, reflecting the paradox of faith and sorrow.

3. **Mary as Intercessor:**

- One of the unique aspects of the poem is the portrayal of Mary as an intercessor for humanity. The stanza 'Amidst this pain my purpose remains, / and my path in love reveals itself' marks a pivotal shift from mourning to mission, illustrating that Mary's grief fuels her compassion for others.
- By referencing the Wedding at Cana, where Mary intercedes on behalf of the guests (John 2:1–11), the poem draws a direct line between Mary's maternal care for Jesus and her enduring love for His followers.
- The inclusion of Rachel's lament (Jeremiah 31:15; Matthew 2:18) further enriches the poem, connecting Mary to the biblical tradition of maternal mourning and advocacy.
- In the Old Testament, Rachel's weeping is a profound symbol of maternal sorrow and intercession.
- Jeremiah 31:15 (NIV) says: 'A voice is heard in Ramah, mourning and great weeping, Rachel weeping for her children and refusing to be comforted, because they are no more.'

- Rachel, as one of the matriarchs of Israel, is depicted metaphorically as weeping for her descendants, symbolizing the collective grief of Israel during their suffering and displacement.
- However, God's response in Jeremiah 31:16–17 reveals the power of maternal intercession: *'Restrain your voice from weeping and your eyes from tears, for your work will be rewarded . . . They will return from the land of the enemy.'*
- This passage demonstrates that God listens to Rachel's sorrow and promises restoration, indicating that maternal advocacy moves the heart of God.
- In the New Testament, Matthew 2:18 references this prophecy when describing Herod's massacre of the innocents:
- *'A voice is heard in Ramah, weeping and great mourning, Rachel weeping for her children and refusing to be comforted, because they are no more.'*
- Here, Rachel's lament is echoed as the mothers of Bethlehem grieve for their slain children, and this lament finds a parallel in Mary's own sorrow at the Cross.
- By comparing Mary to Rachel, the poem emphasizes that Mary's grief is not merely passive suffering but an active, loving force. Just as God listened to Rachel, so too does God respond to Mary's intercession. This parallelism highlights that maternal love, even in sorrow, holds redemptive power.

What I Hope to Convey with This Poem:

I aim to present Mary as a living, evolving figure—not merely a static symbol of suffering but a mother whose love endures beyond loss, a disciple who embraces her divine purpose despite the pain, and an intercessor who continues to advocate for humanity. Through this portrayal, the I invite readers to see Mary not only as a tragic figure at the cross but as a compassionate and proactive mother of all believers.

By drawing on the story of Rachel, the poem also reflects how maternal sorrow throughout biblical history often becomes a channel for God's mercy and intervention. Just as Rachel's tears moved God to respond, Mary's grief becomes an active, loving force that continues to shape the faith community, showing that through loss, *Mary's mission of love and intercession continues.*

Through this nuanced portrayal, I hope that this poem will challenge readers to see Mary's suffering not just as a moment of passive lamentation but as a pivotal point where grief transforms into love that extends to all humanity. In this way, the poem becomes not just a reflection on sorrow but a testament to faith, love, and unending compassion.

MARY: REFLECTION ON MICHELANGELO'S PIETÀ

A sword has pierced my soul—
I was not prepared for this moment.
Just as Simeon foretold—a sword, a wound so deep
With hopeless despair in its wake.

I cradle you, my son—
Rushing waves of anguish
Crashing against the shore of my wounded heart
Tearing it to pieces.

A tide of sorrow floods my heart
A despair only a mother can know.
Once I carried you with joy
I hold you now enveloped in dark despair

I remember Gabriel at the Annunciation
My answer bright with joy—
The Magnificat rose from my lips
Full of grace, full of praise
My heart overflowing with gladness.

I was given a gift from Hashem
To have you by my side.
I know you as the Father
And I, the daughter of the Son—
Still, this grief will not relent.

The years of love we shared—emptied, and now a void—
Only echoes in my arms as I hold you.
Your only crimes: love, truth, compassion—
Healing others and paying this ransom for humanity.

I knew you as your mother
I knew you as my child.
Now I know you as my Savior.
My hands, open to offer you—
Still tremble, longing to hold you near.

Your place on the altar
A vision I wrestled with
Now a reality I cannot bear.
Your life poured out as gift.
You were never mine alone—
You belong to the world
And to eternity.

Amidst this pain my purpose remains
and my path in love reveals itself
By your will, I am Mother for eternity
I will love your flock as my own
As I called out to you in Cana
I will intercede on their behalf.

Just as Rachel wept for her children
And you, Hashem, listened.
So too will I tend your sheep
For I love them as you do

Your breath has left this world
Yet life abundant you bestow
To all who trust and follow.
In sorrow, I am still blessed—
For love eternal flows from you—
A mother's grief, a world's salvation.

Mary: Annotation on Michelangelo's Pietà

The Pietà sculpture by Michelangelo depicts Mary cradling the dead body of Jesus, embodying both maternal grief and divine acceptance. **The open hands convey an anguish of a mother wanting to cling on but at the same time letting go to place Jesus on the altar because that is his mission—to die for us.** The title reflects the poem's meditative nature on Mary's role at the crucifixion.

Stanza 1: Prophetic Grief
A sword has pierced my soul—
I was not prepared for this moment.
Just as Simeon foretold—a sword, a wound so deep,
With hopeless despair in its wake.

Biblical References:

- **Luke 2:34–35**
  'Then Simeon blessed them and said to Mary, his mother: "This child is destined to cause the falling and rising of many in Israel... And a sword will pierce your own soul too".'
  Simeon's prophecy foreshadows Mary's profound sorrow at Jesus' crucifixion.
- **Isaiah 53:3**
  'He was despised and rejected by mankind, a man of suffering, and familiar with pain.'
  Jesus' suffering and rejection are linked to Mary's experience of witnessing His death.

Stanza 2: Waves of Anguish

I cradle you, my son—
Rushing waves of anguish
Break against the shore of my wounded heart,
Tearing it to pieces.

Biblical References:

- *John 19:25:*
  'Near the cross of Jesus stood his mother . . .'
  Mary's presence at the cross, holding her crucified son, mirrors the Pietà's depiction of Mary cradling Jesus.
- *Psalm 22:14:*
  'I am poured out like water, and all my bones are out of joint.'
  Reflects the anguish and physical pain that parallels Mary's emotional suffering.

Stanza 3: Maternal Despair

A tide of sorrow floods my heart,
A despair only a mother can know.
Once I carried you with joy,
I hold you now enveloped in dark despair.

Biblical References:

- *Luke 1:42:*
  'Blessed are you among women, and blessed is the child you will bear!'
  The contrast between the joy of carrying Jesus and the sorrow of holding His lifeless body.
- *John 16:20:*
  'Very truly I tell you, you will weep and mourn while the world rejoices.'
  Jesus' words to His disciples about grief turning to joy, which indirectly reflects Mary's dual experience of joy and despair.

Stanza 4: Memory and Faith

I remember Gabriel at the Annunciation,
My answer bright with joy—
The Magnificat rose from my lips,
Full of grace, full of praise,
My heart overflowing with gladness.

Biblical References:

- **Luke 1:26–38 (Annunciation):**
  The angel Gabriel announces to Mary that she will bear the Son of God.
- **Luke 1:46–55 (The Magnificat):**
  'My soul glorifies the Lord and my spirit rejoices in God my Savior . . .'
  Mary's hymn of praise, expressing her willingness to fulfil God's will.
- **Luke 1:28:**
  'Greetings, you who are highly favoured! The Lord is with you.'
  Reinforces Mary's grace and acceptance of her divine role.

Catholic Doctrine:

Mary recalls the joy of the annunciation, and the Magnificat symbolizes unwavering faith and trust, even in ultimate loss.

Stanza 5: Gift and Grief

I was given a gift from Hashem
To have you by my side.
I know you as the Father
And I, the daughter of the Son—
Still this grief will not relent.

The Word in their Voices | 63

Biblical References:

- *John 1:14:*
  'The Word became flesh and made his dwelling among us.'
  Emphasizes the Incarnation and Mary's role in bearing God in human form.
- *Luke 1:35:*
  'The Holy Spirit will come on you . . . So the holy one to be born will be called the Son of God.'
  Highlights Mary's unique relationship with Jesus as both mother and daughter in the divine plan.
- *Romans 5:8:*
  'But God demonstrates his own love for us in this: While we were still sinners, Christ died for us.'
  Shows the gift of salvation through suffering.

Catholic Doctrine:
Immaculate Conception indicating that Mary was predestined to be mother of God, chosen before all time.

Stanza 6: Eternal Motherhood
By your will, I am mother for eternity.

Biblical References:

- *John 19:27:*
  'Then he said to the disciple, 'Here is your mother.' From that time on, this disciple took her into his home.'
  Jesus establishes Mary as the spiritual mother of all believers.
  Lumen Gentium 62 (Vatican II):
  Mary continues her maternal role as Advocate and Mediatrix in the Church, by God's will and grace.
- *Ephesians 1:4:*
  'For he chose us in him before the creation of the world . . .'
  Implies that Mary's role as Mother of God was predestined by God.

Catholic Doctrine:
This phrase aligns with the Second Vatican Council, Lumen Gentium 62, which teaches that Mary continues to be ab Mother and advocate for the Church.

Stanza 7: Intercessory Role
Just as Rachel wept for her children
And you, Hashem, listened.
So too will I tend to your flock
For I love them as you do.

Biblical References:

- ***Jeremiah 31:15:***
  'A voice is heard in Ramah, mourning and great weeping, Rachel weeping for her children . . .'
  Rachel's grief is a symbol of maternal sorrow and divine empathy.
- ***Matthew 2:18:***
  'A voice is heard in Ramah . . . Rachel weeping for her children.'
  Connects Rachel's mourning to the Massacre of the Innocents, highlighting maternal suffering across generations.
- ***John 2:1–11 (Wedding at Cana):***
  Mary intercedes for the guests, reflecting her role as an intercessor.
- ***John 10:11:***
  'I am the good shepherd. The good shepherd lays down his life for the sheep.'
  Mary's promise to tend to the flock mirrors Jesus' pastoral care for His followers.

Catholic Doctrine:
Both Mary and Rachel are sorrowful intercessors—Rachel for her lost descendants, Mary for her Crucified Son. Both women symbolize God's compassion for suffering, demonstrating that through intercession,

Divine Mercy flows abundantly. This parallel reinforces the idea that Mary, like Rachel, continuously advocates for God's people, and her grief transforms into a channel of grace and blessing

Final Stanza: Grief and Redemption
Your breath has left this world
Yet life abundant you bestow
To all who trust and follow.
In sorrow, I am still blessed—
For love eternal flows from you—
A mother's grief, a world's salvation.

Biblical References:

- ***John 10:10:***
  'I have come that they may have life and have it to the full.'
- ***Romans 8:28:***
  'And we know that in all things God works for the good of those who love him . . .'
- ***1 Peter 1:3:***
  'In his great mercy he has given us new birth into a living hope through the resurrection of Jesus Christ from the dead.'
  Shows that Mary's grief leads to the world's redemption.

GOOD FRIDAY BIBLE STUDY

Seven Reflections on the Passion and Victory of Christ

Each reflection includes the following:

- One Old Testament verse (foreshadowing)
- One New Testament verse (fulfilment)
- A corresponding Psalm (for meditation and worship)
- A thematic image
- Reflections on the readings
- Life Application Questions

'From the Fall to the Final Victory, from the cry of forsakenness to the echo of "It is finished", Christ's work on Good Friday resonates eternally. May each reflection draw you nearer to the heart of our crucified and risen King.'

Introduction to the Good Friday Bible Study

I would like to share the inspiration that sparked its creation. My journey began a year ago but crystallized when I visited the Basilica of St. Mary Major in Rome. Walking through the church, I was captivated by the symbolism embedded in its architecture and art. One detail caught my attention: the forty-two pillars that lead from the entrance to the altar. These pillars represent the three sets of fourteen generations as outlined in the Gospel of Matthew: from Abraham to David, David to the Babylonian exile (specifically marked by King Jeconiah), and from the exile to Christ. This numerical symmetry in the Church reflects the unfolding story of salvation, where every aspect is deeply intentional and imbued with meaning.

Just before reaching the central altar, there is another remarkable detail: a depiction of Melchizedek. This figure, who prefigures Christ as the eternal priest-king, stands as a profound theological symbol. Melchizedek's presence near the altar highlights the continuity between the Old Testament foreshadowing and the New Testament fulfilment in Christ. This inclusion exemplifies the beauty and genius of the architectural design at St. Mary Major, where Marian devotion is crafted to point to and illuminate Jesus Christ. The entire church serves as a harmonious tapestry where prophecy and fulfilment, Old and New Testaments, converge to tell the story of salvation.

Above the pillars, I noticed a striking pattern: on the left side, murals depicting Old Testament prophecies, and on the right, their New Testament fulfilments. The visual dialogue between prophecy and fulfilment resonated deeply with me, and it became clear that the story of salvation is not just a moment on Good Friday but a journey spanning from the dawn of sin to the resurrection of Christ. This realization inspired me to develop a Bible study that embraces this comprehensive vision of salvation history rather than isolating the crucifixion from the broader redemptive arc.

This study is divided into seven reflections, a number chosen deliberately. Seven symbolizes completeness—mirroring the seven days of Creation—suggesting that the story of salvation is a complete and divine work of God. The reflections are arranged using a *Janus structure*, a concept named after the Roman god Janus, who is depicted with two faces looking in opposite directions. In this context, the cross serves as the central pivot: on one side, the narrative moves towards the downfall and death, while on the other, it turns towards resurrection and victory. This duality represents the profound transformation from sin and death to redemption and life.

The poetic framing of this Bible study plays an essential role in setting the tone. It begins with the poem on the cross, followed by the poem on Mary, and ends with the poem on Judas, with the reflections sandwiched in between. The Cross, at the beginning, introduces the profound reality of suffering and sacrifice, while Mary represents the human response of faith and surrender. Judas, at the conclusion, poses a thought-provoking question, reminding us of the gravity of choices and the mystery of grace.

This structure is intended to lead the reader from contemplation to reflection, bookending the Bible study with themes of redemption and betrayal.

The cover image of this Bible study further encapsulates its essence. It features a chalice, symbolizing both the suffering of Christ and the cup of salvation. The chalice depicted in the artwork is located in Bellagio, a charming village on the shores of Lake Como, Italy. The image is part of the ornate decorations in the Church of San Giacomo, located in the central hamlet of Bellagio. This Romanesque church dates back to the twelfth century and is renowned for its harmonious blend of medieval and Baroque styles. The chalice in the artwork, painted with a nuanced interplay of light and shadow, represents the Passion of Christ and serves as a powerful symbol of the Eucharistic mystery. It draws our attention to the ultimate sacrifice that is both historical and ever-present in the life of the Church. The left branch represents wheat used for making bread, and the right branch represents grapes used for making wine.

This Bible study invites you not just to remember Good Friday but to enter into it—understanding it as the culmination of a redemptive journey that began when humanity first fell and found its fulfilment in Christ's resurrection. I hope that as you move through these reflections, you will find a deeper understanding of the cross and the victory that follows, and that the juxtaposition of the Cross, Mary, and Judas will challenge you to consider your own place in this ongoing story of salvation.

Good Friday Bible Study: Seven Reflections

Reflection 1: The Fall: Our Need for Redemption

Old Testament (Genesis 3:6–7) : 'So when the woman saw that the tree was good for food, and that it was a delight to the eyes, and that the tree was to be desired to make one wise, she took of its fruit and ate, and she also gave some to her husband who was with her, and he ate. Then the eyes of both of them were opened, and they realized they were naked; so they sewed fig leaves together and made coverings for themselves.'

New Testament (Romans 5:12, 17–19): 'Therefore, just as sin came into the world through one man, and death through sin, and so death spread to all men because all sinned—', For if, by the trespass of the one man, death reigned through that one man, how much more will those who receive God's abundant provision of grace and of the gift of righteousness reign in life through the one man, Jesus Christ! Consequently, just as one trespass resulted in condemnation for all people, so also one righteous act resulted in justification and life for all people. For just as through the disobedience of the one man the many were made sinners, so also through the obedience of the one man the many will be made righteous.

Psalm (Psalm 51:5): 'Behold, I was brought forth in iniquity, and in sin did my mother conceive me.'

The Story of the Fall: In the Garden of Eden, Adam and Eve disobeyed God's command, bringing sin into God's perfect creation. The Genesis verse above narrates the very moment of the Fall, when our first parents chose their own way over God's way. This original sin had catastrophic consequences: as Romans teaches, through one man (Adam), sin entered the world, and death came as the result of sin. From that point on, every human life has been touched by sin and death. We inherit a fallen nature—the Psalmist David acknowledges this by confessing that from the very start of life, from conception, we are corrupted by sin. Historically and theologically, this doctrine is known as *original sin*: the idea that the guilt and corruption of Adam's sin extend to all humanity. Because of the Fall, we live in a broken world, *separated from the Holy God* and unable to save ourselves. Our need for redemption is absolute—if God does not intervene, we *remain dead in sin*.

Their eyes were opened: Appears both in Genesis and in the Gospel of Luke when Jesus breaks bread with two disciples after His resurrection. In Genesis, when Adam and Eve eat the forbidden fruit, their eyes are opened to their own nakedness, *symbolizing the loss of innocence and a new awareness of good and evil*. This opening leads to shame and separation from God. This is because humanity will turn to themselves to define good and evil. *In contrast*, in Luke 24:30–31, when Jesus breaks bread with the disciples on the road to Emmaus, *their eyes are opened*, and they recognize Him. This moment is one of revelation, joy, and restored connection, transforming their understanding and filling them with hope. While both accounts involve an 'opening' of eyes, the former brings knowledge intertwined with existential burden, whereas the latter unveils divine presence and comprehension of truth, resulting in spiritual enlightenment. And a burning in their hearts to know God.

The Consequences of Sin: Doctrinally, the Fall explains why evil, suffering, and death exist.'Death spread to all men because all sinned'—not only do we inherit sin, but we also *willingly* commit our own sins. We see this truth in our experience: every inclination of the natural human heart is selfish and prone to stray from God. Psalm 51:5 poetically describes this inherited sinful condition, emphasizing that *every person needs God's forgiveness* from their very origin. As we reflect on our own lives, we realize we have repeated Adam and Eve's mistake in various ways—*choosing our will over God's*. This humbling truth is the beginning of the Good Friday journey: understanding why the cross was necessary. If the story ended with the Fall, it would be a tragedy with no hope. But even here, God's grace is already at work. *Knowing our need* prepares our hearts to grasp the greatness of God's solution.

Life Application Questions:

- In what ways do you see the effects of the Fall (sin and brokenness) in your own life and in the world around you?
- How does the promise of redemption shape your daily hope?

Reflection 2: The Promise – God's Plan of Redemption

Old Testament (Genesis 3:15): 'I will put enmity between you and the woman, and between your offspring and her offspring; he shall bruise your head, and you shall bruise his heel.'

New Testament (Galatians 4:4–5): 'But when the fullness of time had come, God sent forth his Son, born of woman, born under the law, to redeem those who were under the law, so that we might receive adoption as sons.'

Psalm (Psalm 130:7–8): 'O Israel, hope in the LORD! For with the LORD there is steadfast love, and with him is plentiful redemption. And he will redeem Israel from all his iniquities.'

God's Promise in the Garden: Amazingly, at the very scene of humanity's fall, God speaks a word of hope. In Genesis 3:15, often called the *protoevangelium* ('first gospel'), God promises that the offspring of the woman will one day crush the serpent's head. This cryptic promise is the earliest proclamation of the Gospel: it foreshadows a coming Saviour, born of a woman, who will deal a fatal blow to Satan (the serpent) even while suffering in the process (a bruised heel).

The Word in their Voices | 75

Historically, faithful readers of Scripture have seen this as a messianic prophecy—a beacon of hope that God would not abandon His creation to sin and death. Right after pronouncing judgments for sin, God's grace shines through in this promise. This shows God's character: even in judgment, He delights in mercy. From the beginning, He set in motion a plan to redeem what was lost. This starts with Abraham and Isaac. Abraham utters the words that will give meaning and make Calvary a reality. Genesis 22:7–8: *Isaac spoke up and said to his father Abraham, 'Father?' 'Yes, my son?' Abraham replied.'The fire and wood are here,' Isaac said, 'but where is the lamb for the burnt offering?' Abraham answered, 'God himself will provide the lamb for the burnt offering, my son.' And the two of them went on together.*

Promise Fulfilled in Christ: Fast-forward to the New Testament. Galatians 4:4–5 proclaims the fulfilment of that ancient promise—when the time was exactly right, God sent His Son, Jesus, born of a woman (echoing "her offspring" from Genesis) to redeem us . Jesus is that promised offspring who would crush the serpent. The "bruising" He endured was the suffering of the cross, but by that sacrifice He defeated Satan, sin, and death. Doctrinally, this is the heart of the Gospel: *God himself provided the solution to our Fall.* Over centuries, God reiterated his promise (through Abraham, Moses, David, and the prophets), gradually unveiling the coming of a Messiah. Galatians emphasizes that Jesus came 'under the law' to redeem those under the law—meaning he fully identified with humanity, obeyed God's law perfectly where we could not, and then died to free us from the law's curse. Through Jesus, we can be adopted as God's children instead of remaining enemies of God.

Hope and Redemption: The Psalmist in Psalm 130 cries out from the depths but finds hope in God's promise of plentiful redemption. 'He will redeem Israel from all his iniquities'—this faithful expectation kept believers looking forward to the Redeemer. Devotionally, we are invited to share that hope. Even before Christ came, believers were assured of God's steadfast love and awaited His salvation. Now, living after Christ's coming, we have even greater confidence. God kept His word: Jesus has come, and *by His death and resurrection, the head of the serpent is crushed.* Good Friday, though a scene of suffering, is also the outworking of God's loving promise made from the beginning of history. We learn that our hope has a sure foundation—*God always had a plan to rescue us, and no human sin or failure could thwart his promise.* In our personal lives, this means we can trust God to keep His promises found in Scripture. *The darkest circumstances (like the tragedy of Eden or the agony of the cross) can become the stage upon which God's faithfulness is displayed.*

Life Application Questions:

- How does knowing that God planned our redemption from the very beginning encourage you when you face the consequences of sin? What does it mean for me to call Jesus Lamb of God?
- In what ways can you live with hope, trusting in God's promises that he will provide, even before you see their fulfilment?

Reflection 3: The Suffering Servant—Prophecy of Atonement

Old Testament (Isaiah 53:5): 'But he was pierced for our transgressions; he was crushed for our iniquities; upon him was the chastisement that brought us peace, and with his wounds we are healed.'

New Testament (Mark 10:45): 'For even the Son of Man came not to be served but to serve, and to give his life as a ransom for many.'

Psalm (Psalm 22:16): For dogs encompass me; a company of evildoers encircles me; they have pierced my hands and feet—'

Prophecy of the Suffering Saviour: Centuries before Jesus, God spoke through the prophet Isaiah about a mysterious 'Servant' who would suffer on behalf of His people. *Isaiah 53:5 is a pinnacle of those prophecies*; it vividly describes an individual who is pierced and crushed for the sins of others. The language of 'pierced for our transgressions' directly connects to what Jesus endured on the cross (His hands and feet pierced by nails) and the purpose behind it—our sins (transgressions, iniquities) were the cause. The verse goes on to declare that this Servant's suffering brings peace and healing to us.

Historically, this passage was perplexing: Who was this sufferer? Why would the Messiah (expected to be a king) suffer such humiliation? Christians understand that Isaiah was foretelling Jesus' atoning death. He is the Lamb led to slaughter, who willingly takes the punishment that we deserved so we could be reconciled to God. The Psalm 22:16 verse likewise is a prophetic foreshadowing: King David describes enemies surrounding him and piercing his hands and feet, an eerily accurate prediction of crucifixion (a method of execution not invented until later). Such prophecies build our confidence that Jesus' suffering was not an accident of history, but the sovereign plan of God foretold long before.

Christ's Willing Sacrifice: In Mark 10:45, Jesus Himself explains His mission in light of the suffering servant role: He came to serve and to give His life as a *ransom* for many. A *'ransom'* is a price paid to free captives or slaves. Doctrinally, this points to *substitutionary atonement—Jesus taking our place*, paying the price (his life's blood) to free us from bondage to sin and death. Every lash of the whip, every nail, and every insult he endured was carrying our sins. This was foreshadowed in the Old Testament sacrificial system (the Passover lamb, the sin offerings), but Jesus is the fulfilment—the real Lamb of God who takes away the sin of the world. It's important to reflect that Christ did this *voluntarily*. Mark's Gospel emphasizes Jesus' intent: He came for this very purpose. No one took his life from him against his will; he laid it down for us out of love. Historically, this sets Jesus apart from any notion of a reluctant martyr—he is a willing Saviour. Devotionally, this should deeply humble and move us. Isaiah's prophecy says 'the chastisement that brought us peace was upon him'—Jesus took our *chastisement (punishment)* to give us the gift of *peace with God*. By *'his wounds we are healed'*, meaning the wound of sin in our souls is cured by his suffering.

Love Beyond Measure: As we consider these prophecies and their fulfilment, we encounter the *profound love of God*. The Holy One was willing to be counted among transgressors and to be treated as guilty so that the guilty (us) could be treated as righteous. When Jesus hung on the cross, *Psalm 22 (which he would quote from the cross) was being fulfilled line by line.* The very detail 'they have pierced my hands and feet' reminds us that the crucifixion was the plan all along—God's way of dealing with sin. This was necessary for our atonement. In a doctrinal sense, *God's justice and mercy meet at the cross:* justice in that sin was punished, mercy in that the punishment fell on the innocent Christ and not on us. For our personal reflection, this challenges us: do we understand the weight of our sin and, in the same breath, the depth of Christ's love? Good Friday invites us to gaze upon the suffering Servant and realize those wounds were for us. It's a call to repentance (recognizing our sins put him there) and a call to grateful faith (recognizing he willingly went there because he loves us).

Life Application Questions:

- When you read Isaiah 53:5, what personal meaning does 'pierced for our transgressions' take on for you? How does Christ's suffering change how I view my own pain?
- Jesus came to serve and give His life. What lessons do I draw from the suffering that Jesus endured for me?

Reflection 4: The Crucifixion – Christ's Sacrifice on the Cross

Old Testament (Zechariah 12:10): 'And I will pour out on the house of David and the inhabitants of Jerusalem a spirit of grace and pleas for mercy, so that, when they look on me, on him whom they have pierced, they shall mourn for him, as one mourns for an only child, and weep bitterly over him, as one weeps over a firstborn.'

New Testament (Luke 23:33): 'And when they came to the place that is called The Skull, there they crucified him, and the criminals, one on his right and one on his left.'

Psalm (Psalm 22:1): 'My God, my God, why have you forsaken me? Why are you so far from saving me, from the words of my groaning?'

Golgotha—The Place of Sacrifice: In this central reflection, *we stand at Calvary (Golgotha)*, beholding the crucifixion of Jesus. Luke 23:33 states it with painful simplicity: 'there they crucified him.' With those few words, the Gospels describe the most momentous event in history. Jesus, the sinless Son of God, was nailed to a wooden cross and executed like a criminal. Crucifixion was a brutal, humiliating, and excruciating way to die. But even greater than the physical torment was the spiritual weight He bore – taking on Himself the sin of the world.

The Pierced One: Zechariah 12:10 is a striking prophecy, centuries before Jesus, foretelling a day when the people of Jerusalem would look *'on him whom they have pierced'* and mourn deeply. Christians have long understood this to be fulfilled in Jesus' crucifixion. He was the one pierced—by nails, by a spear—and one day, many who rejected Him would realize with sorrow who He truly was. At the cross, this prophecy began to unfold as onlookers, soldiers, and even a centurion started to recognize the gravity of what was happening. Devotionally, this verse draws us into a personal response: *we too must 'look upon the one we have pierced'* —not merely physically, but spiritually, with our sins. Mourning over Him like a firstborn is the kind of deep repentance and love that Good Friday calls forth. It's not just historical mourning, but personal: *My sin put Him there.*

Forsaken for Us: Jesus' cry from the cross, recorded in Psalm 22:1 and quoted in Matthew 27:46, reveals the depth of His suffering: *'My God, my God, why have you forsaken me?'* In that moment, He bore the full weight of sin and its consequence—separation from God. Though the Father never ceased loving the Son, the experience of divine abandonment was real. This forsakenness was for us. Jesus took our place, so we would never be forsaken. *This is the heart of substitutionary atonement—Christ became a curse so we could be blessed. He endured wrath so we could receive mercy.*

Looking Upon the Cross: Zechariah's prophecy about people looking upon the pierced One echoes the scene at Golgotha, where some looked with hatred, others with sorrow, and some with awakening faith. The proper response to the cross is not indifference. It's worship, repentance, and surrender. Jesus was not just dying for humanity—*He was dying for me.* Psalm 22, which begins in anguish, ends in praise—*'He* has done it' (v.31). *That arc from agony to victory mirrors the journey of the crucifixion. The cross is both the place of mourning and the fountain of mercy.*

The Cross and Me: Good Friday is called 'good' because of what it accomplished. Through the piercing, the forsakenness, and the death of Jesus, salvation was secured. Zechariah's vision of people mourning is not the end of the story—it is the beginning of grace. God pours out a 'spirit of grace and supplication', leading to repentance and healing. When we 'look upon the one we pierced,' and respond with genuine sorrow and faith, that is the moment of transformation. The cross becomes personal—not just a historical event, but my redemption. Devotionally, this is the invitation of Good Friday: to look, to mourn, and to be changed.

Life Application Questions:

- As you imagine the scene at Calvary, what emotions and thoughts stir in your heart? How does Jesus' cry 'Why have you forsaken me?' deepen your understanding of what He endured for you?
- Zechariah prophesied that people would look upon the One they pierced and mourn. How does this verse challenge your own response to Christ's crucifixion?

Reflection 5: 'It Is Finished' – Atonement Accomplished

Revelation 12:10–11:

Then I heard a loud voice in heaven say,

'Now have come the salvation and the power
    and the kingdom of our God,
    and the authority of his Messiah.
For the accuser of our brothers and sisters,
    who accuses them before our God day and night,
    has been hurled down.
They triumphed over him
    by the blood of the Lamb
    and by the word of their testimony;
they did not love their lives so much
    as to shrink from death.

Old Testament (Zechariah 3:9): 'See, the stone I have set in front of Joshua! There are seven eyes on that one stone, and I will engrave an inscription on it,' says the Lord Almighty, 'and I will remove the sin of this land in a single day.'

New Testament (John 19:30): 'When Jesus had received the sour wine, he said, 'It is finished,' and he bowed his head and gave up his spirit.'

Psalm (Psalm 22:31): 'They shall come and proclaim his righteousness to a people yet unborn, that he has done it.'

One Day, One Sacrifice: The Old Testament is filled with sacrifices offered day after day, year after year, in an attempt to deal with Israel's sins—but they were never sufficient to permanently remove sin (Hebrews 10:4). Zechariah 3:9 contains a stunning promise: God would *'remove the iniquity of the land in a single day'*. For those practicing the perpetual sacrifices, the idea of sin being dealt with once for all in a single day would be incredible. We see the fulfilment of this on Good Friday, the day of Jesus' crucifixion. On that single day, on a hill outside Jerusalem, the cumulative burden of the world's iniquity was laid on Jesus, and by the merit of His divine person, fully paid for. This is why, as John 19:30 records, Jesus triumphantly declared,

'It is finished.' In the original language (Greek: *tetelestai*), this phrase can mean 'paid in full.' Doctrinally, this signifies Christ's atonement was fully sufficient to cover all our sins. *He accomplished in that single day what all of humanity's religious efforts could never do.* At the moment Jesus gave up His spirit, the mission the Father gave Him—to save the world—was completed. *The curtain tearing in the temple and the earth shaking were divine signs that the old order of things had ended, and a new covenant was established in Christ's blood. Exodus 26:33—'The curtain will separate the Holy Place from the Most Holy Place.'*

Forgiveness and Freedom: What does 'It is finished' mean for us? *It means the work needed for our salvation is fully done by Christ, not by the works defined in the Law of Moses.* We can rest in the finished work of Jesus. The Psalm 22:31 verse reflects this, ending the Psalm on a note of victory: *'He has done it.'* (Some translations: 'He has performed it' or 'He has finished it.') Written a thousand years before Calvary, those words anticipate the cross' finality. Because Jesus 'has done it,' our role is to believe and receive. Historically, when people grasped this, it led to great rejoicing. Consider the Apostle Peter on Pentecost, preaching that everyone who repents and believes in Jesus receives forgiveness – no ifs, ands, or buts, and that salvation is by grace through faith, not by penance or merit which manifests as the fruits of the spirit—*Galatians 5:22–23: But the fruit of the Spirit is love, joy, peace, patience, kindness, goodness, faithfulness, gentleness, self-control; against such things there is no law.*

If you trust in Christ, your sins (past, present, future) were nailed to the cross and removed 'in a single day', once and for all. You stand righteous ('proclaim his righteousness to a people yet unborn'—His righteousness, not ours). As Jesus died, He ransomed us, and 'there is therefore now no condemnation for those in Christ Jesus' (Romans 8:1). This is the start of our sanctification and through Grace and faith we walk in Christ with the guidance of the Holy Spirit. *In our Catholic faith, the synergistic relationship between God's grace and human cooperation is foundational.*

The Word in their Voices

Living in the Finished Work: While Jesus' saving work is finished, *our response to it is ongoing.* We are called to live in the good of that finished work—to 'walk in newness of life' with gratitude. *We do not serve God to get saved; we serve because we are saved.* Knowing that the debt is paid produces love and loyalty in our hearts—the relief and gratitude fuel a changed life. Psalm 22:31 envisions future generations hearing of this victory and worshiping God for it. We are those people. We have the privilege to 'proclaim His righteousness'—to tell others that God has provided the righteousness we lack through the cross. Good Friday's message, 'It is finished', gives us peace: we don't have to live in fear wondering if we've done enough to be right with God. *Jesus has done enough, done it all. Our part is to trust in that and let it transform us from the inside out.* We confess, 'Jesus, You finished the work for me; I will live for You in light of that'. The certainty of the finished atonement gives us confidence to draw near to God (Hebrews 10:19–22) 'Therefore, brothers, since we have confidence to enter the holy places by the blood of Jesus, by the new and living way *that he opened for us through the curtain,* that is, through his flesh, and since we have a great priest over the house of God, let us draw near with a true heart in full assurance of faith, with our hearts sprinkled clean from an evil conscience and our bodies washed with pure water.' and to resist Satan's accusations, knowing they have been answered by the blood of the Lamb (Revelation 12:10–11).

Life Application Questions:

- How does the torn veil affect how I approach God in prayer? If lingering guilt or fear remains, how can Jesus' words 'It is finished' bring you freedom and peace?
- Am I living as if I still need access, or am I walking in the freedom Jesus provided?

Reflection 6: The Sabbath Rest – Hope in the Silence

Old Testament (Genesis 2:2): 'And on the seventh day God finished his work that he had done, and he rested on the seventh day from all his work that he had done.'

New Testament (Luke 23:55–56): 'The women who had come with him from Galilee followed and saw the tomb and how his body was laid. Then they returned and prepared spices and ointments. On the Sabbath they rested according to the commandment.'

Psalm (Psalm 4:8): 'In peace I will both lie down and sleep; for you alone, O LORD, make me dwell in safety.'

A Holy Pause: After Jesus died on Friday, His body was placed in a tomb, and the next day was the Jewish Sabbath (Saturday). Luke notes that the women who loved Jesus 'rested on the Sabbath according to the commandment', after the harrowing events of crucifixion day. This Sabbath was unlike any other—the Lord of the Sabbath (Jesus) lay in repose in the grave. In a profound way, Jesus was keeping Sabbath after accomplishing the work of redemption. This mirrors God's rest in Genesis 2:2: after finishing the work of creation in six days, God 'rested on the seventh day'. Now, after the six hours on the cross (often noted from roughly the sixth to the ninth hour, noon to 3:00 p.m.), Jesus had finished the new creation work (redemption) and observed a Sabbath rest in the tomb. This Janus moment (looking back and forward) connects the Old and New: The original creation was finished and God rested; the new creation (our salvation) was finished and the Son rested. Historically, Holy Saturday (the day between crucifixion and resurrection) is a day of quiet reflection for Catholics—a day of waiting. The Bible doesn't detail what happened to Jesus' human soul on that day (beyond references to Him proclaiming victory to spirits in prison, 1 Peter 3:19), but outwardly, it was a day of silence and stillness. The disciples were scattered, grieving, and confused, forced into inactivity by the Sabbath law, perhaps sitting with their sorrow. *And yet in that silence, God was still at work behind the scenes, preparing for the dawn of resurrection.*

Entering God's Rest: The Sabbath theme carries a deep spiritual meaning. Hebrews 4 describes a 'Sabbath rest' for the people of God, tied to ceasing from works and trusting in God's work. Because of Jesus' completed work, believers are invited to rest in Christ. This doesn't mean inactivity in life, but a rest of soul—ceasing to strive for our own salvation and resting in His grace. *On that first Holy Saturday, the world couldn't do anything to contribute to salvation; it was entirely in God's hands.* Likewise, we are called to trust and be still. Psalm 4:8 captures a personal application: David is able to lie down and sleep in peace, trusting the Lord for safety. In times of darkness or uncertainty, we too can find rest knowing God is our security. The disciples were in despair that Saturday—their hopes seemed dead and buried. Yet God knew that Sunday was coming. As Fulton Sheen said, 'There can be no Easter Sunday without a Good Friday'. In our lives, we sometimes experience 'in-between' moments: after a crisis, before we see God's deliverance. *We pray and have to wait.* Holy Saturday teaches us hopeful waiting. *God may seem late, but he is always on time.* God's silence is not his absence. As Jesus 'slept' in death, the Psalm's promise that the Lord makes us 'dwell in safety' was still true. In fact, Jesus' body lay in a tomb guarded by Roman soldiers and under seal—ironically testifying that God would not let anything prevent the coming resurrection.

Resting as an Act of Faith: Observing the Sabbath rest was an act of obedience and faith for the women and disciples—they wanted to anoint Jesus' body more (hence preparing spices) but refrained from work, honouring God's command. This shows that *even in grief, they submitted to God*. Similarly, sometimes our act of faith is to rest, to wait patiently for the Lord when everything in us wants to anxiously do something. *Resting in God can be a form of worship, a declaration that he is God and we are not.* For us, 'Sabbath' can mean carving out regular time to be with God, cease our busyness, and trust Him with what's unfinished. It can also mean internally resting from anxiety because we know God is faithful. Holy Saturday ended with no visible miracle yet, but the faithful still honoured God. In our timeline, we know that after the rest comes victory. The eternal 'rest' that Christ secured is not the rest of a corpse, but *the joyful rest of a completed rescue*. Revelation 14:13 echoes, 'Blessed are the dead who die in the Lord . . . they rest from their labours, for their deeds follow them.' Because of Jesus, even death for a believer is transformed into a peaceful sleep and entry into God's rest, not a fearful unknown. Therefore we can lie down in peace each night (Psalm 4:8) knowing our lives are safely in his hands. *The silence of God is not absence; it is often the prelude to a greater revelation of his power.*

Life Application Questions:

- Have you ever experienced a 'silent Saturday' season in your life—a time between crisis and resolution when God seemed quiet? How did you (or how can you) practice trusting and resting in God during that waiting period?
- In what practical ways can you build a rhythm of rest into your life that demonstrates your confidence in God's finished work (for example: observing a Sabbath day, setting aside time for prayer and reflection, or mentally releasing control of a situation to God)?

Reflection 7: Eternal Rest and Victory – Resurrection and New Creation

Old Testament (Isaiah 25:8): 'He will swallow up death forever; and the Lord GOD will wipe away tears from all faces, and the reproach of his people he will take away from all the earth, for the LORD has spoken.'

New Testament (1 Corinthians 15:57): 'But thanks be to God, who gives us the victory through our Lord Jesus Christ.'

Psalm (Psalm 16:10): 'For you will not abandon my soul to Sheol, or let your holy one see corruption.'

The Dawn of Victory: Early Sunday morning, *the third day*, the quiet of the tomb was shattered—Jesus rose from the dead, conquering death itself. Everything Jesus accomplished on the cross is validated and amplified by the resurrection. The Psalmist had foretold, 'You will not abandon my soul to Sheol (the grave), or let your Holy One see corruption (decay)'. He was raised to life in glory. This event is the ultimate victory moment in God's salvation story. Paul exults in 1 Corinthians 15: 'Thanks be to God, who gives us the victory through our Lord Jesus Christ!' . The 'victory' here specifically refers to *victory over sin and death*. Because Jesus lives, death has lost its sting for those who are in him. Historically, the resurrection turned scared disciples into bold witnesses and has been the cornerstone of Christian faith ever since. It is God's vindication of His Son and the proof that the atonement was accepted. Jesus is the *first fruits* of those who have fallen asleep—meaning His resurrection is the first of many. We too will share in a resurrection because of Him. This is why Isaiah 25:8's prophecy is so powerful: *'He will swallow up death forever'*. Through Christ, this has been set in motion. Death was swallowed in victory on that Easter morning; and when Christ comes again, that victory will be universally manifest—no more death, no more tears.

Eternal Rest in God's Presence: *The phrase 'eternal rest' doesn't imply idleness or boredom; it means the fullness of peace and wholeness in God's presence.* Because Jesus defeated death, believers look forward to entering God's eternal rest—a state of perfect joy, where all strivings cease and every wound is healed. Revelation 21:4 echoes Isaiah: God will wipe every tear from our eyes, and mourning, pain, and crying will be no more. The resurrection of Jesus is the guarantee of our eternal future. Psalm 16:10 is followed by verse 11, which rejoices, 'In your presence there is fullness of joy; at your right hand are pleasures forevermore.' *This is the eternal rest and victory—unbroken fellowship with God in a renewed creation.* Paul in 1 Corinthians 15:55–57 taunts death: 'O death, where is your victory? O death, where is your sting?' The sting of death is sin, and the power of sin is the law. But thanks be to God, who gives us the victory through our Lord Jesus Christ. Death is now a defeated foe. We will still die physically (unless Christ returns first), but death for us is like sleep—we awake to new life at the last day and we do not fear the grave. Eternal life isn't just length of life, but a quality of life—knowing God (John 17:3: 'And this is eternal life, that they know you, the only true God, and Jesus Christ whom you have sent')—that starts now and carries on into eternity.

Living in Victory: The resurrection calls us to live victoriously. 'Thanks be to God!' is a cry of praise—we didn't achieve this victory; God gave it to us in Christ. Therefore our lives should be marked by gratitude and confidence. We fight our battles (whether against sin, despair, or external opposition) not for victory, *but from a place of victory*. We know the ending of the story: Jesus wins, and in him, we win too. This gives us courage to persevere. After 1 Corinthians 15:57, Paul immediately says, 'Therefore . . . be steadfast, immovable, always abounding in the work of the Lord, knowing that in the Lord your labour is not in vain.' Because of the resurrection, anything done for Christ has eternal significance. Easter Sunday fills our hearts with hope. *The darkest Friday led to the brightest Sunday.* So in our darkest moments, we cling to the hope of resurrection. Eternal rest and victory also comfort us as we think of loved ones in Christ who have died—we know we will see them again, restored, because Jesus' tomb is empty. Isaiah's prophecy of God wiping away tears reminds us that whatever sorrows we carry, God will ultimately redeem. He will right every wrong and dry every tear. *Our destiny in Christ is not an endless grave, but a new heaven and new earth where righteousness dwells.* Thus we end this Good Friday study not in sorrow, but in triumph and anticipation. The cross and the empty tomb together tell us that all that was lost in the Fall will be restored and more. Eden will be eclipsed by the glory of New Creation. We will enjoy eternal Sabbath rest—celebrating God's completed work—and share forever in Christ's victory.

Life Application Questions:

- How does the reality of Jesus' resurrection influence the way you face fear or discouragement? Can you identify areas in your life where you need to apply the truth of Christ's victory?
- In what ways can you live as an Easter person, demonstrating hope, joy, and 'victory through our Lord Jesus Christ' in your daily life, especially in a world that still experiences death and tears?
- What do I need to surrender in order to rest in God's Final victory?

Introduction to Judas

Who am I
What am I
If a single kiss can unmake a soul?
My life not ordained; I made a choice.

The figure of Judas Iscariot looms large in the collective imagination—a name synonymous with betrayal and treachery. Yet behind the infamous act lies a human story, one marked by disillusionment, pride, regret, and ultimately, despair. In writing *'Judas'*, I sought to explore this complex character, not to excuse his actions, but to give voice to his inner turmoil and the theological weight of his choices. This is an extremely complex theological and moral and spiritual dilemma involving an equally complex character who saw 'good' for his people in a way that was expected in those times but radically different from Christ's vision. Authors over 2,000 years have grappled with him. I have tried bringing to you his story in a simple demystified way. I do not take sides, and I leave it to you to draw your own conclusions. It is the most challenging poem I have written to date. I also invite you into a theological meditation on free will, destiny, and redemption.

This poem unfolds as a journey through the mind of Judas after his act of betrayal, tracing his descent from misguided zeal to devastating self-awareness. It is not a confession seeking redemption, but a lament shaped by the collision of idealism and tragic error. Judas, the revolutionary, failed to grasp that the kingdom Jesus preached was not one of political revolt but of transformative love. In the end, the kiss meant to signify devotion became the mark of ultimate betrayal.

One of the central tensions in this poem is the juxtaposition of Judas' hopes and Jesus' teachings—his desire for liberation through force against Christ's call to humility and mercy. Judas' tragic flaw is not merely his act of betrayal but his fundamental misunderstanding of the Messiah he followed. The poem's structure reflects this unravelling:

from panic to remorse, from defiance to a shattered realization of his moral blindness.

The inclusion of the Shema at the poem's conclusion was deliberate. In that final breath, Judas does not appeal for forgiveness directly, but he returns to the foundational prayer of his faith, suggesting that even in the depth of despair, the echo of belief persists. It leaves the question open: Can one who has betrayed Love itself still find a place within the embrace of divine mercy? I explore this further at the end of this introduction. It is necessary to understand it from the Jewish perspective as it gives a further insight into Judas' tortured soul wrestling with his Jewish faith.

The potter's wheel metaphor referencing both Jeremiah and Romans is discussed in more detail in the annotations after the poem. I added this stanza as it changes the poem into a more hopeful coda, pointing out that even Judas' brokenness and for that matter our own brokenness, no matter how severe, is not beyond divine transformation

The final line—'Am I finished?'—is both startling and profound. Instead of closing with resignation, it opens a space for reflection, asking whether Judas' fate is sealed or whether grace might yet reach him. It challenges you, the reader to consider whether even the most grievous betrayal can be beyond redemption. By leaving the conclusion open-ended, I invite readers to sit with the discomfort of that uncertainty—a discomfort that mirrors Judas' own tortured soul but with a hope that the potter sees all and can mend and save all with his limitless compassion and love.

By giving Judas this voice, I do not seek to redeem his actions, but to acknowledge his humanity—the flawed, frail soul caught between conviction and catastrophe. In his final moments, Judas' cry becomes a mirror for all who have wrestled with guilt and the longing for forgiveness. It is a poetic meditation on the cost of pride, the blindness of zeal, and the tragedy of realizing the truth too late.

I invite you to read this monologue not as a defence, but as a solemn exploration of remorse—a voice from the shadows that still seeks, perhaps vainly, the light it once knew.

The following reflections is important to understand my reason for structuring the poem the way I did, adding the stanza on the potter's wheel and the Shema Prayer:

1. Judas and the Master Potter: A Reflection on Free Will and Divine Providence

Judas Iscariot, the disciple who betrayed Christ, did so not because he was ordained or predestined to do so. Rather his betrayal was an act of his own free will. This concept is often difficult for us to comprehend because, as human beings, we are bound within the universe and the linear flow of time. God, however, exists beyond this temporal realm—outside the arrow of time—and, in his infinite wisdom, grants humanity the gift of free will.

In this divine framework, Judas always had the choice to betray or to remain faithful. God, respecting the autonomy he has given to humankind, did not force Judas to act in any specific way. Yet once Judas made his choice, God—like a master potter—used that decision as part of his larger redemptive plan.

This idea can be better understood through the analogy of the potter's wheel. Imagine the potter's wheel as the universe, constantly moving and evolving. The clay on the wheel represents humanity and all creation, shaped by the movements of time. God, the potter, skilfully moulds the clay as the wheel turns. If the clay develops a flaw—a dent, an imperfection—the potter does not discard it. Instead, he reshapes and remoulds it, ensuring that the final vessel still fulfils its intended purpose.

Similarly, God did not stop the betrayal, just as he did not stop Joseph from being sold into slavery by his brothers. In both cases, human actions stemmed from personal choices. However, once those choices were made, God, with his masterful hands, transformed the consequences into opportunities for good. Joseph's betrayal led to the preservation of his family and the salvation of many during a famine. Judas' betrayal, though a tragic moral failure, became the catalyst for the Passion, ultimately leading to the salvation of humanity through Christ's death and resurrection. While God foreknew the betrayal, he did not force Judas' hand, preserving both divine omniscience and human accountability.

Had Judas not chosen betrayal, God would have found another way to accomplish his redemptive plan. However, Judas' decision became the reality; and God, in his sovereignty, used even that betrayal for a greater purpose. If even the betrayal of the Son of God can be woven into the tapestry of salvation, it implies that no personal failure is irredeemable. In this sense, while Judas bears responsibility for his choice, God's providence remains supreme, ensuring that even flawed human decisions can be transformed into part of his divine masterpiece.

2. The Shema (שְׁמַע יִשְׂרָאֵל, 'Hear, O Israel')

This is a central declaration of faith in Judaism, expressing the fundamental belief in the oneness of God. It is traditionally recited twice daily (morning and evening) and is also recited at the end of one's life. Here are the key reasons why it is recited before death:

A. Affirmation of Faith:

- The Shema is essentially a declaration of the absolute unity and sovereignty of God:

    'Hear, O Israel: the Lord our God, the Lord is one.' (Deuteronomy 6:4)

- By reciting the Shema at the moment of death, a Jewish person reaffirms their lifelong faith in God. It is an ultimate expression of loyalty to God, even in the face of death.

B. A Connection to Martyrdom and Sacrifice:

- The Talmud recounts that Rabbi Akiva, while being tortured to death by the Romans, recited the Shema as his final words. When his students asked him how he could endure the pain, he explained that he had always desired to fulfil the commandment to love God with all his soul, even if it meant sacrificing his life (Berakhot 61b).
- This story has deeply influenced Jewish tradition, making the recitation of the Shema at the time of death symbolic of the ultimate act of devotion.

C. A Tradition Rooted in Scripture:

- The Shema itself contains the command to recite these words 'when you lie down and when you rise up' (Deuteronomy 6:7). This has been interpreted as encompassing the entirety of life, including the final moments.
- The recitation of Shema before death is seen as fulfilling the biblical injunction to always have God's unity on one's lips and heart.

D. A Proclamation of God's Kingship:

- In Jewish thought, the acknowledgment of God's kingship at death is significant because it signifies acceptance of God's will, including the passage from life to death.
- The Shema proclaims God's eternal rule, reinforcing the belief that life and death are under divine sovereignty.

E. Comfort and Spiritual Readiness:

- Saying the Shema can bring comfort, as it is familiar and connects the dying person to their lifelong practices.
- It serves as a final preparation for the soul's departure, reflecting the hope of returning to God.

F. Unity of the Jewish People:

- Since the Shema is a communal declaration, reciting it at death symbolizes unity with the entire Jewish people across generations.
- It links the individual with those who have recited it before, both in daily life and at the moment of death.

Summary:

Reciting the Shema before death is a profound act of faith, affirming God's oneness and sovereignty. It is inspired by biblical commandments, the example of martyrs, and the desire to enter the next world with a declaration of devotion. This tradition, deeply rooted in Jewish liturgy and practice, serves as a spiritual anchor at life's end.

JUDAS

Who what am I
What am I
If a single kiss can unmake a soul?
My life not ordained; I made a choice.

I run—
as fast as I can
as far as I can go.
There is no hiding place for me
no corner for my soul to rest.
Even if I flee to the ends of the Earth.

I have failed the cause I fought for.
I lost my way into a dark void.
The path I chose, which seemed straight and right
This was the path of death.
but now I know, as it is written
only God sees the end.

I shouted for freedom
but chose myself over others.
I fought against tyranny
but sought only to advance myself.

I agitated and disrupted without a plan—
no vision beyond the moment.
Into the pit I descended.
Thus, I betrayed the One
who came to save us all.

I tried, I judged, I sentenced, and I betrayed—
for thirty coins of silver
when I should have listened

loved, and prayed.
With one kiss, I stripped away my humanity.
My crime—
I sentenced Love to die.

I run and run
I hide and I fall.
But where can I flee
from the Living God?

My thoughts race, my soul aches.
If only I had turned from pride
perhaps I would have seen the light.
Perhaps the true path—
the truth—
would have revealed itself.

Why, Lord, did I not understand?
I cried for salvation—
but you said, 'Blessed are the meek'.
I longed for freedom from oppression—
but you said, 'Love your enemies'.

I wanted to rise and fight—
but you called peacemakers sons of God.
I sought to be as cunning as the Romans—
but you preached righteousness
and mercy.

Your kingdom—
it overturned every kingdom I had imagined.
You were not the King I waited for
I could not understand
that love would win the war.
Misguided in looking for a warrior

I should have sought the Messiah—Hashem
With arrogance and hubris, I looked inward to myself.

The Scriptures were hollow empty words.
I turned away from them
They had foretold this
They had revealed Him—
but pride blinded me.
Like a veil in front of me, I could not see
that true freedom
comes not through fight or fury
but through humility
love
and sacrifice
The word of God is the true sword that pierces all.

I see it now—
I have cast an abyss before me
wide and eternal.
No bridge can span it.
No road returns.

This life is not meant for me.
I have no refuge.
The Son of Man I betrayed
now walks the road I should have taken.

I did not understand that your mission
Was winning the war over evil
with redemption, salvation, and eternal life as your gift.
All the while I was obsessed
with winning a single battle.

Future generations will judge me.
Let my life be a lesson:
that anger, agitation, and hate
even when cloaked in noble cause
or righteous fire
will always dissolve
into misery.

I am not worthy of the gift of life
to bear His image
to be in His likeness.

As I gaze upon the valley of the shadow of death
I have no comfort—only misery.
And when I am gone
It will be called Akeldama—
The field of blood.

I am a mistake that must be erased.
To remove myself from eternity
to pay the price of betrayal
with my final breath.

My Lord, my God—
why did I forsake You?
I return the silver
but the deed cannot be undone.
I was the beast that surrounded You.
I am the evil You came to conquer.

In this last act
I return the gift of life I am not worthy of.
Where you send me, I accept.
To Sheol I will go.

Better death
than undeserved life.

Forgive me . . .
if forgiveness still lives for me.
But I knew not what I had done.

Shema Israel, Elohim, Eloheinu, Echad.

The wheel turns—time's relentless hand
Clay spinning, flawed, within His plan.
The potter sees each crack and mar,
Yet moulds the vessel as it scars.

Am I finished?

Annotation

Opening: The Flight and the Fall

I run—
as fast as I can
as far as I can go.
There is no hiding place for me
no corner for my soul to rest.

Biblical Reference: Psalm 139:7–8

'Where can I go from your Spirit? Where can I flee from your presence? If I go up to the heavens, you are there; if I make my bed in the depths, you are there.'

- These lines reflect Judas' futile attempt to escape divine justice and his own guilt. They echo David's realization that one cannot hide from God, highlighting the inescapable presence of the divine even in guilt.

The Cause Betrayed: Idealism Gone Wrong

I have failed the cause I fought for.
I lost my way into a dark void.
The path I chose, which seemed straight and right
This was the path of death.
but now I know, as it is written
only God sees the end.

Biblical Reference: Proverbs 14:12

'There is a way that appears to be right, but in the end it leads to death.'

- Judas, in his zeal for political freedom and justice, chose a path that seemed righteous but led to betrayal and death. The line highlights the danger of human certainty when separated from divine wisdom.

Misguided Zeal and Selfish Ambition

I shouted for freedom,
but chose myself over others.
I fought against tyranny
but sought only to advance myself.

Biblical Reference: John 12:4–6

Judas criticizes the use of expensive perfume, not out of concern for the poor but because he was a thief.

- Judas' political ambitions and selfish motives are revealed. This stanza examines his fundamental flaw: placing personal gain above communal good, contrasting with Jesus' self-giving love.

Descent and Betrayal

I agitated and disrupted without a plan—
no vision beyond the moment.
Into the pit I descended.
Thus, I betrayed the One
who came to save us all.

Biblical Reference: Matthew 26:14–16

'Then one of the Twelve—the one called Judas Iscariot—went to the chief priests and asked, "What are you willing to give me if I deliver him over to you?" So they counted out for him thirty pieces of silver.'

- The poem captures Judas' impulsiveness and lack of foresight, aligning with the biblical narrative where Judas acts hastily and without considering the eternal consequences.

The Kiss of Betrayal

With one kiss, I stripped away my humanity.
My crime—
I sentenced Love to die.

Biblical Reference: Matthew 26:48–50

'Now the betrayer had arranged a signal with them: "The one I kiss is the man; arrest him".'

- The kiss, meant to be a sign of intimacy and friendship, becomes the act of ultimate treachery. Judas' admission that he stripped away his humanity with this act reflects the profound moral corruption involved.

Fleeing from God

I run and run
I hide and I fall.
But where can I flee
from the Living God?

Biblical Reference: Psalm 139:11–12

'If I say, "Surely the darkness will hide me", the night will shine like the day.'

- Judas' flight mirrors the universal human desire to escape guilt, but he acknowledges that God's presence is inescapable.

Blindness to Divine Truth

I wanted to rise and fight—
but You called peacemakers sons of God.
I sought to be as cunning as the Romans—
but you preached righteousness
and mercy.

Biblical Reference: Matthew 5:9

'Blessed are the peacemakers, for they will be called children of God.'

- Judas' expectation of a political Messiah clashes with Jesus' teachings on peace and humility. This reflects the misguided zeal that leads to his downfall.

Clarity of Mission

I did not understand that your mission
Was winning the war over evil
with redemption, salvation, and eternal life as your gift.

Biblical references:

1. **John 3:16:** 'For God so Loved the world that he gave his only begotten Son that whoever believes in him shall not perish but have everlasting life.'
2. **Romans 6:23:** 'For the wages of sin is death, but the gift of God is eternal life in Christ Jesus our Lord.'

This shifts from political liberation to the redemptive power of the Cross. Judas failed to grasp this deeper gift from Christ.

Return and Regret

I return the silver,
but the deed cannot be undone.

Biblical Reference: Matthew 27:3–4

'When Judas, who had betrayed him, saw that Jesus was condemned, he was seized with remorse and returned the thirty pieces of silver to the chief priests and the elders.'

- The act of returning the silver is a futile attempt to undo the irreversible. The tragic irony lies in realizing too late that repentance without understanding cannot erase the betrayal.

Seeking a Warrior, Finding a Messiah:

You were not the King I waited for,
I could not understand
that love would win the war.

Biblical Reference: John 18:36

'My kingdom is not of this world.'

- Judas' mistake was in expecting a conquering political leader rather than a spiritual saviour who would conquer through sacrifice.

Looking Inwards

I should have sought the Messiah—Hashem
With arrogance and hubris, I looked inward to myself.

St Augustine described the heart of our fallen state *'incurvatus in se'*, humanity curved in on itself. When our lives are turned inward on ourselves, we embody the curse.

Consequences and Death:

As I gaze upon the valley of the shadow of death
I have no comfort—only misery.
And when I am gone
It will be called Akeldama—
The field of blood.

Biblical References:

1. **Psalm 23:4:** *'Though I walk through the valley of the shadow of death . . .'*
2. **Acts 1:18–19:** Akeldama as the field of blood, where Judas' betrayal and demise are memorialized.
   - The field of blood symbolizes both physical consequence and eternal guilt, marking the place where betrayal meets judgment.

Final Question of Redemption

Shema Israel, Elohim, Eloheinu, Echad. (Hear O Israel, The Lord God is One)
Am I finished?

Biblical Reference:

1. **Deuteronomy 6:4**
   'Hear, O Israel: The Lord our God, the Lord is one.'
   - Judas' last words are a return to the core of Jewish faith, suggesting a final plea for recognition or reconciliation with God.

2. **Jeremiah 18:1–6**
   'Like clay in the hand of the potter, so are you in my hand.'

3. **Romans 9:21**
   'Does not the potter have the right to make out of the same lump of clay some pottery for special purposes and some for common use?'

The potter's wheel serves as a final metaphor between human choice and divine sovereignty. While Judas sees himself as irreparably broken, a vessel marred by betrayal, the image of the potter suggests that even flawed clay can be remoulded and redeemed. It introduces hope that, despite human failure, the Master Potter may still shape the vessel into something of purpose, even through its scars.

The question **"Am I finished?"** transforms Judas' fate from finality to ambiguity, raising the question, *Is divine forgiveness possible, even now?*

FROM LAW TO LIFE : SIN, CONVERSION AND THE FLAME OF THE SPIRIT

From Law to Life : Sin, Conversion and the Flame of the Spirit

This section marks a pivotal passage in the journey of the soul—a theological and spiritual arc that moves from the burden of sin under the Law, to the moment of personal conversion, and finally to the indwelling presence of the Holy Spirit. These three poems—**The Power of Sin Is the Law, Paul: A Life Overturned,** and **The Holy Spirit: The Breath of God Made Life**—are not merely separate meditations. Together, they form a narrative of transformation.

I have placed this section here—just before the poems on the martyrs—to show that we, too, have the power and the will to endure and overcome trials today. The courage of the martyrs was not drawn from themselves, but from the Spirit who lives within. The Word of the Lord is enough—but only when it is truly heard, understood as it was intended, and not filtered through convenience, fear, or cultural distortion. This section is a reminder that the same Spirit who sustained Paul and the other Apostles is offered to us—and that we are called to respond with clarity, courage, and faith.

We begin with the stark reality that even the Law, though holy, can be misused—*The Power of Sin Is the Law* explores how sin hides beneath virtue, how the letter without the Spirit can become a weapon. This poem asks us to confront the truth that religion without love, law without grace, can become a mask for evil. It is the theological foundation and warning: that without the Spirit, even holy things may decay.

Then we meet Paul—*A Life Overturned*—whose journey is our own. From zealous adherence to the Law to his dramatic encounter with Christ, Paul becomes a vessel of grace. His transformation is not instant perfection, but a process of surrender, of being remade. This poem speaks in his voice, but it also speaks for every soul who has ever been called out of blindness into light, from violence into mercy, from control into love.

Finally, *The Holy Spirit: The Breath of God Made Life* invites us into the mystery of the Spirit Himself—the divine Person who sustains us beyond the moment of conversion. It is the Spirit who breathes life into dry bones, who comforts, teaches, sanctifies, and refines. This poem dares to imagine the Spirit's own voice speaking to us, not with thunder, but with patient tenderness. It is here that the journey culminates—not just in salvation, but in communion.

These poems, together, trace the inner pilgrimage of every believer: from the bondage of sin, to the breaking open of the heart, to the burning presence of God within. This is the pattern of grace. This is the path of life in Christ.

May these poems not only be read, but prayed. May they illuminate both your struggles and your longings. And above all, may they lead you to that still, small voice that speaks eternal love into the deepest parts of your soul. I have added reflection questions for each poem.

Introduction to 'The Power of Sin Is the Law'

This poem stands as one of the most important in this collection. It marks a nexus point—where theory meets practice, where theology confronts the human heart. At this pivotal juncture, unless one's heart and mind are truly aligned with God, even something as sacred as the Law can falter. The Law, in its essence, is holy. But without grace, it can become a closed box. The heart aligned to Christ is the key—and when that key is placed into the lock, the box opens, and out pours a life rightly ordered: full of love, compassion, and mercy.

Without that key, however, the Law becomes rigid, lifeless—something that can be used to justify apathy, spiritual isolation, or even hidden sin. This is what Paul means when he says, *'The power of sin is the law'* (1 Corinthians 15:56). Sin misuses what is good. It cloaks itself in righteousness, hiding behind commandments while resisting the transformation that love demands.

Throughout salvation history, this danger has been recognized. Even the greatest of the faithful—Abraham, Habakkuk, Job—wrestled with God, not in rebellion, but in longing to understand divine justice. Abraham pleaded, *'Will not the Judge of all the earth do right'*(Genesis 18:25), daring to question the destruction of the righteous with the wicked. Habakkuk cried out in anguish, *'Why do you tolerate wrongdoing?'*(Habakkuk 1:3). These were not denials of God's goodness but affirmations of it—a desperate appeal that what is done in God's name must reflect His character.

And this is why discernment is essential. Not everything done in the name of God is from God. Scripture itself warns us of false prophets, misapplied law, and hardened hearts. We must constantly seek the Spirit's guidance to know whether what we follow is truly from the Lord—or merely human tradition, fear, or ambition wearing holy robes. The Law without love can become a sword turned inward, cutting down rather than lifting up. But when God's command is truly discerned, it is always rooted in mercy, humility, and the cross.

In our time, the danger remains. Law is often quoted—but twisted, used not to lift burdens, but to avoid responsibility. It becomes an excuse for not acting, a way to retreat into spiritual silos rather than enter into communion with God and others. The Kingdom of God calls us to more than private righteousness; it calls us into community, into communion, and into the full expression of love.

That is why this poem is more than reflection—it is a warning and a plea. It reminds us that Scripture is not a modern novel to be casually interpreted or personalized without context. It belongs to a sacred tradition. That tradition includes a discipline of reading, a humility before the text, and a commitment to bridge the temporal and cultural gap between biblical authors and ourselves. This is the very strategy I have used throughout this book: to inhabit the minds and voices of biblical figures, to bring the reader back to their world, to their suffering, to their hope.

In *The Power of Sin Is the Law*, we are invited to see with Paul's eyes, albeit at a distance, the subtle but devastating ways sin can mask itself in piety. My next poem is a reflection through the 'skin' of Paul.

In more recent times, C.S. Lewis *absolutely* emphasizes in *The Abolition of Man* the need for more than just raw feeling or detached intellect. He argues for the formation of the *chest*—that part of the human person where trained emotion, rightly ordered affection, and reasoned discernment meet. It is this middle element that connects the cerebral mind with the visceral gut: not simply what we *feel*, and not merely what we *think*, but what we *ought to love* and how we ought to respond.

The following three points compare the Abolition of Man by CS Lewis and the poem:-

1. Lewis on Discernment and Ordered Affection

> In *The Abolition of Man*, Lewis critiques the 'Conditioners' of his day for producing 'men without chests'—that is, human beings who are either led solely by appetite or driven only by cold reason, but who lack the cultivated inner faculty to *discern rightly*. He writes:

'The head rules the belly through the chest—the seat of Magnanimity, of emotions organized by trained habit into stable sentiments.'

Lewis argues that proper moral judgment comes from *trained and rightly ordered desires*. He's drawing on the same tradition as Augustine and Aquinas: we must *love what is truly lovable,* and this love must be *formed*, not invented.

2. The Poem's Insight: Law Without Discernment Is Dangerous

In my poem, I show how sin can co-opt the law—twist it, hide behind it, weaponize it. And this is precisely why mere intellectual assent or emotional sympathy is not enough. As I say:

'The Law—its form etched in script,
Empty of Spirit.
Its true intent unmasked only
When pursued in prayer.'

This line is especially telling. It reflects what Lewis (and Paul) warn against: the *letter* of the law kills when it is disconnected from the Spirit. That is, without *discernment*—without the integration of heart, mind, and covenantal love—we are left with either legalism or lawlessness.

3. Faith, Covenantal Love, and Redemption as Discernment Lenses

To rightly interpret and act on Scripture, the poem points out that we must ingest it—not just read it or feel it—but *let it read us* and be transformed. This echoes James 1:22–25 (being not hearers only, but doers), and Hebrews 4:12, where the Word 'discerns the thoughts and attitudes of the heart.' That's the

The Word in their Voices

kind of discernment Lewis believes education should instill—not just "thinking" but *moral vision*.

And in this, the same essential point is made in the poem: *Scripture is not self-interpreting apart from the Spirit.* The Law, unmoored from the Person of Christ, becomes a shell—or worse, a trap.

We are challenged to go beyond legalism and enter into a relationship—where the Law, fulfilled by love, becomes a torch, a song, a path. It is here that the Law, far from being a burden, breathes again—through Christ, and in the Spirit.

THE POWER OF SIN IS THE LAW

'The letter kills, but the Spirit gives life.' (2 Corinthians 3:6)

Law, pure—made for holy order.
Sin, vile—birthed in chaos and revolt.
Two apparent foes—
What strange bedfellows!

Sin, when naked, is revolting.
But dressed in the linen of law
It hides its stench beneath propriety
And makes the unthinkable acceptable.

Cloaked in virtue
Sin walks unrecognized.
The Law becomes its garment,
And evil earns applause.

But beneath the finery
Its marks are indelible—
Etched deep, not of God.
The Law, now only a shadow in its wake.

To say 'Here I am' to God's call,
Is to respond to the Law
with Grace and Love.
Suffering and sacrifice—
The cost of discipleship.

Yet how easy to feign goodwill,
Hiding behind commandments.
The spirit of Law now falls silent
What remains—an empty shell.
In silence, a coward is revealed.

The Law—so often quoted,
So quickly twisted—
A shield for those
Unwilling to act.
'It belongs to another age,' they claim—
A law no longer ours to obey.

The Law meant to guide
Now serves the ends of the indolent.
What was made to save is dimmed—
Now a flicker, its spirit ignored—
Used to sanctify sin.

The shallow obey blindly—
Dotting the i's, crossing the t's—
Never reading the sentence.
Their misplaced zeal forges chains
Their altar, their Baal.

And so, the Law becomes excuse:
No longer a call, but a pause.
What they fear, they bury in doctrine.

They fear the Cross
Afraid of the cost,
They preach the Law
But miss its soul
And stand frozen—
where love should burn

With Love as its soul
Law becomes the torch that
Illumines The Way.
Without it, Law is stone
But with it—Law breathes
It heals. It lifts. It transforms.

The Law completed with Love:
Full of Grace, without conflict
Always in communion—
To bind what sin has torn,
To be set free, not to be shackled again.

Sin recoils when alone—
It prowls in the shadows
Cunning, clothed, prepared
Like a predator—
Ready to devour.

False respectability
when dressed in Law
Sin earns applause—tempting
Like the fruit in Eden.

But its core is rot—
So too our hearts,
When we justify
what we should repent.

The Law—its form etched in script
Empty of Spirit.
It's true intent unmasked only
When pursued in prayer.

By the transforming grace of Christ
The letter turns to love—
Written not on stone, but in the heart
To transform, not to conform.

Then—and only then—
The Law is a song with power.
And that power when sung
Is Love.

The Word in their Voices | 123

ANNOTATIONS : THE POWER OF SIN IS THE LAW

'The letter kills, but the Spirit gives life.' (2 Corinthians 3:6)

- This epigraph echoes the heart of Pauline theology: the Law, when followed without the Spirit, condemns (cf. *Romans 7:9–11*). Paul sees the Law as good (*Romans 7:12*), but when co-opted by sin, it becomes a mechanism for death rather than life. The 'letter' refers to mere external observance; the 'Spirit' refers to inward transformation through grace.
- Augustine comments similarly in *On the Spirit and the Letter* (AD 412):
'The Law was given not to justify, but to convict and make men long for grace.'

Stanza-by-Stanza Annotations

Stanza 1

Law, pure—made for holy order.
Sin, vile—birthed in chaos and revolt.
Two apparent foes—
What strange bedfellows!

- **Scriptural echo:** Romans 7:12 affirms that *'the law is holy, and the commandment is holy, righteous and good.'* Yet sin uses even this good to cause death (Romans 7:10-13).
- **'What strange bedfellows' evokes irony:** law and sin are opposed in essence, yet in fallen humanity, they can cooperate destructively.
- **Augustine (Confessions, Book VII):** Augustine speaks of the 'law of sin' that works within him, even as he knows God's law is good.

- **Ignatian note:** The tension here invites discernment—how can a good be manipulated to evil? This is a central concern in Ignatian spirituality.

Stanza 2

Sin, when naked, is revolting.
But dressed in the linen of law
It hides its stench beneath propriety
And makes the unthinkable acceptable.

- **Literary power:** The image of linen (priestly or ritualistic purity) being used to disguise sin heightens the sense of desecration.
- **Franciscan echo:** St. Francis detested pretense and worldliness disguised as piety. Here, sin uses the garments of ritual to mask its corruption.
- **Biblical link:** Matthew 23:27 – 'whitewashed tombs... beautiful on the outside but full of dead men's bones.'

Stanza 3

Cloaked in virtue
Sin walks unrecognized.
The Law becomes its garment
And evil earns applause.

- **Theme of hypocrisy:** This is a critique not of law per se, but its misuse. Law becomes a costume.
- **Modern resonance:** Sin cloaked in social virtue—justice distorted, morality politicized—wins approval.
- **Augustine's thought:** In *City of God*, he warns that without true justice, states become bands of robbers.

Stanza 4

But beneath the finery
Its marks are indelible—
Etched deep, not of God.
The Law, now only a shadow in its wake.

- **Imagery of engraving:** A contrast to the law written on stone or hearts—this mark is etched by sin.
- **Shadow of the Law:** Colossians 2:17 speaks of the Law as a shadow of things to come, 'the reality, however, is found in Christ.'

Stanza 5

To say 'Here I am' to God's call
Is to respond to the Law
with Grace and Love.
Suffering and sacrifice—
The cost of discipleship.

- **Biblical foundation:** Isaiah 6:8 – 'Here I am, send me.' Also Luke 9:23 – 'take up your cross daily.'
- Law with Grace and Love recalls John 1:17 – 'The law was given through Moses; grace and truth came through Jesus Christ.'
- **Ignatian dimension:** This is sacrificial love over legal compliance. The letter yields to the Spirit; justice yields to discerning mercy; where the follower of Christ becomes not a servant under the Law but a companion of Jesus, walking the way of the Cross out of love, not duty.

Stanza 6

Yet how easy to feign goodwill
Hiding behind commandments.
The spirit of Law now falls silent,
What remains—an empty shell.
In silence, a coward is revealed.

- **Jesus and Pharisees:** Mark 7:6-8 – 'They worship me in vain; their teachings are merely human rules.'
- **Franciscan poverty of spirit:** calls for radical authenticity; this stanza critiques religious cowardice.
- **Augustinian struggle:** Augustine saw his pre-conversion life as a façade of virtue hiding lust and pride.

Stanza 7

The Law—so often quoted
So quickly twisted—
A shield for those
Unwilling to act.
'It belongs to another age,' they claim—
A law no longer ours to obey.

- **Modern relativism:** echoes how moral truth is dismissed as outdated.
- **Romans 10:4** – 'Christ is the culmination of the law...' not its cancellation, but its perfection.
- **Augustine's De Doctrina Christiana:** Scripture must be interpreted in the spirit of love, not used as cover.

Stanza 8

The Law meant to guide
Now serves the ends of the indolent.
What was made to save is dimmed—

The Word in their Voices

Now a flicker, its spirit ignored—
Used to sanctify sin.

- **Galatians 3:24:** 'The law was our guardian until Christ came.'
- Sanctifying sin is the gravest irony—when evil becomes respectable under sacred symbols.
- **Franciscan challenge:** How does one live purely without enabling the misuse of spiritual tools?

Stanza 9

The shallow obey blindly—
Dotting the i's, crossing the t's—
Never reading the sentence.
Their misplaced zeal forges chains
Their altar, their Baal.

- **Powerful allusion:** The golden calf (Exodus 32) represents worship distorted by fear and impatience.
- 'Never reading the sentence' is a cutting image of legalism without comprehension or relationship.
- **Ignatian insight:** False zeal lacks discernment; true obedience listens to the *spirit* of the law.

Stanza 10

And so, the Law becomes excuse:
No longer a call, but a pause.
What they fear, they bury in doctrine.

- **Key insight:** Doctrinal correctness used to delay true conversion or avoid risk.
- **Luke 11:46:** 'You load people down with burdens they can hardly carry…'
- **Augustine:** Truth unites, fear divides. Doctrines become tombs when not enlivened by love.

Stanza 11

They fear the Cross
Afraid of the cost,
They preach the Law,
But miss its soul
And stand frozen—
where love should burn

- **Luke 14:27:** 'Whoever does not carry their cross and follow me cannot be my disciple.'
- The image of being 'frozen' is stark—paralyzed orthodoxy, where fire (love) should kindle action.
- **Ignatian examen:** Where is love absent in our proclamation?

Stanza 12

With Love as its soul,
Law becomes the torch that
Illumines The Way.
Without it, Law is stone.
But with it—Law breathes.
It heals. It lifts. It transforms.

- **Psalm 119:105** – 'Your word is a lamp for my feet, a light on my path.'
- **'Law breathes':** recalls the Spirit (ruach/pneuma) that gives life—Genesis 2:7.
- **Augustine:** Love is the soul of the Law (*Letter 189*, to Fortunatus): *'Love, and do what you will.'*

Stanza 13

The Law completed with Love:
Full of Grace, without conflict
Always in communion—
To bind what sin has torn,
To be set free, not to be shackled again.

- **Romans 13:10:** 'Love is the fulfillment of the law.'
- **Galatians 5:1:** 'It is for freedom that Christ has set us free... do not let yourselves be burdened again.'
- **Franciscan note:** freedom is the fruit of communion, not rebellion.

Stanza 14

Sin recoils when alone—
It prowls in the shadows
Cunning, clothed, prepared
Like a predator—
Ready to devour.

- **1 Peter 5:8:** 'Your enemy the devil prowls around like a roaring lion...'
- **Sin seeks cover:** isolation is the strategy of temptation—separation from light, community, truth.

Stanza 15

False respectability
when dressed in Law,
Sin earns applause—tempting
Like the fruit in Eden.

- **Genesis 3:** 'pleasing to the eye and desirable for gaining wisdom.'

- **Augustine:** Pride is the root sin—seeking to be like God, but without God.
- **Modern relevance:** applause for sin masked as sophistication is a recurring prophetic theme.

Stanza 16

But its core is rot—
So too our hearts
When we justify
what we should repent.

- **Jeremiah 17:9:** 'The heart is deceitful above all things...'
- **True repentance:** requires unmasking justification and naming sin.
- **Ignatian examen:** calls us daily to repentance and to root out rationalization.

Stanza 17

The Law—its form etched in script
Empty of Spirit.
Its true intent unmasked only
When pursued in prayer.

- **2 Corinthians 3:6 (again):** 'the letter kills, but the Spirit gives life.'
- **Lectio Divina:** Prayer is what turns law into life.
- **Augustine:** 'Understanding is the reward of faith. Therefore seek not to understand that you may believe, but believe that you may understand.'

Stanza 18

By the transforming grace of Christ
The letter turns to love—
Written not on stone, but in the heart
To transform, not to conform.

- **Jeremiah 31:33 / Hebrews 8:10:** 'I will write my law on their hearts.'
- **Romans 12:2:** 'Be transformed by the renewing of your mind.'
- **Franciscan emphasis:** Grace renews the heart, not merely behavior.

Stanza 19 (Finale)

Then—and only then—
The Law is a song with power.
And that power when sung
Is Love.

- **Psalm 40:3:** 'He put a new song in my mouth…'
- **Augustinian aesthetics:** beauty and order reflect divine love. The law is not only command—it is harmony.
- **Franciscan joy:** the law is not burden, but melody, when animated by charity.

Reflection Questions

As this poem marks a pivotal hinge in the book—a turning point where the themes explored so far converge—I felt it important to offer a set of reflection questions. This moment serves as a kind of halfway mark: a guide to pause, take stock, and consider not only what we've learned, but where we are being called next.

Theoretical knowledge alone is not enough. Unless it translates into lived faith—into the way we love, serve, and discern—it remains abstract. With this spirit in mind, I offer these reflection questions as an invitation: to enter more deeply into the meaning of this poem, and to allow its insights to shape our journey forward.

1. Personal Alignment and the Heart
- Where in my life do I see a tension between outward obedience and inner surrender to God?
- Have I ever used religious knowledge or rules to avoid the harder demands of love, mercy, or forgiveness?
- What does it mean for my heart and mind to be 'aligned with God'? What blocks this alignment?

2. The Law and Love
- St. Paul says, *'The letter kills, but the Spirit gives life'* (2 Cor. 3:6). How do I understand the difference between following the letter of the law and living in its Spirit?
- How can I allow love to animate the commandments I follow? Is there a commandment I observe without love?
- In what ways do I see the Law of God as a closed box, and what would it look like for it to be opened by grace?

3. Sin Disguised as Righteousness
- The poem speaks of sin "cloaked in virtue" and "dressed in the linen of law." Where might I have mistaken false righteousness for holiness?

- Do I ever hide behind good intentions or religious forms to avoid true conversion or sacrifice?
- Am I tempted to use Scripture or tradition selectively—to justify myself, rather than to be transformed?

4. Community and Communion
- How has my understanding of the Law either isolated me or brought me into deeper communion with others?
- What role does Christian community play in helping me live out the Law as love rather than legalism?
- Do I see God's Law as something that fosters joy, healing, and freedom—or something burdensome?

5. Scripture and Tradition
- Do I approach Scripture as a living Word that speaks through tradition, or as something to be privately interpreted?
- How can I better integrate prayer, tradition, and study when engaging with the Bible?
- Am I willing to inhabit the mindset of biblical figures—to enter their world and learn from their struggles?

6. The Call to Discipleship
- The poem says, *'To bear the Cross of Christ, the cost of discipleship.'* What does bearing the Cross look like in my daily life?
- What am I afraid to lose by following Christ fully? What is the cost I hesitate to pay?

7. The Law as a Song of Love
- The poem ends by saying the Law, when fulfilled by love, becomes a song with power. How do I experience God's Law: as command, constraint, or as music?
- Can I recall a time when obedience to God led me into deeper joy, not just duty?

PAUL

To write this poem, I chose not to stand apart from Paul, but to step inside his voice—to inhabit the anguish and the fire of the apostle, the soul of the man once called Saul. This poetic act is not an exercise in fiction, nor a flight of imagination. It is a form of postulation grounded in truth—truth drawn from Scripture, from historical reality, and from the very human echoes of suffering and redemption that mark the journey of every believer.

In this poem, Paul stands at the threshold of death, about to be beheaded. He is dying in the present, yet his mind traverses the past—revisiting the path that led him from persecutor to apostle, from blindness to vision, from law to grace. Time collapses in this moment. The man reconciles his entire life—its failures, its revelations, its call—beneath the gaze of eternal truth. What unfolds is not just memory, but metanoia: a complete reordering of self in light of Christ.

To inhabit a voice from two thousand years ago is to enter the world that shaped it. Paul's world was not abstract; it was marked by Roman tyranny, cultural fragmentation, religious zeal, and philosophical rivalry. While Scripture gives us the vital contours of Paul's life, it leaves many human details unstated. And so, through prayerful reflection and informed imagination, I have sought to fill in the silences—not to speculate aimlessly, but to deepen our encounter with the man whose letters still shape the Church.

The ideologies of Paul's day—Stoic resignation, Epicurean detachment, the fatalism of fate—whispered despair beneath the surface of an empire. In that world, Paul proclaimed something scandalously new: hope. A hope not grounded in reason or pleasure, but in love, sacrifice, and the Resurrection. His Gospel clashed with both religious legalism and worldly cynicism, and that collision made his mission both daunting and divine.

But Paul's transformation was not sudden or easy. His was a road paved with misunderstanding, betrayal, imprisonment, and opposition. And yet he endured. Why? Because the love of Christ compelled him. Because what he once tried to destroy had become the very reason he lived—and died. His letters, his journeys, and his martyrdom testify to a soul utterly consumed by truth and mercy.

Today, many of us imagine our trials to be unprecedented. But Paul's world was no less hostile to truth. In many ways, his burdens mirror ours: a culture resistant to faith, the temptation to conform, and the loneliness of the one who dares to proclaim a different way. This poem, then, is not merely a reflection on Paul—it is a call to each of us. A call to take on his voice, to enter his struggle, and to allow his unwavering discipleship to shape our own.

To write in Paul's voice is to listen more deeply to our own. It is to remember that we, too, are members of the Body of Christ—and that every age needs its apostles. Let us inhabit these voices not merely to remember them, but to become like them. For in doing so, we step not only into history, but into the heart of the Gospel.

Paul: A Life Overturned

'The martyrs were bound, imprisoned, scourged, racked, burned, rent, butchered—and they multiplied.'
— St. Augustine, Sermon 329

I have journeyed long and far—
From youth shaped by Torah, in the holy tongue
Chanted in the halls of the synagogue.
Then I was called Saul.

While I hunted followers of The Way.
He called me to serve
In blinding light—He spoke to me
His lost sheep drawn to His voice.
He gifted me unblinkered sight.

The Law I once studied—
Now transfigured into living love.
Grace poured out, a balm to my aching soul
A healing oil, softening my hate
The eyes of my heart opened
I beheld the rot within.

My heart belongs
To The Way, The Truth, and The Life.
My prey then are now my sheep—
My kingdom he overturned.

He named me Paul
One letter changed—
A different man born.
My home, now no longer fixed in place.

Broken, that I might be remade;
Blinded, that I might receive sight.
The Lord set me on a path
Guided by the mind's eye—
Journey's end before me now
This wooden block.

I once saw only the Law—narrow, rigid, absolute.
Now I see in fullness: mercy, grace, and the face of Christ.
A revelation dawned:
The power of sin is the Law.
I have embraced this inconvenient truth:
The Author and Perfecter of our faith—
Put to death by those He came to save.
An irony of faithful deference to the mitzvah,
Divine love—answered with human violence.
I share His fate, and wear it with joy.

The pain, the agony—unbearable
Yet I feel joy and peace.
Stephen prayed as I stoned him—
Now my brother, I do the same,
My life and death is tribute
To him,
And all whom I have wronged.

My neck to the wood—steel soon to fall.
My earthly frame will cease, but not my fight.
For my sword has already been wielded—
The word of God, alive and sharp,
Will crush the serpent's head beneath its truth.

At the feet of Gamaliel,
I read and was taught
Of laws, commands, and words.

Augustine Jeyaraj

But Christ unsealed my heart
And showed me love, compassion, mercy.

The fruits of the Spirit—
Elusive to the lawful mind.
Christ shattered the prison
The Law had built within
Freeing me with the Good News.

My destiny:
To reveal the New Covenant of Old,
Written in the hearts
As God revealed to Jeremiah.
Thus, salvation flows from Abraham's promise,
Perfected in Christ, our Lord and Light.

My travels have not been in vain;
much I have written
Proclaiming the evangelion—
Watering hearts with the living word,
Each soul, beloved by Christ.

Emptying Himself to be one of us,
He took on our sins.
What love, to become as we are—
Perfection stepping into our dust.
This—is the love of Christ.

Three times I was chained,
But shackles could not restrain
The Spirit when unleashed.
The doors that God opens
No power can close.

The Word in their Voices | 139

My thorn in the flesh—
Gnawing and tormenting—
Could not bind me or distract me,
For the transforming power of Christ
Was all I needed.

The Gospel is a weapon not seen
Its secret power,
To illumine minds to the truth—
It changes and reforms
Transforms and creates
And makes all things new.

My captivity, my death—
I offer to the Lord.
And I forgive
As he did.

The heat rages, my skin burns.
My head I bow,
Not for my executioner but to God—
Grateful that he chose me
To wield his sword.

I am gifted now with rest and joy
In eternity with our Lord.
At last, I meet face to face.
And now—silence.
All that remains… is glory.
O death, where is thy sting?

ANNOTATIONS: PAUL: A LIFE OVERTURNED

'The martyrs were bound, imprisoned, scourged, racked, burned, rent, butchered—and they multiplied.'
— St. Augustine, *Sermon 329*

This epigraph by Augustine sets the tone: persecution cannot destroy truth—it purifies and multiplies it. Like the blood of the martyrs, Paul's suffering becomes seed for the Church.

I have journeyed long and far—
From youth shaped by Torah, in the holy tongue,
Chanted in the halls of the synagogue.
Then I was called Saul.

This stanza roots Paul in his Jewish heritage: a Pharisee, raised in the Law, trained under Gamaliel (**Acts 22:3**). "Holy tongue" refers to Hebrew, the sacred language of Scripture. The transformation from *Saul* (Hebrew name) to *Paul* (Roman/Greek name) is both literal and symbolic of his mission shift—from Israel to the Gentiles.

While I hunted followers of The Way.
He called me to serve,
In blinding light—He spoke to me
His lost sheep drawn to His voice.
He gifted me unblinkered sight.

A retelling of **Acts 9**. 'The Way' was an early term for Christianity. The juxtaposition of hunting to being called reflects violent opposition transformed into divine vocation. "Lost sheep" (**Luke 15:4**) evokes Christ the Shepherd. 'Unblinkered sight' references not just physical healing but spiritual revelation.

The Law I once studied—
Now transfigured into living love.
Grace poured out, a balm to my aching soul
A healing oil, softening my hate
The eyes of my heart opened
I beheld the rot within.

The Law here is not rejected but transfigured—fulfilled through Christ (**Matthew 5:17**). The imagery of balm and healing oil echoes **Psalm 23:5** and **Isaiah 61:1–3**. 'The eyes of my heart' (**cf. Ephesians 1:18**) implies deeper inner awakening.

My heart belongs
To The Way, The Truth, and The Life.
My prey then are now my sheep—
My kingdom he overturned.

Christ's self-description in **John 14:6** is central here. The reversal of "prey" to 'sheep' mirrors Paul's radical conversion. 'My kingdom he overturned' suggests Paul's inner regime—self, pride, law-centeredness—was replaced with Christ's reign.

He named me Paul,
One letter changed—
A different man born.
My home, now no longer fixed in place.

The name change is poetic license (Scripture never explicitly records Christ changing Saul's name), but symbolically rich—Paul adopts a Gentile name as apostle to the Gentiles. 'No longer fixed' speaks of his itinerant mission and spiritual detachment (**Philippians 3:7–8**).

Broken, that I might be remade;
Blinded, that I might receive sight.
The Lord set me on a path
Guided by the mind's eye—
Journey's end before me now
This wooden block.

Echoes of **Isaiah 64:8** (God as potter). "Mind's eye" refers to spiritual vision. 'Wooden block' subtly evokes Paul's coming martyrdom—likely beheading (a Roman method). It contrasts with the 'path' he walked for Christ.

I once saw only the Law—narrow, rigid, absolute.
Now I see in fullness: mercy, grace, and the face of Christ.
A revelation dawned:
The power of sin is the Law.

Romans 7:8–13 is key here—Paul teaches that sin takes advantage of the Law to produce death. Without the Spirit, the Law becomes an instrument of judgment. The contrast between law and grace is central to Pauline theology.

I have embraced this inconvenient truth:
The Author and Perfecter of our faith—
Put to death by those He came to save.
An irony of faithful deference to the mitzvah,
Divine love—answered with human violence.
I share His fate,
And wear it with joy.

The Word in their Voices | 143

'Inconvenient truth' is modern idiom, but effective. **Hebrews 12:2** names Christ as 'Author and Perfecter.' 'Mitzvah' (commandment) points to the irony of legalistic faith becoming the vehicle for Christ's execution. Paul's joyful martyrdom (**Philippians 1:21; Acts 21:13**) mirrors Christ's.

The pain, the agony—unbearable,
Yet I feel joy and peace.
Stephen prayed as I stoned him—
Now my brother, I do the same,
My life and death is tribute
To him,
And all whom I have wronged.

A powerful reflection on **Acts 7**. Paul (then Saul) approved Stephen's martyrdom. This act of violence becomes a touchstone for his remorse and redemption. 'Tribute' is both personal atonement and ecclesial solidarity.

My neck to the wood—steel soon to fall.
My earthly frame will cease, but not my fight.
For my sword has already been wielded—
The word of God, alive and sharp,
Will crush the serpent's head beneath its truth.

Anticipation of Paul's beheading. The 'sword of the Spirit' (**Ephesians 6:17; Hebrews 4:12**) is the Word. **Genesis 3:15** is invoked: the serpent will be crushed. Paul's martyrdom becomes participation in Christ's victory.

At the feet of Gamaliel,
I read and was taught
Of laws, commands, and words.
But Christ unsealed my heart
And showed me love, compassion, mercy.

Acts 22:3 references Gamaliel. The phrase 'unsealed my heart' contrasts external knowledge with internal transformation. See **2 Corinthians 3:6** ('the letter kills, but the Spirit gives life').

The fruits of the Spirit—
Elusive to the lawful mind.
Christ shattered the prison
The Law had built within,
Freeing me with the Good News.

Galatians 5:22–23 outlines the fruit of the Spirit. The Law is not evil but becomes a prison when misused (**Galatians 3:23–25**). The Gospel liberates from this bondage.

My destiny:
To reveal the new covenant of old,
Written in the hearts,
As God revealed to Jeremiah.
Thus, salvation flows from Abraham's promise,
Perfected in Christ, our Lord and Light.

Jeremiah 31:31–34 promised a new covenant written on hearts, not stone. **Romans 4** shows salvation through Abraham by faith, not the Law. 'Light' echoes **John 1** and **Isaiah 60**.

My travels have not been in vain;
much I have written,
Proclaiming the evangelion—
Watering hearts with the living word,
Each soul, beloved by Christ.

'Evangelion' (Greek for Gospel) honors Paul's original language. The agricultural metaphor (**1 Corinthians 3:6**) links his ministry to sowing and watering. "Beloved" recalls **Romans 8** and the personal care of Paul's letters.

Emptying Himself to be one of us,
He took on our sins.
What love, to become as we are—
Perfection stepping into our dust.
This—is the love of Christ.

Philippians 2:6–8 and **2 Corinthians 5:21** underpin this stanza. The poetic image of 'dust' recalls **Genesis 2:7**, emphasizing incarnation's humility and redemptive descent.

Three times I was chained,
But shackles could not restrain
The Spirit when unleashed.
The doors that God opens,
No power can close.

See **Acts 16:25–26** and **2 Timothy 2:9**: 'The word of God is not chained.' **Revelation 3:7** is paraphrased: what God opens, no one can shut.

My thorn in the flesh—
Gnawing and tormenting—
Could not bind me or distract me,
For the transforming power of Christ
Was all I needed.

2 Corinthians 12:7–9 speaks of Paul's thorn. Its nature is unknown, but the spiritual lesson is central: 'My grace is sufficient for you.'

The Gospel is a weapon not seen
Its secret power,
To illumine minds to the truth—
It changes and reforms,
Transforms and creates,
And makes all things new.

Romans 1:16: the Gospel is 'the power of God for salvation.' The transformation echoes **2 Corinthians 5:17**—"If anyone is in Christ, he is a new creation."

My captivity, my death—
I offer to the Lord.
And I forgive,
As he did.

Like Christ (**Luke 23:34**) and Stephen (**Acts 7:60**), Paul forgives his persecutors. His death becomes Eucharistic—an offering.

The Word in their Voices

The heat rages, my skin burns.
My head I bow,
Not for my executioner but to God—
Grateful that he chose me,
To wield his sword.

Imagery of martyrdom, both physical and spiritual. Bowing signifies not defeat but surrender to divine will. 'His sword' again refers to the Word of God.

I am gifted now with rest and joy,
In eternity with our Lord.
At last, I meet face to face.
And now—silence.
All that remains… is glory.
O death, where is thy sting?*

Final stanza echoes **1 Corinthians 13:12** ('face to face') and **15:55** ('Where, O death, is your sting?'). 'Silence' suggests both physical death and spiritual consummation. Glory remains.

Reflection Questions for "Paul"

1. **Conversion and Identity**

   - What does Paul's transformation from *Saul* to *Paul* reveal about the nature of true conversion?
   - In what ways might God be calling you to change—not just your actions, but your identity?

2. **Law and Grace**

   - The poem describes the Law as both formative and imprisoning. How do you understand the difference between obeying the Law and living in grace?
   - Have you ever experienced a time when rules or religion felt rigid and lifeless—how did the Spirit bring freedom?

3. **Repentance and Redemption**

   - Paul reflects on his role in Stephen's death with sorrow and humility. Who or what in your life needs to be brought to Christ for healing and forgiveness?
   - What does it mean to make one's life a tribute to those we have harmed?

4. **Suffering and Joy**

   - How does Paul's joyful embrace of suffering challenge our modern understanding of discipleship?
   - What suffering in your life might be transformed into an offering or witness?

5. **Vocation and Mission**

   - Paul's mission took him across cultures and boundaries. Where might God be calling you to speak the Gospel—perhaps outside your comfort zone?
   - How can your words become "the sword of the Spirit" that heals, convicts, and sets others free?

6. **Forgiveness and Martyrdom**

   - Paul forgives as Christ forgave. How are you invited to forgive those who have harmed you, even when it feels unjust?
   - Martyrdom may not be physical, but have you faced forms of sacrifice or rejection for your faith?

7. **Silence and Glory**

   - The poem ends in silence and glory. What does it mean to you to 'meet face to face' with God at the end of your life?
   - How do you envision eternity—not as escape, but as fulfillment?

8. **Legacy and the Word**

   - Paul's "'word' is the living Word. What legacy do you hope your life and words will leave behind?
   - How are you proclaiming the *evangelion* in your daily life—whether in speech, writing, or action?

HOLY SPIRIT

Introduction to Holy Spirit

This poem is an intimate theological meditation voiced by the Holy Spirit—a kind of *Confessions* of the Third Person of the Trinity. It draws deeply from Scripture, patristic wisdom (especially Augustine and Aquinas), and mystical theology. Through layered metaphors—breath, bridge, fire, mother, dance—it reveals a divine Person both eternal and near, gentle and powerful, elusive and yet always waiting.

Whereas other poems in this volume explore the mystery of God through the eyes of biblical figures—Paul, Mary, Stephen, or even Judas—this poem stands apart as a theological self-revelation. It gives voice to the Holy Spirit Himself. Not in spectacle or thunder, but in quiet love, the Spirit speaks directly to us. It is a monologue, but also a summons: to listen, to open, to be transformed.

This poem was born from the desire to give voice to the One who is often the most hidden Person of the Trinity. Though fully God, the Holy Spirit is frequently overlooked, remaining unnamed or abstract in many hearts. Yet He has been present from the very beginning—hovering over the waters of creation, speaking through the prophets, descending at Pentecost, and abiding in the Church and the human soul.

In composing this meditation, I sought to imagine what the Spirit might say if He were to speak to us plainly—not in grand declarations, but in the quiet clarity of divine love. Scripture tells us that the Spirit hovered, descended, filled, and inspired. He glorifies the Son and draws us to the Father. Through these stanzas, I have attempted to trace the Spirit's movement across creation, covenant, Church, and conscience—showing that He is not a mere force, but a divine Person who sanctifies, strengthens, refines, and comforts. He dwells in silence, yet He is ever near. If this poem opens even the smallest space of stillness in which the Spirit may be heard, then it has fulfilled its purpose.

This poem holds a central place in the arc of this book. While others may serve as hinges or narrative turning points, this one is foundational—because it speaks of how God mediates His life into ours. The Spirit is the bridge between the Godhead and humanity. He is the liaison, the indwelling flame, the One who brings the life of the Trinity into our mortal lives. The voice I have given Him is bold, yes—but it is rooted in reverent imagination, aimed at prompting intense meditation. What does the Spirit truly desire of us? How does His presence change us once received? And how does His indwelling love manifest in the world?

To enrich the theological texture of this poem, I also wove in references that invite deeper study. For instance, I mention the word ***Bereishit***—the Hebrew title for the Book of Genesis, meaning "In the beginning." This was how the ancient Israelites named their scrolls: by the first significant word of the text. ***Shemot*** ('Names') for Exodus, ***Vayikra*** ('He called') for Leviticus, ***Bamidbar*** ('In the desert') for Numbers, and ***Devarim*** ('Words') for Deuteronomy. Understanding this tradition reminds us that Scripture was not a codex of segmented chapters, but a living, unfolding word in scrolls—meant to be heard, remembered, and responded to.

When Jesus cried from the Cross, "My God, my God, why have you forsaken me?" He was not expressing despair, but pointing us to the first line of Psalm 22—a scroll named by its opening, inviting us to an encounter with the Psalm. In the same spirit, this poem names the Spirit—not to define Him, but to invite encounter. Augustine and Aquinas both wrote profoundly on the Holy Spirit, and while I have drawn from their insights, I have tried here to offer a simplified doorway into their wisdom.

If this poem offers you a gentle entry point into the vast treasury of the Church's teaching on the Spirit—if it helps you understand, feel, and respond to the Spirit's presence—then it will have done what poetry, at its best, can do: awaken the soul to God.

If you hear Me, open.
If you thirst, come.
If you long, surrender.
I do not force.
I wait—eternal, patient, near.

THE HOLY SPIRIT – THE BREATH OF GOD MADE LIFE.

'Now the earth was formless and empty... and the Spirit of God was hovering over the waters.'
— *Genesis 1:2*

'But the Advocate, the Holy Spirit, whom the Father will send in my name, will teach you all things and will remind you of everything I have said to you.'— *John 14:26*

Call me the Advocate,
Many names have graced My breath.
In days of old, I was known as
Ruach Elohim—the Spirit of God.

With the Father and the Son, I created.
We are Three, yet One.
We exist beyond time and space.
Moses wrote of Me in *Bereishit*—
The Spirit of God hovering over the waters.

In creation, I am the bridge
Between two realities
Between what is and what will be
The link from Source to Summit—
Unseen, unbroken, eternal.

I have been poured out upon many,
Found a home in hearts willing to receive.
Rejected by some
Yet I remain—present, though unseen
Waiting to enter the contrite heart.

I am the breath behind the Law's true fruit.
Where love is, there I am.

I am *Vinculum Amoris*—
The bond of love that unites Father and Son.

Where compassion lives, I dwell.
Where hope endures, I give it.
To will the good of the other—
This is the faithful's witness of Me.
This is the mark of those who love with Us.

In ancient days, I nurtured,
Comforted, and called.
At Babel, man's pride I humbled,
By scattering tongues in love.
I parted the Red Sea for the Israelites.

Like a loving mother to Israel, I sheltered and led.
In Egypt, My embrace—
a shield and protector—
From the Angel of Death at Passover.

I am the womb of mercy in the breath of God,
Veiled in tenderness, strength without striving—
Presence shaped in grace, not might.
Soft yet unyielding,
Caring, nurturing, near.

In Us, the Trinity holds,
Both Fatherhood, the Son and Mercy—
Perfectly One.

For the early Church, I was sent by the Son—
The Paraclete—to forgive sins,
To proclaim the Gospel,
To dwell in the hearts of believers.

I have been felt and seen in many forms—
The wind, the fire, the storm, the lightning.
Through prophets I have spoken.
To hearts attuned, I lavish
Mercy, compassion, and every fruit.

The Law stands like a hollow stone,
When hearts are emptied of Me.
Cracked and crumbling,
Beneath the weight of life.

But where I dwell, Grace overflows—
Just as Mary received the *Summum Bonum*—
The Highest Good: Love Incarnate, Christ Himself.
I become the cornerstone within,
The seal of union in flesh and Spirit,
A glimpse of eternal love made manifest.

You cannot grasp Me,
But you can know Me.
In silence, in prayer, in love—
There I am—
Like a dance, I draw you in
And lead to the music of the Gospel.

Prayer tunes the soul to Me.
It clears the noise.
Only in stillness am I known,
Only in the heart am I felt.

Bonum diffusivum sui—
The Good pours itself outward.
This is My power,
And My gift to all who ask.

At Pentecost, My fire fell—
For they believed
Their hearts aligned with the Son.
And so, I came as the son promised.

I am ever present——
Waiting to enter hearts and minds
Of those who seek
Who knock
Who ask.

You'll know them by their quiet strength—
Faithful in trials, patient in storms.
They curb the anger born of pain,
And practice self-control with grace.

I may seem slow to answer
But I answer in time.
I give not what is desired
But what is needed.

I am love
The breath that draws you home—
A flame that does not consume
But refines you like silver.
I lead beyond what eyes can see—
To union, rest, and life in God.

If you hear Me, open.
If you thirst, come.
If you long, surrender.
I do not force.
I wait—eternal, patient, near.

Full Annotation of Holy Spirit

Holy Spirit

Title Significance:
The poem takes its name directly from the Third Person of the Holy Trinity—the Holy Spirit—emphasizing intimacy and reverence. By giving the Spirit a speaking voice, the poem invites the reader into a direct contemplative encounter. The Spirit is not explained or described from a distance but speaks from within, in the tradition of prophetic utterance and interior dialogue.

Epigraphs:

'Now the earth was formless and empty... and the Spirit of God was hovering over the waters.' – Genesis 1:2
This alludes to the Spirit's primal role in *creation*, before form or order emerged—underscoring the Spirit's role as divine breath, origin of all becoming. The Hebrew **ruach** (רוּחַ) means both *wind* and *spirit*, carrying the resonance of motion, mystery, and life-giving presence. This the first biblical designation of the Spirit, pointing to the Spirit's presence at the beginning of all things.

'But the Advocate, the Holy Spirit, whom the Father will send in my name...' – John 14:26
This points to the Spirit's role in *revelation* and *remembrance*, as Jesus promises the Spirit to His disciples for comfort, instruction, and empowerment. The Spirit is the divine anamnesis—the power by which the Church remembers Christ rightly.

Stanza-by-Stanza Commentary:

1. *Call me the Advocate... Ruach Elohim—the Spirit of God.*

The Spirit identifies itself with the Paraclete (Greek *Paraklētos*), translated as Advocate, Counselor, or Comforter (cf. John 14:26). The naming here traces both the Old Testament origin (Ruach Elohim) and the New Testament mission, setting the tone for a poem that unites the Testaments through the Spirit's continuity.

The phrase *'Many names have graced My breath'* is rich in theological subtlety—it suggests that the Spirit's breath (or *pneuma, ruach*) is the medium by which divine names, identities, and callings are revealed across salvation history.

A clear Trinitarian declaration: 'We are Three, yet One', echoing the Nicene Creed and the *filioque* clause: 'Who proceeds from the Father and the Son.' The Spirit hovers 'over the waters' (Genesis 1:2), signaling divine preparation before creation—the threshold between chaos and cosmos. 'Hovering' (מְרַחֶפֶת, *merachefet*)—a verb evoking maternal protection, like a bird over its young (cf. Deut. 32:11).This stanza presents the Spirit as eternally active and co-eternal with Father and Son.

3. In creation, I am the bridge... eternal.

The metaphor of the Spirit as a bridge reveals a deeply mystical theology: the Spirit connects temporal creation with eternal origin. "Source to Summit" mirrors mystical ascent theology (e.g., Dionysius the Areopagite), showing the Spirit as both initiator and finisher of sanctification. The line *"unseen, unbroken, eternal"* evokes the Spirit's invisible yet faithful presence.

The Spirit is portrayed as a liminal presence, mediating between eternity and time, divine and human, spirit and matter. The phrase *"from Source to Summit"* recalls both mystical theology (e.g., Bonaventure's *Itinerarium*) and Trinitarian origin and return. This is the Spirit as both *Alpha and Omega* in our journey to God.

4. I have been poured out upon many... the contrite heart.

This stanza recalls Joel 2:28 and Acts 2, where the Spirit is "poured out upon all flesh." The distinction between reception and rejection highlights the freedom of the Spirit's indwelling—affirming that though God is always near, the human heart must respond. "The contrite heart" references Psalm 51:17, showing where the Spirit finds a fitting temple.

5. I am the breath behind the Law's true fruit...

This section integrates Romans 8:2 and Galatians 5:22–23: the Spirit gives life, love, and spiritual fruit that fulfill the Law's true purpose. The Latin **Vinculum Amoris** (**Bond of Love**), drawn from St. Augustine (**De Trinitate**) and St. Thomas Aquinas, describing the Holy Spirit as the love-bond between the Father and the Son (*Summa Theologiae* I, q. 37, a. 1)—not just a passive link, but active, personal love that overflows.

6. Where compassion lives, I dwell... the mark of those who love with Us.

This stanza beautifully aligns with Ignatian spirituality and Aquinas' definition of love as *willing the good of the other* (*Summa Theologia I–II.26.4*).—to "will the good of the other" is to enact *agape*, the divine love that mirrors God. This marks true discipleship: not in emotional fervor, but in intentional, Spirit-filled love.

7–8. In ancient days, I nurtured... at Passover.

This draws from salvation history:
- Babel: Genesis 11 – Spirit humbles pride through dispersion, in contrast to Pentecost's unifying tongues.
- Red Sea: Exodus 14 – Spirit as deliverer and liberator.
- Passover: Exodus 12 – Spirit shields in judgment.

This portion reflects maternal imagery—the Spirit as a motherly presence, aligning with patristic sources like St. Ephrem and medieval mystics who depicted the Spirit in feminine imagery (cf. *Shekinah*, Sophia traditions).

9. Like a loving mother to Israel,...

The Spirit's feminine portrayal continues here, affirming divine tenderness and caregiving.
Here the Spirit is imaged maternally, in continuity with Isaiah 66:13 and Deuteronomy 32:11. The Spirit's protective role during Passover evokes the Shekinah—God's indwelling presence—and the hovering imagery from Genesis.
See Footnote*

10. I am the womb of mercy in the breath of God

This stanza expresses the Spirit in feminine, maternal, and mystical terms without gendering her explicitly. "Womb of mercy" echoes Divine Mercy theology and Luke 1:35—the Spirit overshadowing Mary. The tone reflects St. John of the Cross and Julian of Norwich: God's love as both fierce and tender.

11. In Us, the Trinity holds,...

This is a poetic formulation of Trinitarian theology: Father, Son, and Spirit (named "Mercy") are one essence. "Mercy" as a title for the Spirit recalls Titus 3:5 and Divine Mercy devotion, in which the Spirit is the one through whom mercy flows from the Father and Son.

12. For the early Church, I was sent by the Son—

References John 20:22, Acts 2, and Luke 24:49—the Spirit is the missionary flame, the divine empowerment for the Church to forgive, proclaim, and indwell. *Paraclete* returns, this time in a more ecclesial context.

The Word in their Voices | 163

13. I have been felt and seen... lavish mercy...

The Spirit is visible in elements and prophets (cf. Elijah's wind in 1 Kings 19; Ezekiel's vision). The poetic triplet *"wind, fire, storm, lightning"* evokes Pentecost and Theophanies. "Lavish" recalls Titus 3:5–6, where the Spirit is "poured out generously."

Imagery from Acts 2:2–4 (wind and fire), Exodus 19:16 (storm and lightning), and 1 Kings 19 (still small voice). The phrase "hearts attuned" reflects 1 Corinthians 2:10–16, where the Spirit reveals what the natural mind cannot perceive.

14. The Law stands like a hollow stone...

An echo of 2 Corinthians 3:6—"the letter kills, but the Spirit gives life." Without the Spirit, even holy tings become burdensome. "Cracked and crumbling" evokes the stone tablets and how the Law without love becomes oppressive.

15. But where I dwell, Grace overflows... cornerstone within.

Mary's "Yes" (Luke 1:38) becomes the model of perfect receptivity. "Summum Bonum"—the Highest Good (a Thomistic phrase)—is God Himself. Christ as *Love Incarnate* makes Mary the first *temple of the Spirit*. The Spirit becomes the "cornerstone"—language used of Christ (Psalm 118:22), here extended to the indwelling Spirit that stabilizes the soul and Ephesians 2:20, where Christ is the cornerstone of the Church—and the Spirit seals this union (Eph. 1:13)

16. You cannot grasp Me... the music of the Gospel.

The Spirit is not fully comprehensible (*mysterium*), yet deeply knowable (cf. Romans 8:26, John 3:8). This mystical language echoes St. John of the Cross and Gregory of Nyssa: the Spirit draws us like a dance— known not by force, but by attraction. *'The music of the Gospel'* suggests a harmony of grace, echoing Psalm 40:3: 'He put a new song in my mouth.'

16. *Prayer tunes the soul to Me... only in the heart am I felt.*

This section is deeply Ignatian: interior stillness reveals divine presence. *'Prayer tunes'* is a musical metaphor—the soul must be *attuned* to discern the Spirit. The reference to 'clearing the noise' mirrors Elijah's encounter in the "still, small voice" (1 Kings 19:12). Echoes Psalm 46:10: *'Be still and know that I am God'*, and 1 Kings 19—Elijah hearing God not in noise, but in stillness. Also reflects St. Ignatius's spirituality—discernment begins in silence.

17. *Bonum diffusivum sui...*

The Thomistic axiom (Summa Theologia I, q.6, a.2) is a classic Scholastic formula: *'The good is self-diffusive.'* God, being Good, necessarily pours Himself out. This line is the philosophical anchor of the poem: the Spirit is not just the energy of God—but the self-outpouring of divine goodness into creation.

18. *At Pentecost, My fire fell...*

Rooted in Acts 2, this moment is the birth of the Church. The fire descends because the hearts of the apostles were prepared. 'Aligned with the Son' echoes John 15: abiding in Christ prepares one to receive the Spirit.

19. *I am ever present...*

Echoes Matthew 7:7—'ask, seek, knock.' The Spirit is gentle but always available, honoring human freedom while drawing the soul into communion.

20. You'll know them by their quiet strength...

A fruits-of-the-Spirit stanza (cf. Galatians 5:22–23). The tone is pastoral—showing how the Spirit is known not by spectacle but by *gentle resilience and love in trial.*

21. I may seem slow to answer...

This stanza reflects divine wisdom: God's answers come not on demand but in Kairos (God's time). It recalls Romans 8:26–27—the Spirit intercedes with wisdom and discernment beyond human asking.

22. I am love... to union, rest, and life in God.

The poem's closing crescendo:
- 'I am love' (cf. 1 John 4:8),
- 'Refines you like silver' (cf. Malachi 3:3),
- 'leads beyond what eyes can see' (cf. 1 Corinthians 2:9).

It ends with invitation: 'If you hear Me, open.' Like Revelation 3:20, the Spirit knocks but does not force. *'Eternal, patient, near'*—the poem closes on divine gentleness and availability.

* Notes :- Ruach Elohim and the Feminine Imagery of the Spirit
'Ruach Elohim' (רוּחַ אֱלֹהִים) is a Hebrew phrase meaning 'Spirit of God', first appearing in *Genesis 1:2*:

'And the Spirit of God was hovering over the waters.'
In Hebrew, the word "ruach" (רוּחַ) means breath, wind, or spirit and is grammatically feminine often being referred to as 'she' or 'her'. This does not indicate that the Spirit is a 'woman' or has gender in the human sense, but it has led many Jewish and Christian thinkers to speak of the Spirit in maternal or nurturing metaphors.

In early Christian writings, especially among the Syriac Fathers (e.g., St. Ephrem the Syrian), the Spirit is often referred to in feminine terms.

Ephrem calls the Holy Spirit "she who brooded over the waters"—linking Genesis with maternal imagery. The early church also saw the Spirit as comforter, indweller, and sanctifier—roles that involve protection, nourishment, and inner transformation.

In Christian theology, God transcends gender. While the Father is revealed in masculine terms, and the Son was incarnated male, the Spirit is often described with qualities traditionally associated with both motherhood and fatherhood—gentleness, indwelling presence, creativity, and fire.

The Catechism of the Catholic Church affirms this poetic richness: *'God's parental tenderness can also be expressed by the image of motherhood...'* (CCC §239)

Thus, poetic references to the Spirit as "like a mother" or "sheltering in feminine form" are theologically acceptable when understood metaphorically, rooted in the Spirit's scriptural role as life-giver, advocate, and guide.

Note to the Reader

The Holy Spirit: The Breath of God Made Life is a poem that invites not just reading, but dwelling. Of all the poems in this book, this one perhaps requires the most silence and the most interior stillness. The Holy Spirit does not clamor for attention—He moves like breath, speaks in whispers, and waits in love. He is the most hidden Person of the Trinity, yet He is the one who lives within us, who prays when we cannot pray, who teaches us to love as Christ loved.

That is why I felt it important to include a set of reflection questions for this poem—not as a theological examination, but as a personal invitation. As I've often said, theological insight is only one part of engaging with Scripture. The real test of faith is not in how much we know, but in how we live. It is when the rubber meets the road—when belief must become action, and knowledge must become love—that we are truly called to follow Christ.

Even Peter, who walked with Jesus, struggled when faith met fear. He denied the Lord—not once, but three times. And yet, that failure was not the end of his story. His relationship with Christ grew. It deepened. In time, Peter gave his life for the Gospel, crucified upside down for the name he once denied. That is the journey we are all on: from fragile beginnings to faithful endings, carried not by our own strength but by the Spirit who sustains us.

These reflection questions are meant to guide you on that same path. They are not designed to test your intellect, but to prompt your heart. They ask you to distill what you have learned through Scripture into the realities of daily life—into your decisions, your relationships, your sorrows, your joys. They ask: *What would Jesus do?* But more importantly: *What is the Spirit prompting you to do, now, today, in this specific moment of your life?*

The Holy Spirit never forces.
He does not shout.
He invites.
He teaches.
He waits—eternal, patient, near.

If these questions help you pause, reflect, and grow—if they help you take even one step forward in becoming the person God created you to be—then this poem has done what it was meant to do. It has opened a space for transformation.

Thank you for reading. May the Spirit breathe through your life with wisdom, strength, and peace. And now enjoy the reflection questions

Reflection Questions for The Holy Spirit: The Breath of God Made Life

1. Encountering the Spirit as a Person
- How do you usually relate to the Holy Spirit—more as an abstract force, or as a divine Person?
- In what ways does this poem shift or deepen your understanding of the Spirit's personality and presence?

2. Creation and Re-Creation
- The Spirit is described as the breath that hovers over the waters and gives life. Where in your life do you feel formless or empty—waiting for God's breath?
- How is the Holy Spirit still at work in the 'new creation' of your heart, your relationships, your vocation?

3. The Spirit as Bridge and Bond
- The poem calls the Spirit 'the bridge between two realities' and *Vinculum Amoris,* the bond of love. What do these metaphors reveal about the Spirit's role in your relationship with God and others?
- Are there areas of your life where reconciliation or unity is needed—and could the Spirit be inviting you to be that bridge?

4. Maternal Imagery and Tender Mercy
- The Holy Spirit is poetically described as nurturing, comforting, and sheltering 'like a mother.' Does this maternal imagery offer you a new or healing way to understand God?
- How have you experienced the Spirit's comfort during times of fear, grief, or loneliness?

5. The Spirit and the Law
- 'The Law stands like a hollow stone when hearts are emptied of Me.' Have you ever followed faith as a set of rules rather than a relationship? What helped restore life to your spiritual practice?
- How do you discern the difference between actions driven by legalism and those animated by the Spirit?

6. Hearing the Spirit's Voice
- The poem speaks of the Spirit being known 'only in silence, in prayer, in love.' What practices help you still your heart enough to hear the Spirit's promptings?
- Have you ever experienced a time when the Spirit spoke clearly to you—not in words, but in clarity, peace, or conviction?

7. Receiving the Gifts and Fruits
- Which fruits of the Spirit (Galatians 5:22–23) are most evident in your life? Which ones do you feel called to grow in?
- How can you open yourself more fully to the Spirit's refining presence—allowing Him to make you 'like silver'?

8. Surrender and Invitation
- The closing lines offer a gentle call: *'If you hear Me, open… I wait—eternal, patient, near.'* What is one area of your life where the Spirit is knocking but you haven't yet opened the door?
- What would it look like today to say 'yes' to the Spirit—not just in word, but in trust and surrender?

9. Living in the Spirit
- How does the Spirit guide your decisions, animate your prayer, or inspire your service?
- In what ways are you allowing the Spirit to make your life a living testimony—a breath of God made visible in the world?

MARTYRDOM FOR CHRIST: STILL VERY MUCH ALIVE

Introduction to the Seven Reflections and Poem of St Stephen

Martyrdom is not a relic of the past, confined to the dusty pages of ancient Scripture or the distant memories of early Church history. It is, tragically and heroically, a reality of the present Church. Even today, men and women across the world give up their lives for the Christian faith they hold dear. These are not mere legends; they are real people, living witnesses to a truth they deemed more valuable than their own breath.

In this segment of the book, I present *seven Bible study reflections*—drawing from both Old and New Testament periods, as well as recent examples of martyrdom in the modern world. These reflections are not intended to glorify death, but to honour the *depth of conviction and profound intimacy with God* that compels someone to stand firm even unto death. In their stories, we do not see a thirst for suffering, but rather a love for Christ so real, so transformative, that not even death could silence it.

This study begins where Christian martyrdom begins with *St Stephen*, the Church's first martyr. I introduce him not just as a historical figure, but as a voice. In the poem that follows, I attempt to give words to what Stephen might have felt in those final moments—the isolation, the courage, the forgiveness, the surrender. His story sets the tone for all that follows, a reminder that *true faith does not die*; it endures, even in the face of stones.

Yet martyrdom is not only about literal death. It is also a *spiritual and existential pattern* woven into the very fabric of life: *the cycle of Good Friday and Easter Sunday, crucifixion and resurrection.* This cycle is not confined to a calendar or to a single historical moment—it plays out repeatedly in our lives. We all encounter moments of *loss, betrayal, failure, and grief.* These are our personal Good Fridays. But the Christian faith—our Catholic faith—teaches us to look beyond the tomb. It reminds us that every Good Friday carries within it the promise of *an Easter Sunday.* Christ's death and resurrection are not only historical facts; they are *a living metaphor for our human condition,* for the pattern of suffering and redemption that repeats in every heart that seeks God.

Without faith, this cycle may appear senseless pain without purpose. But with Christ as our compass, we begin to understand there is *resurrection after loss, light after darkness, hope after despair.* This Bible study seeks to awaken that understanding. The life of the martyr makes this cycle most visible. Though their earthly lives ended in violence, *the good they stood for continued, and their personal Easter was eternity with God.*

It is not martyrdom itself that we are called to seek, but the depth of faith it represents. Faith that is willing to endure. Faith that knows God not as an idea, but as a person, alive and present. Faith that remains steadfast, even in the darkest of hours. This is the kind of faith to which we are all invited. We may not be called to die for Christ, but we are all called to *live for Him with the same courage.*

The examples included in this study are but a handful of the countless men and women—known and unknown—who have lived and died for the sake of the Gospel. Many stories remain untold. Many names will never be recorded. Yet their faith shines, and their witness continues.

I have put St Stephen's poem after Paul. The impact of St Stephen's Prayer of Forgiveness transformed Paul through the grace of the Holy Spirit and its really understood here fully after the previous section (missing rib the word).

To deepen the reflection, I have also included *annotations to the poem of St Stephen*, drawing upon *Scripture,* and the spiritual insights of *St Augustine* and *St Francis of Assisi.* These voices from the past—like Stephen's—continue to speak into the present.

May their words, and their lives, challenge us, strengthen us, and awaken in us a deeper desire to walk in the footsteps of Christ—through the valleys of Good Friday, into the glory of Easter Sunday.

St Stephen: The First Martyr

I stand apart from them.
I see it now: though only steps divide us
An abyss of darkness stretches between—
A chasm only love can cross.

My heart races, my heart pounds—
Dragged here by cruel hands
Like the lion they surround me.
They gather to feast on my fear and see me break.
But my Lord is with me; I will not yield.
His voice, my peace; his light, my all.

Hands in chains, legs shackled
I stand alone, accused by evil—
Cowardice masked as righteousness—
Twisted minds whose fear demand my end.
Preaching love, proclaiming truth—my hideous crimes.

They point their fingers to condemn
They scream and shout
With anger unbridled.
But I stand calm—I hold my ground—
For my Lord is with me, his rod and staff
My guard and my comfort

In silence lies my strength in God.
I pray for them—and then, I see him.
As they prepare to stone and maul
There stands a man—the one called Saul.

My death, my blood, my persecution—
I offer as prayer for his redemption.
His soul, one day, the Father shall win
To carry the torch when mine is dimmed.

If this is the price I must pay
I accept with grace this final plan.
For He sees beyond, and knows all good—
And I, like Isaac, am the willing lamb.

I kneel not in fear, but in prayer.
Those words He said, I repeat:
'Forgive them, for they know not what they do.'
Then pain and hurt rain down.

I use my hands to soothe the wounds—
Blood flows as stones are hurled
My garments soaked as I fall.
But upwards I gaze—beyond pain, beyond stone—
Into Your hands, my Lord, I come home.'

Annotations: St Stephen

(Annotated with Biblical and Patristic References)

I stand apart from them.
I see it now: though only steps divide us,
An abyss of darkness stretches between—
A chasm only love can cross.

Annotation:
- This stanza expresses spiritual alienation. Though physically close, Stephen recognizes a moral and spiritual gulf between him and his accusers.
- **Biblical parallel:** *Luke 16:26*—'Between us and you a great chasm has been fixed . . .' (parable of Lazarus).
- **Theological resonance:** Stephen sees clearly that only love (*agapē*) can bridge the hatred they carry—a foreshadowing of his forgiveness.
- **St Francis of Assisi:** 'Where there is hatred, let me sow love' (*Prayer of St Francis*)—Stephen embodies this here.

My heart races, my heart pounds—
Dragged here by cruel hands
Like the lion they surround me.
They gather to feast on my fear and see me break.
But my Lord is with me; I will not yield.
His voice, my peace; his light, my all.

Annotation:
- The intensity of persecution is palpable; the lion imagery echoes **Psalm 22:13**—'They open wide their mouths at me, like a ravening and roaring lion.'
- **Psalm 23:4 is directly invoked:** 'Even though I walk through the valley of the shadow of death . . . your rod and your staff, they comfort me.'

The Word in their Voices | 179

- **'His light, my all'** recalls John 8:12: 'I am the light of the world. Whoever follows me will never walk in darkness.'
- **St Augustine:** 'Our hearts are restless until they rest in Thee' (*Confessions I.1*)—Stephen finds peace in Christ even as the world rages around him.

Hands in chains, legs shackled
I stand alone, accused by evil—
Cowardice masked as righteousness—
Twisted minds whose fear demand my end.
Preaching love, proclaiming truth—my hideous crimes.

Annotation:
- Stephen is literally bound, yet morally free. His accusers are morally bound, though externally powerful.
- **Acts 6:13:** 'They set up false witnesses . . .' aligns with the charge of evil wearing a mask of righteousness.
- **Isaiah 5:20:** 'Woe to those who call evil good and good evil . . .'
- **St Augustine:** 'They love the truth when it enlightens them but hate it when it accuses them' (*Confessions X.23*)—a fitting lens for Stephen's situation.

They point their fingers to condemn
They scream and shout
With anger unbridled.
But I stand calm—I hold my ground—
For my Lord is with me, His rod and staff
My guard and my comfort.

Annotation:
- **This section dramatizes the mob frenzy of Acts 7:57:** 'They covered their ears and, yelling at the top of their voices, they all rushed at him.'
- **The calmness echoes Isaiah 53:7:** 'He was oppressed and afflicted, yet he did not open his mouth . . .'

- **Psalm 23:4 again:** 'Your rod and staff, they comfort me.'
- **St Francis:** 'True patience and humility are not disturbed by the anger of others.'

In silence lies my strength in God.
I pray for them—and then, I see Him.
As they prepare to stone and maul
There stands a man—the one called Saul.

Annotation:
- 'In silence lies my strength' is a reference to Christ-like endurance (cf. Isaiah 30:15– 'In quietness and trust is your strength.').
- **Acts 7:55–58:** Stephen sees Jesus standing at the right hand of God; Saul (later Paul) is present, approving of his execution.
- The structure moves from prayer to vision—a prophetic moment, as Stephen's martyrdom becomes a seed of Paul's future mission.
- **St Augustine (on Stephen's prayer for Saul):** 'If Stephen had not prayed, the Church would not have Paul.' (*Sermon 315*)

My death, my blood, my persecution—
I offer as prayer for his redemption.
His soul, one day, the Father shall win
To carry the torch when mine is dimmed.

Annotation:
- This stanza reflects the theology of redemptive suffering: offering one's pain for another's conversion.
- **Acts 9:15** – The Lord says of Saul, 'He is a chosen instrument of mine.'
- **'Carry the torch'** subtly alludes to 2 Timothy 4:7: 'I have fought the good fight . . .'
- **St Augustine:** 'The blood of the martyrs is the seed of the Church.'

The Word in their Voices

If this is the price I must pay,
I accept with grace this final plan.
For He sees beyond, and knows all good—
And I, like Isaac, am the willing lamb.

Annotation:
- **Genesis 22:** Isaac as a type of Christ—and now Stephen consciously steps into that typology.
- **Romans 8:28:** – 'We know that in all things God works for the good of those who love him.'
- **St Augustine (on God's providence):** 'What then is time? If no one asks me, I know what it is. But if I wish to explain it . . . I do not' (*Confessions XI.14*)—Stephen trusts the 'plan' even when it is incomprehensible.
- **St Francis:** 'It is in dying that we are born to eternal life.' (Prayer attributed to him)

I kneel not in fear, but in prayer.
Those words he said, I repeat:
'Forgive them, for they know not what they do.'
Then pain and hurt rain down.

Annotation:
- **Luke 23:34:** Jesus' words from the Cross.
- **Acts 7:60:** 'Lord, do not hold this sin against them.' Stephen directly imitates Christ.
- This is the moral summit of the poem: radical forgiveness in the face of violence.
- **St Augustine:** 'What is perfection in love? To love your enemies and pray for them.'

I use my hands to soothe the wounds—
Blood flows as stones are hurled
My garments soaked as I fall.
But upwards I gaze—beyond pain, beyond stone—
'Into Your hands, my Lord, I come home.'

Annotation:
- **Luke 23:46:** 'Father, into your hands I commit my spirit.'
- **Acts 7:59:** 'Lord Jesus, receive my spirit.'
- The poem ends with a gaze—not down at death, but upward, toward union.
- 'Come home' evokes a return to God (cf. *Luke 15*, the Prodigal Son)—Stephen, now fully conformed to Christ, is received into glory.

Martyrs: The Church is Very Much Alive in the Present

Reflection 1: Faithfulness Unto Death
Daniel and Dietrich Bonhoeffer

Biblical Example:
Daniel

Daniel was a Hebrew noble taken captive to Babylon during the exile (sixth century BC). Despite being immersed in a pagan empire, Daniel remained unshakably faithful to God. His life of integrity gained him favour with kings, but it also stirred jealousy among political rivals. Under King Darius, jealous officials manipulated the king into signing a decree forbidding prayer to anyone but the king himself for thirty days. Daniel, knowing the cost, continued to pray three times a day, just as he had always done (Daniel 6:10).

His loyalty led to his being thrown into a den of lions. Yet God shut the mouths of the lions and preserved Daniel. The next morning Daniel declared,

'My God sent his angel and shut the lions' mouths, and they have not harmed me, because I was found blameless before him' (Daniel 6:22, ESV).

Daniel's deliverance led to the public glorification of the God of Israel throughout the empire. The broader context shows us how exile, political corruption, and spiritual fidelity interwove—but Daniel's private prayer life became the source of his public victory.

Modern Example:
Dietrich Bonhoeffer

Born in 1906 into an aristocratic German family, Dietrich Bonhoeffer was a brilliant theologian and pastor. At a time when the German church was largely co-opted by Hitler's regime, Bonhoeffer helped establish the Confessing Church, resisting Nazism's attempt to control Christianity. He was also involved in efforts to rescue Jews and resist the Nazi government. Bonhoeffer was arrested in 1943 and spent two years in prison. Even there, he wrote letters and prayers encouraging faith under trial. His famous words summarize his theology of costly discipleship:

'When Christ calls a man, he bids him come and die.'

In April 1945, just weeks before the Nazi defeat, Bonhoeffer was executed by hanging at Flossenbürg concentration camp. His calm courage at the gallows, witnessed by others, spoke powerfully:

'This is the end—for me, the beginning of life.'

The political context of Nazi Germany demanded conformity, but Bonhoeffer's life stands as a beacon of faithful resistance to evil, rooted in a living relationship with Christ, even unto death.

Spiritual Lesson

Daniel and Bonhoeffer teach us that faithfulness often demands sacrifice. Obedience to God sometimes brings us face-to-face with hostile powers, but trust in God's sovereignty and ultimate vindication enables believers to stand firm. Daniel was willing to risk death for prayer; Bonhoeffer was willing to risk death for truth and justice.

Both show us that even when human powers seem overwhelming, God honours those who honour Him (1 Samuel 2:30).

Faithfulness in private—prayer, integrity, obedience—prepares us for faithfulness in public trials.

Whether we are delivered (like Daniel) or we die in faith (like Bonhoeffer), our victory is assured in Christ.

Old Testament Reading

Daniel 6:10–23 (ESV, abridged excerpt)

When Daniel knew that the document had been signed, he went to his house where he had windows in his upper chamber open toward Jerusalem. He got down on his knees three times a day and prayed and gave thanks before his God, as he had done previously.

Then these men came by agreement and found Daniel making petition and plea before his God. [. . .]

Then the king commanded, and Daniel was brought and cast into the den of lions. [. . .]

Then Daniel said to the king, 'O king, live forever! My God sent his angel and shut the lions' mouths, and they have not harmed me, because I was found blameless before him; and also before you, O king, I have done no harm.'

Then the king was exceedingly glad, and commanded that Daniel be taken up out of the den. So Daniel was taken up out of the den, and no kind of harm was found on him, because he had trusted in his God.

New Testament Reading

1 Peter 4:12–14 (ESV)

Beloved, do not be surprised at the fiery trial when it comes upon you to test you, as though something strange were happening to you.

But rejoice insofar as you share Christ's sufferings, that you may also rejoice and be glad when his glory is revealed.

If you are insulted for the name of Christ, you are blessed, because the Spirit of glory and of God rests upon you.

Short Prayer

Lord, grant me courage to stand firm in faith when trials come. Teach me to trust you whether you deliver me now or vindicate me in eternity. Help me to pray and obey you faithfully, as Daniel and Bonhoeffer did, knowing that you are with me in every lion's den and every trial. Amen.

Reflection Questions

- Faithfulness in small things: Daniel's public courage flowed from his daily habit of private prayer. What habits are you cultivating now that will sustain you when trials come?
- Costly obedience: Bonhoeffer said, 'When Christ calls a man, he bids him come and die.' How does this challenge the way you think about following Christ?
- Facing fear: Are there areas where you are tempted to compromise your faith under pressure? How can Daniel and Bonhoeffer's examples strengthen you to remain faithful?

Reflection 2: Witness in Martyrdom
Stephen and Oscar Romero

Expanded Story
Biblical Example:
Stephen

Stephen was one of the first deacons appointed by the apostles to care for the growing Christian community in Jerusalem (Acts 6). Described as 'full of faith and of the Holy Spirit' (Acts 6:5), Stephen was a man of deep devotion, wisdom, and power. His preaching about Jesus Christ stirred fierce opposition from members of various synagogues. Unable to defeat his wisdom, his enemies resorted to false accusations of blasphemy.

Stephen was brought before the Sanhedrin, where he delivered a powerful speech recounting Israel's history of rejecting God's messengers. His bold declaration, 'Behold, I see the heavens opened, and the Son of Man standing at the right hand of God,' (Acts 7:56) enraged the council. They dragged him out of the city and stoned him. As he died, Stephen prayed, 'Lord Jesus, receive my spirit,' and 'Lord, do not hold this sin against them' (Acts 7:59–60), echoing Jesus' own words from the Cross.

Stephen's martyrdom ignited a severe persecution, scattering the early believers beyond Jerusalem — but that scattering spread the Gospel further, fulfilling Jesus' command to be witnesses 'to the ends of the earth' (Acts 1:8). His death also deeply impacted a young man named Saul (later the Apostle Paul), who witnessed and approved of Stephen's execution.

Modern Example:
Oscar Romero

Oscar Romero, Archbishop of San Salvador, lived during a time of great turmoil in El Salvador in the 1970s to 1980s, when military repression, death squads, and civil war ravaged the country. Initially seen as a quiet, conservative choice for bishop, Romero underwent a profound transformation after the assassination of his friend, Father Rutilio Grande, a priest who spoke out for the poor.

Moved by injustice and the cries of the oppressed, Romero became the 'voice of the voiceless', fearlessly denouncing violence, government abuses, and social injustice from the pulpit and through radio broadcasts. In his final homily, he boldly called on soldiers to obey God's higher law rather than unjust orders,

'In the name of God, and in the name of this suffering people, I beg you, I beseech you, I command you in the name of God: stop the repression!'

On March 24, 1980, while celebrating Mass in a hospital chapel, Romero was assassinated — a sniper's bullet struck him at the altar, just after he consecrated the bread and wine. His death electrified El Salvador and the world.

Though silenced by human hands, Romero's voice lives on. He famously said before his death,

'If they kill me, I will rise again in the Salvadoran people.'

Pope Francis canonized Oscar Romero as a saint in 2018, recognizing him as a martyr who 'shed his blood for the love of God and the service of his brothers.'

Historical Context

- Stephen: The early Jerusalem church faced hostility from the Jewish religious authorities who saw the new Jesus movement as a dangerous sect. The Sanhedrin sought to preserve religious order and viewed Christians as blasphemous.

Stephen's martyrdom marked the first bloodshed of Christian persecution.

- Oscar Romero: El Salvador in the late twentieth century was mired in violent conflict. The government, backed by military and oligarchic elites, brutally suppressed dissent. The Church was divided—some supported the regime, others sided with the poor. Romero's prophetic stand came at enormous personal risk during this political repression.

Spiritual Lesson

Stephen and Romero embody what it means to witness faithfully even unto death.

Both faced violent opposition not because they were political revolutionaries, but because they bore witness to the kingdom of God—a kingdom where justice, truth, and mercy reign over fear, oppression, and lies.

Both forgave their killers. Both died during acts of worship: Stephen while praying, Romero while offering the Eucharist. Both deaths bore unexpected fruit—Stephen's death led to the Gospel's spread through the diaspora; Romero's martyrdom ignited movements for justice and inspired Christians globally.

They remind us that martyrdom is not defeat but victory. As Jesus said,

'Blessed are those who are persecuted for righteousness' sake, for theirs is the kingdom of heaven' (Matthew 5:10).

Even when earthly powers strike down the faithful, their witness lives on.

Suffering borne for Christ's sake becomes a seed that multiplies into new life.

Old Testament Reading

Isaiah 53:7–11 (ESV)
He was oppressed, and he was afflicted, yet he opened not his mouth.

Like a lamb that is led to the slaughter, and like a sheep that before its shearers is silent, so he opened not his mouth.

By oppression and judgment, he was taken away.

And as for his generation, who considered that he was cut off out of the land of the living,

stricken for the transgression of my people?

And they made his grave with the wicked and with a rich man in his death, although he had done no violence, and there was no deceit in his mouth.

Yet it was the will of the LORD to crush him; he has put him to grief.

when his soul makes an offering for guilt, he shall see his offspring; he shall prolong his days.

The will of the LORD shall prosper in his hand.

Out of the anguish of his soul he shall see and be satisfied.

By his knowledge shall the righteous one, my servant, make many to be accounted righteous, and he shall bear their iniquities.

New Testament Reading

Acts 7:54–60 (ESV)
Now when they heard these things they were enraged, and they ground their teeth at him.

But he, full of the Holy Spirit, gazed into heaven and saw the glory of God, and Jesus standing at the right hand of God.

And he said, 'Behold, I see the heavens opened, and the Son of Man standing at the right hand of God.'

But they cried out with a loud voice and stopped their ears and rushed together at him.

Then they cast him out of the city and stoned him.

And the witnesses laid down their garments at the feet of a young man named Saul.

And as they were stoning Stephen, he called out, 'Lord Jesus, receive my spirit.'

And falling to his knees he cried out with a loud voice, 'Lord, do not hold this sin against them.'

And when he had said this, he fell asleep.

Short Prayer

Lord Jesus, give us the courage to speak your truth boldly and to forgive as you forgave. When trials come, help us to see the heavens opened and trust that you stand with us. May our lives be faithful witnesses to your resurrection life. Amen.

Reflection Questions

- Forgiving enemies: Stephen and Romero forgave those who killed them. Is there someone you need to forgive today, trusting God to be your vindicator?
- Speaking truth: Both men spoke hard truths with love. Where in your life might God be calling you to stand for truth or justice, even at personal risk?
- Martyrdom mindset: Are you prepared, spiritually and emotionally, to suffer for your faith if necessary? What habits or prayers could strengthen you for such a witness?

Reflection 3: Apostolic Courage (The Apostles and the Coptic Martyrs of Libya)
The Apostles and Modern Martyrs

In the early days of the Church, the Apostles stood fearless in the face of deadly opposition. After Jesus' resurrection, Peter and John were warned by authorities to stop preaching, yet they replied boldly, 'We must obey God rather than men' (Acts 5:29, ESV). Despite imprisonment and beatings, the Apostles rejoiced that they 'had been counted worthy to suffer dishonour for the name' of Jesus. They went on teaching and preaching Christ openly, empowered by the Holy Spirit and undeterred by threats. Their courage birthed a movement that spread the Gospel across the world.

Fast forward to 2015: on a remote Libyan beach, a line of twenty-one Christian men—twenty Egyptian Copts and one Ghanaian—knelt before masked extremists. They had been kidnapped by ISIS and pressured to renounce Christ. Like the Apostles, these modern believers would not deny their Lord. In the moments before their execution, some cried out 'Ya Rab Yasu!' ('O Lord Jesus!'). Refusing a final chance to save their lives by conversion, they entrusted themselves to Jesus. These Coptic martyrs were beheaded for their faith, dying with the name of Christ on their lips. Their story stunned the world—a stark, modern echo of apostolic-era courage and faithfulness unto death.

Historical Context

The Apostles' courage was forged in a time of persecution. In the first century, proclaiming Jesus as Lord often meant defying both Jewish leaders and the Roman Empire. One by one, most of the Apostles eventually suffered martyrdom for their witness. Tradition holds that Peter was crucified upside-down in Rome, Thomas was speared in India, and others likewise gave their lives. They had seen the risen Christ and were filled with the Holy Spirit, emboldened to 'obey God rather than men' no matter the cost. Their fearless preaching under persecution helped spread Christianity like wildfire across the ancient world.

The Coptic Christians of Libya in 2015 likewise lived in a context of danger. As migrant workers in a volatile region, they were targeted for their faith. ISIS militants viewed them as 'people of the Cross' and sought to terrorize Christians. The twenty-one men who were killed became instant martyrs in the eyes of the Church. In fact, the Coptic Orthodox Pope declared them martyrs and saints soon after their deaths. Even the Catholic Church later honoured them in its martyrology as an ecumenical gesture of respect. Their sacrifice is part of a long history of persecution in the Middle East—a modern chapter in the book of Christian martyrdom that dates back to the Apostles. Knowing this context deepens our appreciation: these were ordinary believers—fishermen of Galilee, labourers from Egypt—who displayed extraordinary faith when tested.

Spiritual Lesson

Courage through Christ: The Apostles and the Coptic martyrs show that true courage is rooted in faith in Christ. They feared God more than men. They believed Jesus' promise of eternal life, which made them bold in the face of death. Such apostolic courage is not brash confidence in oneself, but steadfast trust in God. When threatened, Peter and John prayed for even more boldness to keep speaking about Jesus. Similarly, the Libyan martyrs, trusting in Jesus' name, did not yield even as swords hovered over their necks. Their example challenges us to stand firm in our convictions. We may not face execution, but we all encounter moments to either confess Christ or stay silent. In those moments, remembering these witnesses can inspire us to choose faith over fear.

The Power of Witness: There is a saying that 'the blood of the martyrs is the seed of the Church.' When believers show unflinching faith, it profoundly impacts others. The Apostles' bold stand fuelled the young church with zeal. In our time, the testimony of the Coptic martyrs has encouraged Christians worldwide to live less fearfully and more faithfully. Their story has been told in churches, books, and films, spreading the message of fidelity to Christ. God can use even our suffering as a witness that draws others to Jesus. Apostolic courage, old and new, reminds us that Christ is worth any cost. As Jesus said, 'Do not fear those who kill the body but cannot kill the soul' (Matthew 10:28, ESV). If we believe this, we find strength to face our own trials with grace. The presence of Christ with us—just as he stood with Stephen and others—gives us peace in persecution.

Bible Readings (ESV)

Old Testament Reading:
'If this be so, our God whom we serve is able to deliver us from the burning fiery furnace, and he will deliver us out of your hand, O king. But if not, be it known to you, O king, that we will not serve your gods or worship the golden image that you have set up' (Daniel 3:17–18, ESV).

New Testament Reading:

'But Peter and the apostles answered, 'We must obey God rather than men' (Acts 5:29, ESV).

Short Prayer

Lord, you are the strength of those who trust in You. Thank you for the courageous examples of the Apostles and modern martyrs. Please give us a share of that bold faith. When we are afraid, fill us with your Spirit to stand firm and speak truth in love. Help us to remember that our lives are in your hands and that eternity with you outweighs every trial. In Jesus' name we pray. Amen.

Reflection Questions
- Where in your life are you feeling pressure to stay quiet about your faith? How do the Apostles' and martyrs' examples encourage you to respond?
- What fears most often keep you from obeying God boldly? What truths about God's presence or eternity can help you overcome those fears?
- The Coptic martyrs died saying, 'Lord Jesus.' What might it look like for you to call on Jesus' name in the face of daily challenges or opposition?
- How can you support believers in hostile environments today who exhibit 'apostolic courage'? What can you learn from their faithfulness?

Reflection 4: Obedience Despite Fear (Abraham and Jim Elliot)
Abraham's Surrender and a Modern Missionary's Resolve

A lone figure stands on a mountain in Moriah, heart pounding, knife in hand. Abraham gazes at his beloved son Isaac, bound on an altar of wood. Years earlier, God had promised that through Isaac would come countless descendants—yet now, God was asking Abraham to sacrifice that very son. Trembling yet resolute, Abraham raises the blade. In that moment of supreme obedience, an angel calls out to stop him. God provides a ram in Isaac's place, honouring Abraham's faith. Abraham proved willing to obey God despite overwhelming fear and grief, trusting that God could even raise the dead to keep his promise (cf. Hebrews 11:17–19). Because Abraham did not withhold his only son, God richly blessed him, and through Isaac came the nation of Israel. Abraham's obedience, though tested by fear, became a model of faith for generations.

Now consider Jim Elliot standing on a riverbank in Ecuador in 1956, about to make contact with the Huaorani (Waodani) people. Jim was a young missionary pilot who, with four friends, felt called to bring the love of Christ to this isolated tribe. The Huaorani were known for violence against outsiders—surely Jim felt fear at times. He was newly married, and his wife Elisabeth had just given birth to their daughter. Yet Jim's heart echoed Abraham's resolve: he would obey God's call despite the risks. After weeks of friendly gift exchanges by air, Jim and his team finally camped on the ground to meet the tribesmen. Tragically, the Huaorani warriors attacked, and Jim and the other missionaries were speared to death. It was a shocking end—five young men martyred. Yet Jim Elliot had written in his journal not long before, 'He is no fool who gives what he cannot keep to gain what he cannot lose'. Like Abraham, Jim surrendered everything—even life itself—in obedience to God, believing the eternal reward outweighed the cost. His death was not in vain: years later, his wife and others returned to befriend the tribe, and many Huaorani came to faith in

Christ. Jim's courageous obedience, in the face of fear, opened the door for God's grace to reach an entire people group.

Historical Context

Abraham's test on Mount Moriah (Genesis 22) occurred around 4,000 years ago in the region of Canaan. Child sacrifice was practiced by some pagan cultures of that era, but God abhorred such sacrifices—this was a unique command meant to prove Abraham's devotion. The emotional and spiritual weight of this test is almost unimaginable. Abraham had left his homeland in Mesopotamia at God's command, journeying to an unknown land with only a promise. Throughout his life, he learned to obey God step by step: leaving home, believing for a son in old age, and finally this—offering that miracle son back to God. Hebrews 11:19 reveals Abraham's reasoning: he 'considered that God was able even to raise him from the dead.' In context, Abraham's obedience became a foundational example of faith (he is called the *father of faith*). His story set a precedent that trusting God sometimes means not understanding fully yet choosing to obey.

Jim Elliot's story takes us to the jungles of twentieth-century Ecuador. After World War II, a wave of young missionaries felt called to unreached peoples. Jim and his friends were part of this movement. They knew the risks—a few years earlier, shell oil workers had been speared by Huaorani hunters, which is why the area was considered so dangerous. Jim and the team spent months preparing, learning some phrases, dropping gifts from Jim's small plane, trying to show friendly intent. Their faith was not blind to danger; they simply valued obedience to the Great Commission above personal safety. In the historical aftermath, their martyrdom in 1956 sparked an outpouring of new missionaries and inspired countless people to dedicate their lives to Christ's service. The very tribe that killed them later welcomed Jim's wife Elisabeth and fellow missionary Rachel Saint. This led to remarkable reconciliation—some of the men who participated in the killing eventually became believers and were baptized. The legacy of Jim Elliot stands in missionary history as a testament that obedience to God's call can bear fruit even through one's death. His famous quote is often repeated because it distils the biblical truth that our earthly life is not ours to keep anyway, and yielding it to God's purposes is ultimately wise, not foolish.

Spiritual Lesson

Obedience Over Comfort: Abraham and Jim Elliot both teach us that truly following God means obeying Him even when we are afraid or when obedience costs us dearly. It's natural to feel fear—Abraham surely felt anguish and confusion; Jim likely felt apprehension about leaving his young family to approach a hostile tribe. Yet they didn't allow fear to stop their obedience. The lesson for us is that faith is not the absence of fear, but the resolve to act in trust despite fear. God understands our fears and doubts, but he calls us to move forward in faith one step at a time. When we choose obedience in the face of fear, we declare through our actions that we trust God's character and his promises more than our feelings. Jim Elliot's life motto—'Give what you cannot keep to gain what you cannot lose'—echoes Jesus' words that whoever loses his life for Christ's sake will save it. We may not be called to literal martyrdom or such dramatic tests, but daily obedience often requires little 'deaths' to our comfort and control. It might mean standing up for what's right at work, risking reputation, or surrendering our plans to God's will. The courage to obey comes from knowing that God is faithful and His rewards are eternal.

God's Greater Plan: Another lesson is that our obedience is never in vain. Abraham couldn't have foreseen how God would provide a ram, or that his act of surrender would become a prophetic picture of God's own heart (for God so loved the world that he did not withhold his only Son but gave him for us all). In hindsight we see that Mount Moriah pointed to Calvary, where God provided the Lamb—Jesus—in our place. Abraham's obedience was part of a much greater redemption story. In Jim Elliot's case, his death seemed senseless at first. But God brought amazing good out of it: an entire tribe encountering Christ's love and countless Christians inspired to bold missionary service.

When we obey God, we join in a story much larger than ourselves. We may not see the outcome immediately. Abraham walked back down Moriah with Isaac alive, but the full scope of God's oath to bless all nations through his offspring unfolded over centuries. Similarly, we may not know the ripple effects of our obedience, but we can trust that God will use it. Our task is surrender; God's task is results. Even in apparent failures or losses, God can bring triumph—even life from death.

Bible Readings (ESV)
Old Testament Reading:

'He [God] said, "Take your son, your only son Isaac, whom you love, and go to the land of Moriah, and offer him there as a burnt offering on one of the mountains of which I shall tell you." So Abraham rose early in the morning, saddled his donkey, and took two of his young men with him, and his son Isaac . . . and went to the place of which God had told him' (Genesis 22:2–3, ESV).

New Testament Reading:

'For whoever would save his life will lose it, but whoever loses his life for my sake will save it' (Luke 9:24, ESV).

Short Prayer
Father God, thank you for the examples of Abraham and Jim Elliot, who obeyed your voice even when it was hard. You know our fears and how we cling to what is comfortable. Help us to surrender our lives into your loving hands. Give us faith to trust you with what we hold dearest, knowing that you will provide and that your plans are good. May we obey your leading promptly and fully, as Abraham did, and leave the results to you. Strengthen us to say 'yes' to your call today, through Jesus Christ our Lord. Amen.

Reflection Questions

- What is something you sense God has been asking you to do that you find fearful or costly? What would obedience look like, and what encouragement do you draw from Abraham's story?
- How do you typically respond when you feel God nudging you out of your comfort zone? In what ways does Jim Elliot's example challenge your perspective on safety and risk for the sake of the Gospel?
- Jim Elliot wrote, 'He is no fool who gives what he cannot keep to gain what he cannot lose.' What 'earthly' things might God be calling you to hold more loosely? What eternal gains might he be offering in return?
- Can you recall a time when obedience to God brought an outcome you didn't expect, perhaps even after a period of trial or loss? How does that memory encourage you to trust him now?

Reflection 5: Silent Faithfulness (Women at the Cross and Fr. Jacques Hamel)
Devoted Women and a Faithful Priest

On a dark Friday afternoon in Jerusalem, a small group of women stood near Jesus as he hung on the cross. Among them were Mary Magdalene, Mary the mother of Jesus, and other faithful women (John 19:25). Their hearts were shattered, their teacher and Lord brutally crucified. Unlike most of the disciples who fled in fear, these women remained present—silent but steadfast. Under the shadow of the cross, they could do very little outwardly; yet their very presence spoke volumes of love, loyalty, and faith. They did not run from the horror or hide from association with Jesus. Instead, they stayed, weeping and watching, offering the comfort of their nearness. After Jesus' death, it was these same women who prepared spices and went early to the tomb (Luke 23:55–56, 24:1). They were the first witnesses of the resurrection. Their silent faithfulness in the darkest hour was honoured by God with the greatest news of all. Sometimes love is demonstrated not in words or miracles, but in quiet endurance and devotion. The women at the cross exemplified this kind of faithful presence.

In our own time, an elderly priest in France demonstrated a similar quiet faithfulness. Father Jacques Hamel was eighty-five years old, a humble parish priest who had retired but still helped with daily Mass at his local church. On July 26, 2016, as Fr Hamel was celebrating morning Mass in the town of Saint-Étienne-du-Rouvray, two young extremists suddenly burst into the church. In an instant, this routine act of worship turned into a scene of terror. The attackers seized the priest and several worshippers. In that moment, Fr Hamel's decades of faithful service were put to the ultimate test. Eyewitnesses say he resisted evil with the only weapon he had: the words 'Be gone, Satan!' He spoke those words twice, refusing to yield to the assailants' demands. The terrorists took his life, slitting his throat at the very altar where he was serving God. Fr Jacques fell as a martyr in the middle of the liturgy he had performed countless times. He died in silence after that brief rebuke of evil—a quiet, faithful shepherd laying down his life for his flock. In life, he was known as a gentle, unassuming man who 'did his job to the very end'. In death, his blood mingled with the sacrifice of Christ's altar, a powerful testimony that stunned France and the world. Fr Hamel's story, like that of the women at the cross, shows faithfulness that doesn't call attention to itself yet stands firm when it counts.

Historical Context

The women who remained at Golgotha had followed Jesus during his ministry in Galilee. In a time when women's testimony was often undervalued, the Gospels highlight their presence at the cross and the tomb. Culturally, most of Jesus' male followers fled for fear of arrest, but these women braved the potential danger simply to be with Jesus. Mary Magdalene had been delivered by Jesus from seven demons—her life transformed, she could not abandon him now. Mary, Jesus' mother, had heard Simeon's prophecy thirty-three years earlier that a sword would pierce her own soul (Luke 2:35). On Calvary, that prophecy was fulfilled as she watched her son suffer. Yet Mary stayed, embodying a mother's love and a believer's devotion even when God's plan was utterly bewildering. Historically, their silent vigil might seem insignificant compared to preaching or miracles. But in God's eyes, it was precious. The faithfulness of these women became part of the Resurrection story—in all four Gospels, women are the first to learn that Jesus is risen. Their reward for silent faithfulness was the joy of being messengers of the greatest hope. This underlines a key historical lesson: God often uses those who quietly persevere to be the initial bearers of his victory.

Father Jacques Hamel's context was a small parish in secularized France. By 2016, Europe had experienced a number of terror attacks, but the murder of a priest during Mass was particularly shocking. Normandy, where Fr Hamel served, is a quiet region—not a place one would expect martyrdom. Fr Hamel was born in 1930 and lived through World War II. He was ordained in 1958 and spent nearly sixty years serving in local parishes. In a time when fewer people in France attend church, he was known for his dedication to those who did—baptizing infants, visiting the elderly, faithfully saying Mass every day. On that summer morning, there were perhaps only a handful of worshippers (including nuns) present. The attackers targeted him because he was a symbol of faith. Yet this 'good, meek man' stood his ground spiritually. The eyewitness account (later shared by the archbishop of Rouen) noted that Fr Hamel tried to push the knife-wielding attackers with his feet and spoke the words 'Go away, Satan' even as he was being mortally wounded. These words hark back to Jesus' own words rebuking Satan (Matthew 4:10). After his death, Fr Hamel was widely honored—even Pope Francis referred to him as a martyr and held a special Mass in his memory. In historical perspective, Fr Hamel's martyrdom is seen as a testimony to faith thriving in unexpected places. He did not seek fame; he was not on a grand missionary endeavour abroad; he was simply faithful in the routine of parish life. Yet when evil struck, that lifetime of quiet devotion shone in a moment of courageous witness.

Spiritual Lesson

The Strength of Presence: The women at the cross and Fr Hamel illustrate that faithfulness is often demonstrated by simply being there and not abandoning our post. There is great spiritual strength in a loving presence. When others fled, the women stayed with Jesus—they couldn't stop the crucifixion, but their love refused to leave him alone in his suffering. In our lives, we sometimes underestimate the ministry of presence. Whether it's staying by a sick loved one's bedside, standing with a friend in crisis, or remaining true to God when it's unpopular—silent support is a powerful witness. Fr Hamel was doing just that: he was present for his small flock, doing what God had called him to do that morning. Even as danger approached, he didn't run; he kept doing his duty, up to his final breath. Our culture often celebrates the loud and the spectacular, but God values steadfast loyalty even if it's quiet. As 1 Corinthians 4:2 says, 'It is required of stewards that they be found faithful'—and faithful means consistently present and reliable. We learn that we don't have to be famous or perform great feats to honour God; often he asks us simply to stay, to show up, to not quit when it's hard. Your silent faithfulness in a tough situation might be the very thing that speaks to someone's heart about the love of Christ.

Speaking Truth in Love (When Necessary): Another lesson is that there is a time to speak and a time to remain silent, and both can glorify God. The women at Golgotha said little or nothing that is recorded—their silence was fitting in the face of Jesus' suffering. Sometimes words fail, and what matters is the heart's posture. Yet later, these same women did speak—announcing the resurrection to the disciples. Fr Hamel, on the other hand, was mostly quiet in his final moment except for a short, firm declaration against evil: 'Go away, Satan.' There is a beautiful balance here. A life of silent faithfulness prepares us to speak truth in love at the critical moment. Fr Hamel's brief words were backed up by a lifetime of living for Christ, which gave them weight. We too should cultivate a daily faithfulness so that if and when we must speak up—whether to confront evil, to defend our faith, or to comfort others—our words carry the power of integrity. Moreover, Fr Hamel's words remind us that our struggle is not against flesh and blood, but against spiritual forces of evil (Ephesians 6:12). He recognized the true enemy—Satan—and opposed him even as he himself was being overcome physically. His example encourages us to view our challenges through spiritual lenses and respond with prayerful authority when needed. Most of the time, our calling is to persist in quiet goodness; occasionally, God may call us to a bold proclamation. In both cases, a heart anchored in Christ is essential.

Bible Readings (ESV)

Old Testament Reading:
'The LORD will fight for you, and you have only to be silent' (Exodus 14:14, ESV).

New Testament Reading:

'Be faithful unto death, and I will give you the crown of life' (Revelation 2:10, ESV).

(The first reading reminds us that in moments of fear, God often calls us to trust quietly in him. The second reading is Christ's promise to those who remain faithful even to the point of death.)

Short Prayer

Dear Lord, thank you for the quiet heroes of faith—the women who stayed by your cross and servants like Father Hamel who stayed at their post. Teach me the beauty of steadfast love that doesn't need spotlight or praise. In my small daily duties, help me to be faithful. When evil or hardship comes, strengthen me to stand firm with grace, whether in silence or in speaking truth. I pray for the courage to simply be present for others as You are present with me. May my life, even in its quiet moments, honour you. In Jesus' name. Amen.

Reflection Questions

- Can you think of a time when someone's quiet presence made a big difference in your life during a trial? How does that encourage you to offer the same kind of presence to others?
- In what areas of your life has God placed you to 'stand by the cross'—to be a faithful witness or support even if you feel powerless to change the situation? What can you learn from the women at Calvary about this?
- Father Hamel continued his routine of prayer and worship despite potential danger. Are there routines of faith (prayer, worship, service) that you are tempted to abandon when facing opposition or inconvenience? How does his example challenge you?
- What might 'silent faithfulness' look like for you this week? Are there situations where you sense God calling you to simply remain steadfast and trust him to fight for you (Exodus 14:14)?

Reflection 6: Female Martyrs: Strength and Surrender (Perpetua, Felicity, and Modern Christian Women)
Ancient Resolve and Contemporary Courage

In the year 203 AD, in a North African arena, two young women stood hand in hand facing death. Perpetua, a twenty-two-year-old noblewoman and new mother, and Felicity, her slave who had just given birth days before, had been condemned to die because they were Christians. As the crowd roared, the Roman authorities sent wild beasts against them—a raging heifer meant to maul these defiant women. Thrown and gored by the animal, Perpetua and Felicity were bruised and bloodied, yet remarkably, they remained standing together, encouraging each other. According to Perpetua's own prison diary, she and her companions refused to renounce Christ despite pleas from family. When Felicity was in labour in prison, she cried out in pain. A guard mocked her, asking how she would handle the beasts if childbirth made her scream. Felicity answered quietly, 'Now I suffer what I suffer; but then there will be Another in me who will suffer for me, because I am to suffer for Him'. Her meaning was clear: God would give her strength in the arena, just as He was with her in childbirth. In the end, after surviving the heifer's attack, Perpetua and Felicity were killed by the sword. It's recorded that the executioner's hand trembled so much that Perpetua had to guide the sword to her throat—an extraordinary image of surrender and strength. They died serenely, faces shining with faith, choosing death over denying Christ. Their martyrdom became one of the most celebrated stories in the early Church, inspiring believers for centuries.

Now picture a modern scene: a young Christian woman in a hostile environment—perhaps in North Korea, or northern Nigeria, or a Middle Eastern village—who decides to follow Jesus. She knows that this decision might cost her life or her freedom or separation from family. Yet like Perpetua and Felicity, she presses on with courage and surrender. Consider Deborah, a university student in Nigeria (one of many real examples), who refuses to hide her Christian faith even as extremist threats loom on campus. Or the group of Missionaries of Charity nuns in Yemen who in 2016 chose to stay and care for the elderly and disabled despite a civil war. Gunmen stormed their facility, and these four Catholic sisters were murdered for their faith and service. These modern women joined the honoured ranks of martyrs—some well-known, most nameless to us—who met hatred with love and death with unyielding faith. They share a kinship with Perpetua and Felicity across time: a profound inner strength coupled with a surrender to God's will. In them we see that martyrdom is not a relic of the past; the same strength and surrender displayed in the arena of Carthage in 203 AD can be found in the hearts of women today who hold fast to Christ under persecution.

Historical Context

Perpetua and Felicity's story comes from the early third century during Roman persecutions of Christians. Their account is particularly valuable because Perpetua herself wrote part of it from prison—a rare firsthand testimony by a young woman in the ancient world. They were living in Carthage (modern-day Tunisia) under the rule of Emperor Septimius Severus, who had issued laws against conversion to Christianity. Perpetua came from a wealthy pagan family; her father begged her repeatedly to renounce her faith and save herself, but she calmly refused, saying, 'I am a Christian'. The firmness of her identity in Christ enraged the authorities. Felicity, her servant, was eight months pregnant when imprisoned. Roman law forbade executing pregnant women (showing even the empire had some limits), so Felicity prayed to give birth before the planned execution date so she could die with her friends and not alone later. God granted that prayer—she delivered a healthy baby girl in prison, who was secretly adopted by fellow Christians. The day of the execution, eyewitnesses noted how the martyrs appeared joyful, as if going to a wedding feast rather than death. They treated their executioners with kindness and concern. This historical record shattered stereotypes of the time: women were typically seen as weak, but here were two women exhibiting immense courage and spiritual strength. The early Church held Perpetua and Felicity in high honour; their feast day (March 7) was celebrated from very early on. Their story gave strength to other persecuted Christians: if these young mothers could conquer fear, others could as well. It emphasized that in Christ there is no distinction in valour between male or female—the Holy Spirit empowers all believers to witness, even unto death.

In modern times, persecution of Christians sadly continues, and often women face unique horrors. For instance, in some regions, Christian women are targeted for kidnapping, forced marriage, or violence as a way to intimidate the community. Yet we have numerous accounts of remarkable faith. In the late twentieth and early twenty-first centuries, many women in communist or extremist-controlled countries have suffered imprisonment or martyrdom. One example: Sister Annel, a Coptic Christian in Egypt, was killed in 2017 by a terrorist while she was serving the poor—she died praying for her attacker. Another: Leah Sharibu, a Nigerian schoolgirl (age fourteen) abducted by Boko Haram in 2018, who refused to renounce Jesus and convert to Islam, so she was not released with her classmates. Years later, she remains in captivity, reportedly enslaved—yet reports say she remains steadfast in faith. Such stories show the double burden on women—not only targeted for being Christian, but also vulnerable as females in cruel hands. And yet, like Perpetua and Felicity, so many Christian women display astounding resilience and grace. The Missionaries of Charity nuns in Yemen knowingly stayed in a dangerous place because of their surrender to God's call to serve 'the least of these'. They were executed by militants while at the bedside of the helpless. The Church today regards them as martyrs of charity. Looking at the broad historical context, we see a lineage of brave Christian women: from biblical times (like Esther risking her life, or the women who defied the king's edict in Exodus 1) to the early martyrs like Perpetua, to countless unsung heroines in every era. The constancy of their witness under fire is a powerful testament that the same Holy Spirit who filled believers at Pentecost is still at work.

Spiritual Lesson

Strength in Surrender: At first glance, *strength* and *surrender* might seem opposites; but in God's kingdom, they go hand in hand. The women martyrs teach us that yielding one's life to God is the ultimate act of strength. Perpetua and Felicity were physically weaker than the armed gladiators and beasts, yet spiritually, they were unbreakable. Their strength came from surrendering their fate to God's will. Jesus modelled this paradox too—in Gethsemane, his surrender ('Not my will, but yours be done') was his strength to face the cross. For us, we may not face martyrdom, but we are called to 'take up our cross daily' (Luke 9:23). That means daily surrender of our will, and in that surrender, we find the Holy Spirit's strength to do what we cannot do on our own. When we yield to God—be it in a small act of obedience or a monumental sacrifice—his power rests on us. The apostle Paul learned that when he was weak, then he was strong, because Christ's grace was sufficient (2 Corinthians 12:9–10). Female martyrs exemplify this truth vividly. They also show that courage is not the absence of fear, but the resolve to not let fear win. It's okay to feel afraid. Surely Perpetua felt fear as a young mother, Felicity worried about her baby, modern women tremble before threats, but they set their eyes on Jesus beyond the fear. Their surrendered hearts gave them a vision of glory that outshone the terror in front of them. We can draw inspiration from them for our struggles: When we face trials or hostile pressure for our faith, we can pray for the same grace to surrender our lives into God's hands and stand firm.

The Witness of Women: Another lesson is the unique witness that female martyrs and sufferers bring to the Church. In many societies, women are expected to be silent or secondary. But God often uses the 'weak' to shame the strong (1 Corinthians 1:27). The testimony of women who endure persecution can soften even the hardest of hearts. There are stories of jailers and even executioners converted by the gracious endurance of Christian women prisoners. Why? Perhaps because in such women, the beauty of Christ's character shines—compassion, forgiveness, peacefulness. For example, Perpetua prayed for her brother and even for her persecutors while in prison. Modern Christian women who forgive their tormentors or continue to serve others under oppression show an otherworldly love. This echoes Jesus forgiving his killers from the cross. It's a witness that arguments or sermons alone often can't achieve.

We learn from this that our character under duress is one of the most powerful testimonies we have. Whether man or woman, when we respond to hatred with love, to injustice with forgiveness, we display the reality of Christ in us. Female martyrs also remind us that no one is too 'ordinary' to make a profound impact for Christ. Perpetua was a young mom; she became a beacon. A Pakistani housewife on death row for blasphemy (like Asia Bibi) becomes a witness to millions by her steadfast faith. You, too, in your context—perhaps as a mother, a student, a professional—can shine for Christ in trials. God's strength is made perfect in your weakness and daily faithfulness. Lastly, these stories call us to support and remember the persecuted church, especially our sisters in Christ who suffer. The Bible urges us to 'remember those who are in prison, as though in prison with them' (Hebrews 13:3). We can pray for modern Perpetuas and Felicitys—women in hostile places—that God would fill them with strength and comfort. And we can allow their witness to embolden our own faith, knowing that if they can stand firm, by God's grace so can we.

Bible Readings (ESV)

Old Testament Reading:

'Then Esther told them to reply to Mordecai, " . . . I and my young women will also fast as you do. Then I will go to the king, though it is against the law, and if I perish, I perish".' (Esther 4:15–16, ESV)

New Testament Reading:

'Do not fear what you are about to suffer. . . . Be faithful unto death, and I will give you the crown of life.' (Revelation 2:10, ESV)

Short Prayer

O God, you gave courage to Perpetua, Felicity, and so many women who have faced death rather than deny you. We praise you for empowering the weak to be strong. Infuse us with the same strength in our own trials. May we surrender our lives daily into your care, trusting you completely. We pray for our sisters around the world who are in danger for following Jesus—please uphold them, let them feel your presence as 'another' suffering in and with them, just as Felicity believed. Help us to learn from their example to live with brave faith and gentle surrender. In the name of Jesus, who is our strength and our hope. Amen.

Reflection Questions

- Consider the phrase 'strength in surrender.' Can you recall a situation wherein giving up control to God actually made you stronger or more at peace? What does Perpetua's and Felicity's example teach you about surrendering outcomes to God?
- Esther said, 'If I perish, I perish.' What might an 'if I perish' attitude look like in your life? In what areas do you sense God calling you to deeper trust, even if there's a risk or cost?
- How do stories of persecuted Christian women today impact your faith? Think of one specific modern example you've heard (perhaps from mission news or church). How does their witness challenge you in your context, where the pressures might be different?
- In what ways can you support or remember the persecuted Church, especially women who suffer for Christ? Are there practical steps (prayer, advocacy, giving) you feel led to take as a result of reflecting on these stories?

Reflection 7: New Life from Death (Asia Bibi, Leah Sharibu, and the Persecuted Church)
Trials Turned to Testimony

A humble Pakistani woman named Asia Bibi spent nearly a decade on death row, and through that living 'death' found a new life and a global ministry she never expected. In 2009, Asia (a Christian farm worker and mother of five) was accused under Pakistan's harsh blasphemy laws after an argument over a cup of water. She was convicted and sentenced to hang. Locked in a prison cell awaiting death, Asia passed through a great darkness of the soul. Yet she clung to Jesus. She later said that at her lowest point, she dreamed of Christ reaching out to her, reassuring her of his presence. Strengthened by faith, Asia refused to renounce Jesus in exchange for her freedom. International pressure mounted for her release, and finally in 2018, her conviction was overturned. She walked out of prison—a free woman—in 2019. It was as if she had been resurrected from the grave. After years in solitary confinement, Asia Bibi emerged with her faith intact and her face radiant. She forgave those who accused her and thanked God for sustaining her. Now living in exile, she advocates for others facing persecution. In Asia Bibi's story, we see new life from death: her death sentence was not carried out, and instead, God turned her ordeal into a testimony of his deliverance. Her name, once associated only with a small village incident, is now known worldwide as a symbol of steadfast faith. Her suffering birthed a new mission—speaking on behalf of the persecuted and testifying to Christ's grace under pressure.

On another continent, a young Nigerian girl named Leah Sharibu embodies the hope of new life even amid continuing captivity. In February 2018, fourteen-year-old Leah was among 110 girls abducted by Boko Haram terrorists from their school in Dapchi, Nigeria. After a month, the jihadists released the other surviving girls—except Leah. The reason? Leah refused to convert to Islam. Witnesses say her captors gave her one last chance to say the Islamic creed and save her life, but she chose to remain a Christian, even if it meant not going home.

For Leah, this was a kind of living death: she remained a prisoner, isolated from her family and the world. In the years since, reports have surfaced that Leah is still alive, now a young woman possibly forced into marriage in captivity. Though her physical freedom has not yet been achieved, Leah's spirit remains unbroken. Her family recounts how, even at fourteen, Leah was devout and courageous. She loved to sing hymns and was active in her church youth group. In captivity, she sent word through released classmates, asking her mother to 'pray for me' and reassuring, 'I am not afraid'—powerful words from a teenager. Leah's story is still unfinished, but even now, it has brought forth immense fruit. She has become a rallying figure for the persecuted church in Nigeria and beyond. Many have come to a stronger faith seeing her faith. We pray and trust that, like Asia Bibi, Leah will one day be freed—a symbol of new life emerging from what was meant for evil. And even if, God forbid, her earthly life is cut short, Leah's hope is anchored in the resurrection. In Christ, no martyr ever truly dies; they live forever. Leah's steadfastness points to that reality—that our ultimate life cannot be taken by any captor.

Historical Context

Asia Bibi's ordeal unfolded in a contemporary context of severe persecution of minority Christians in parts of the Muslim world. Pakistan's blasphemy laws (originating from British colonial laws but made more extreme in the 1980s) have often been misused to settle personal scores or incite mobs. Asia's case is one of the most famous, but tragically not unique. Two Pakistani officials who spoke out in her defence—Governor Salman Taseer and Minister Shahbaz Bhatti—were assassinated in 2011. Asia spent about nine years on death row under constant threat; even after acquittal, radical groups demanded her execution. It took great political courage and international advocacy to finally secure her release and safe passage out of Pakistan. Historically, her story highlights how the global Church can unite in prayer and action to help a sister in chains. Asia Bibi's eventual freedom in 2019 was seen as a significant victory for religious liberty. It reminds us of biblical accounts like Peter being miraculously freed from prison (Acts 12)—an entire community had been praying earnestly for Asia, and God made a way where there was none. Today, Asia lives in Canada quietly with her family, but she has written a memoir of her experience and continues to speak (through interviews or messages) about faith under fire. She stands in a long line of persecuted believers whose suffering brought attention to injustice and stirred others to faith.

Leah Sharibu's context is the ongoing conflict in northern Nigeria, where Islamic extremist groups (Boko Haram and ISWAP) have targeted Christians. Leah's abduction in 2018 is reminiscent of the infamous Chibok kidnapping of schoolgirls in 2014. These kidnappings are used as leverage by terrorists and as a means to terrorize Christian communities. Historically, many kidnapped girls are forced to renounce their faith, and those who refuse face enslavement or death. Leah's refusal is extraordinarily brave for a child. Her stance drew comparisons to early Christian martyrs who, when pressured to deny Christ, chose suffering instead. The Nigerian government has claimed efforts to negotiate her release, but years have passed without success. Leah's family, and Christians worldwide, continue to pray for her. In a wider historical sense, her story illustrates the price that many in the persecuted church today are paying, especially in Sub-Saharan Africa and parts of Asia. Yet it also highlights a truth seen throughout church history: persecution often strengthens the Church rather than destroying it. Reports from Nigeria indicate that Leah's testimony has emboldened other believers not to give up their faith. Church gatherings commemorate her, songs have been written about her courage, and her name is remembered in prayers across the globe. This mirrors the early church, where stories of martyrs like Polycarp or Blandina fortified the believers. Tertullian's ancient statement that 'the blood of the martyrs is the seed of the Church' seems to hold true—the more the church is pressured, the more resilient and rooted it becomes. In places like China, Iran, or Nigeria, where oppression is intense, Christianity often grows in depth and number, as people witness genuine faith under trial.

Spiritual Lesson

Resurrection Hope: The theme 'New Life from Death' is ultimately a gospel theme. Jesus Himself through death brought forth resurrection life. For Asia Bibi and Leah Sharibu, as well as countless persecuted Christians, the hope of resurrection is what fuels endurance. They teach us about hope. Asia, in her cell, clung to the hope that God had not abandoned her, whether she lived or died. Leah holds on to Jesus in captivity because she has the hope of eternal life—a promise that outlasts any earthly pain. The persecuted church reminds those of us who live in relative safety that Christianity is a faith of living hope beyond the grave. We often get comfortable and focus on this life, but their experiences refocus us on the reality of heaven. Paul wrote, 'If we have died with him, we will also live with him; if we endure, we will also reign with him' (2 Timothy 2:11–12). Do we believe this? Our brothers and sisters facing death for Christ certainly do, and their lives challenge us to rekindle that hope in our hearts. We learn that no situation is truly hopeless when Christ is present. Asia's release was against all odds—a reminder that God still works deliverances today. But even when deliverance hasn't come yet (as with Leah), God is sustaining His children in miraculous ways. Many persecuted Christians speak of an inexplicable peace or the sense of Christ standing with them in the fire (like the fourth figure in Daniel 3:25). Their stories encourage us to trust God's promises deeply: He will either rescue from death or give new life through death. Either way, victory is assured.

The Seed that Grows: Another spiritual principle here is that God can bring great fruit from our trials. Jesus used the analogy: 'Unless a grain of wheat falls into the earth and dies, it remains alone; but if it dies, it bears much fruit' (John 12:24). The suffering of the persecuted church is like seed planted in the ground. It looks like a tragedy, but God uses it to produce a harvest of faith. In Asia Bibi's case, her imprisonment mobilized believers worldwide to pray, to speak out against injustice, and likely stirred many Pakistani Christians to be bold. In Leah's case, her testimony reverberates especially among young people: if a fourteen-year-old can stand for Jesus, others are inspired to stand strong too. We see 'new life' in the sense of renewed faith, new believers coming to Christ (there are accounts of extremists converting after witnessing the faith of Christians they persecuted), and new unity in the Body of Christ. Persecuted Christians often pray not just for themselves, but for the church to be revived. Their prayers and sacrifices are like rain on dry ground for the global church. For us, the lesson is to not squander the freedom and blessings we have but rather use them fruitfully. The courage of Asia and Leah can spur us to die to our own complacency and live more fully for God. Perhaps we can 'die' to fear of others' opinions, or 'die' to materialism or selfishness—and in doing so, bear fruit in love, generosity, and witness. Also, we are reminded to engage with the persecuted church, for we are one body (1 Corinthians 12:26 says if one part suffers, all suffer together). When we connect with their stories, it breathes new spiritual life into us. Their perspective can shake us from spiritual slumber and ignite fresh passion for Christ.

Bible Readings (ESV)
Old Testament Reading:

'Those who sow in tears shall reap with shouts of joy!' (Psalm 126:5, ESV).

New Testament Reading:

'Truly, truly, I say to you, unless a grain of wheat falls into the earth and dies, it remains alone; but if it dies, it bears much fruit' (John 12:24, ESV).

Short Prayer

Lord Jesus, you are the Resurrection and the Life. We thank you for the living hope you gave to Asia Bibi, to Leah Sharibu, and to all in your persecuted Church. What the enemy intends for evil, you can turn to good. Strengthen our suffering brethren; let them experience new life even in the midst of death and darkness. May chains break and captives be freed, but even before that day, fill their hearts with joy and peace that surpass understanding. Teach us through their example to hold fast to the hope of the resurrection. Help us to die to sin and self, that we might bear much fruit for your kingdom. We pray for the persecutors as well—that the light of Christ in believers like Asia and Leah would soften hearts and lead many to salvation. Keep us united with our persecuted family in prayer and love. In your powerful name, Jesus. Amen.

Reflection Questions

- Psalm 126:5 speaks of sowing in tears and reaping in joy. Can you identify an area in your life where you have experienced (or need to trust for) this principle—that your present tears could lead to future joy? How does the story of Asia Bibi reinforce this promise?
- Jesus' image of the grain of wheat (John 12:24) implies that apparent loss can lead to greater gain. What might God be asking you to 'die' to (let go of or endure) in order to bring new spiritual fruit in your life or community?
- When you think of Leah Sharibu's unwavering faith at fourteen, what emotions or thoughts stir in you? Does her example prompt you to reevaluate the seriousness with which you live out your own faith? In what way?
- The persecuted Church often prays for believers in comfortable countries to wake up and grow in faith. What steps can you take to answer that call? For instance, how can you actively remember persecuted Christians in your prayer life or support organizations that help them? What impact might that also have on your personal spiritual growth?

WRITINGS:
Reflective Meditations

Introduction to 'When Evil Hides Behind a Smile'

In the modern world, sin no longer shouts—it whispers behind causes that appear noble. It hides itself beneath words like justice, compassion, and truth, but often serves only vanity, pride, or self-interest. As Ecclesiastes reminds us, everything has a season, and hidden motives will be revealed in time.

This poem is a reflection on the deceptive face of evil, especially in an age when discernment is rare, and appearances are everything. When someone espouses a seemingly virtuous cause, we must ask: What is their true reason? Who are they serving? For even good words, when they are misused, can cloak dangerous intentions.

We live in a time when masking civility and borrowed nobility are used to manipulate others and disguise selfish aims. Those who are honest, who seem to lose the battles of popularity or worldly success, are often the ones who win the deeper war—because their lives are built on solid ground, not shifting sand. Their strength lies in God, not ego.

In this poem, I explore the age-old struggle between good and evil, not as abstract forces but as real and present powers that demand our vigilance. Discernment, now more than ever, is essential—to separate light from darkness, truth from illusion. God must be at the centre of our lives, and we must be clear: Who is calling us? And whom are we answering? If it is not God, it may be our pride. This is evils calling card. We give in to evil without realizing it

'When Evil Hides Behind a Smile' is both a warning and a hope—that even when evil masquerades as good, it fears love and truth for in these, it dies.

WHEN EVIL HIDES BEHIND A SMILE

It has been so
Since Abel fell to Cain—
A sin so hideous
Played out in paradise.

To Cain, Hashem had warned;
A beast lies crouched at the door
A predator poised to devour—
That is sin that can be tamed.

Iniquity brings despair
Madness, chaos, and death.
Yet sin, though fierce as fire
Can be broken like a wild horse.

For what is stronger than sin?
Not more wrath, nor more force, nor more might
The very tools it knows too well.
But love
Kindness
Compassion.

Against these
Evil has no response.
It fears love
For in love, it dies.

Jealousy, hatred, malice—
Fruits of the beast—
Vanish like vapor
Pierced by mercy's flame.

Beware! Evil adapts!
It finds a new disguise:
In false nobility
In false humility
In false compassion, and
In false mercy.

It speaks in twisted tongues
Confuses right and wrong.
Faith is used to persecute
Love is used to hate.
Compassion is wielded
To demean.

Evil prides itself in hubris
It loves the sound of its lies.
But its gain is short
A fleeting mirage
A whisper next to divine truth.

But steadfast love
and Divine mercy
Are the armour and shield
Of God's elect.

Even when masked
Evil brings ruin.
But love—pure and undiluted—
Brings peace that endures.

The ones who yield to the beast
Will have their day.

But those who surrender to Christ
Shall rise.
For death has lost its sting
And peace is now
And forever.

Annotated Version: When Evil Hides Behind a Smile

Annotated Edition

It has been so
Since Abel fell to Cain—
A sin so hideous,
Played out in paradise.

Genesis 4:8: The first murder, rooted in jealousy and rejected offering.
Theological note: This stanza signals the primordial entrance of evil not in a world already broken, but within the echoes of paradise itself— where the first human relationships are corrupted by sin.

To Cain, Hashem had warned;
A beast lies crouched at the door
A predator poised to devour—
That is sin that can be tamed.

Genesis 4:7: 'Sin is crouching at your door; it desires to have you, but you must rule over it.'
Hashem—Hebrew for 'The Name,' a reverent reference to YHWH.
Theological note: Sin is personified as a predator—*alive, active, and dangerous*—but it can be mastered, implying human freedom and God's grace.

Iniquity brings despair,
Madness, chaos, and death.
Yet sin, though fierce as fire,
Can be broken like a wild horse.

James 1:15: 'After desire has conceived, it gives birth to sin; and sin . . . gives birth to death.'

The Word in their Voices

Imagery: The 'wild horse' represents unbridled impulse—the potential of human energy either to destroy or be transformed through discipline and grace (cf. Ignatian mastery of desire).

For what is stronger than sin?
Not more wrath, nor more force, nor more might,
The very tools it knows too well.
But love,
Kindness,
Compassion.

Romans 12:21: 'Do not be overcome by evil, but overcome evil with good.'
1 Peter 4:8: 'Love covers over a multitude of sins.'
Theological note: Sin cannot be defeated with its own weapons. Divine love—not brute force—undoes evil's power. This is the paradox of the Cross.

Against these
Evil has no response.
It fears love
For in love, it dies.

1 John 4:18: 'There is no fear in love. But perfect love drives out fear.'
Augustine: *'Love, and do what you will.'* Love rightly ordered destroys sin at its root.

Jealousy, hatred, malice—
Fruits of the beast—
Vanish like vapor
Pierced by mercy's flame.

Galatians 5:19–21: Lists the 'acts of the flesh' (including hatred, jealousy, etc.) as opposed to the fruits of the Spirit.

Luke 1:78: 'Because of the tender mercy of our God . . . the rising sun will come to us from heaven.'
Imagery: God's mercy is depicted as a cleansing, burning flame that dissolves evil, not through violence, but through light.

Beware! Evil adapts!
It finds a new disguise:
In false nobility
In false humility
In false compassion, and
In false mercy.

Isaiah 5:20: 'Woe to those who call evil good and good evil.'
2 Corinthians 11:14: 'Satan himself masquerades as an angel of light.'
Theological note: Evil is not always violent—it is often subtle, moral-looking, and cloaked in virtue. This is a major theme in modern Catholic moral theology.

It speaks in twisted tongues
Confuses right and wrong.
Faith is used to persecute
Love is used to hate.
Compassion is wielded
To demean.

Romans 1:25: 'They exchanged the truth about God for a lie.'
St. Augustine: Warns against *splendid vices*: when virtue is perverted by pride or ideology.
Ignatian discernment: Evil may disguise itself in what appears to be good; discernment is needed to distinguish true consolation from false consolation.

Evil prides itself in hubris,
It loves the sound of its lies.
But its gain is short
A fleeting mirage
A whisper next to divine truth.

Psalm 73:18–20: The wicked seem to prosper but are quickly swept away.
John 8:44: Satan is 'the father of lies.'
1 Kings 19:12: God's presence is not in thunder, but in the 'still small voice'—the divine truth that outlasts deception.

But steadfast love
and Divine mercy,
Are the armour and shield
Of God's elect.

Ephesians 6:10–18: *'Put on the full armour of God.'*
Psalm 91:4: 'His faithfulness will be your shield and rampart.'
Theological note: This stanza provides a counter-armour to evil's disguise. The weapons of the faithful are interior, not exterior—rooted in grace.

Even when masked
Evil brings ruin.
But love—pure and undiluted—
Brings peace that endures.

John 14:27: 'Peace I leave with you . . . not as the world gives.'
Franciscan spirituality: True peace is born from humility, mercy, and simplicity, not worldly compromise.

The ones who yield to the beast
Will have their day.

Revelation 13: The 'beast' is the archetype of worldly power opposed to God.
Theological note: Evil has temporary authority—it may triumph for a moment—but its time is limited.

But those who surrender to Christ
Shall rise.
For death has lost its sting,
And peace is now
And forever.

1 Corinthians 15:55–57: 'Where, O death, is your victory? Where, O death, is your sting?'
Romans 6:4–5: We share in Christ's death to also share in His resurrection.
Augustine: *'Our hearts are restless until they rest in You.'*

Final Reflections:

- This poem journeys through salvation history in poetic form: from Genesis to Revelation, from sin's deception to Christ's redemption.
- It reflects the Ignatian call to discernment, the Augustinian understanding of rightly ordered love, and the Franciscan peace through humility.
- It could serve as a contemplative meditation, a theological teaching, or a devotional reading—it is that complete.

Introduction to 'The Unknown Saint'

This poem was born out of two quiet yet unforgettable encounters with goodness.

The first was in Loreto, where my wife and I met a kind priest who, despite being busy, took time to guide us to the reconstructed Holy House of Mary in the Basilica. We were really two lost souls in a crowd, and he knew instinctively what we needed. There was no fanfare, no sense of burden—just grace and peace radiating from a soul rooted in Christ. The second moment came unexpectedly in Sri Lanka, when my family, caught in the rain, asked to use the washroom facilities of a hotel. The humble keeper welcomed all six of us, refusing any compensation. Though we had brought in mud and water from the storm, he simply smiled. His kindness lingered with us long after we left.

These encounters made me reflect: in a world loud with cruelty, noise, and outrage—especially on social media and in the news—we often fail to notice the quiet saints among us. Their love does not announce itself. It does not trend. But it is real. It is found in the simplest acts, in the most unassuming souls.

'The Unknown Saint' stands in a long poetic and spiritual tradition that celebrates the hidden holiness of everyday souls—those who reflect Christ not through title or proclamation, but through quiet acts of mercy and love.

This poem echoes the spirit of St. Francis of Assisi, whose 'Prayer for Peace' asks to be a channel of God's love, sowing compassion where there is hatred. It shares the theological interiority of St. Augustine, who taught that God's law is written not merely in Scripture, but upon the heart. And it embodies the Ignatian way of seeing God in all things, especially in the humble and unrecognized.

Where some poetry dazzles with complexity, in the 'The Unknown Saint', I want to offer a different kind of beauty: clarity, peace, and truth. I want to invite you the reader to recognize the divine in the soft-spoken, the kind-hearted, and the uncelebrated—the ones who walk humbly, love softly, and carry forward love's gentle flame.

In this poem, I use the Hebrew word *chesed*—a rich and deeply biblical term that appears often in the Old Testament. Though it is commonly translated as 'steadfast love', 'lovingkindness', or 'mercy', no single English word fully captures its depth.

Chesed refers to a covenantal, faithful love—the kind of love God shows to his people: unearned, unwavering, and enduring. It is the love behind every act of divine mercy, the kind that does not abandon, even when betrayed.

When I speak of the unknown saint's *chesed*, I mean more than kindness or goodness. I mean a love that reflects God's own nature—a love that binds itself to others not out of duty, but out of faithfulness, grace, and self-giving compassion.

This one word, *chesed*, holds within it the spirit of the poem: quiet, enduring love that reveals the face of Christ.

Do we live this kind of love—in our homes, our workplaces, our service to the Church?

Words and works must go together. We need to hold a mirror to our own hearts and ask: *Am I a reflection of this quiet holiness?*

To become a saint to others, we must first put out into the deep. That is the call of Christ.

The Word in their Voices | 231

The Unknown Saint

He sits alone, set apart—
Unknown to all
A man thought small
His stature unassuming.

Yet this saint exists
In places unexpected
At times most needed
Filled with grace and reflecting Christ.

His heart is close to God
Yet in demeanour weak and simple.
In his quiet way, his love is pure—
His humble disposition belies
A quiet depth of compassion.

His kindness is freely given;
No coin will he accept
His currency is love
His only concern, that you are well.
He is a giant—
A mighty man of moral worth.

When paths do cross
Kindness greets, and his heart is made known.
Then it dawns, as his *chesed* shines forth
This is as it was with Christ.

The saint is not the lofty;
He is the man who loves softly.
He is not a man who relishes wealth—
His only concern: your health.

His life is not bound by moral codes
Or by laws so vast and studied.
No dogma, creed, or scholar's clause
Can taint the sincerity of this gentle soul.

He bears no title, no religious name—
The law of grace is written in his heart.
He acts justly and he loves mercy
and walks humbly.
He carries forward love's gentle flame.

When you meet this saint
Your heart will stir—your eyes gently opened.
You will be moved by joy inscrutable
For in the simplest acts
Come the greatest gifts.

Annotated Version of 'The Unknown Saint

He sits alone, set apart—
Unknown to all
A man thought small
His stature unassuming.

- **Luke 9:48 (NIV):** 'For it is the one who is least among you all who is the greatest.'
- This opening evokes the Gospel paradox: the true saints are often unnoticed, ordinary in appearance, and overlooked by the world.
- **St. Francis of Assisi:** His spirituality embraced being a *minor*—a 'lesser brother.' This stanza mirrors the Franciscan ideal: to be hidden in Christ.
- **Ignatian Echo:** The saint lives what Ignatius calls *holy indifference*—no concern for status, only the will of God.

Yet this saint exists
In places unexpected
At times most needed
Filled with grace and reflecting Christ.

- **John 1:14 (NIV):** 'The Word became flesh . . . full of grace and truth.'
- The saint's hidden presence is a quiet incarnation of Christ's love in the world.
- **Augustine (Confessions):** 'You were within me, but I was outside myself . . .'—the divine often shows up in unexpected ways and people.

'His heart is close to God
Yet in demeanour weak and simple.
In his quiet way, his love is pure—

- **1 Samuel 16:7 (NIV):** 'People look at the outward appearance, but the Lord looks at the heart.'
- The juxtaposition of *'weak and simple'* with *'close to God'* reflects Christian humility—echoing Christ's own hiddenness.
- **Ignatian Spirituality:** God's presence is often experienced in gentle, inner movements—not dramatic signs.

His humble disposition belies
A quiet depth of compassion

- **Matthew 11:29 (NIV):** 'I am gentle and humble in heart . . .'
- *Belies* is a powerful word here. It signals that the saint's outward gentleness conceals a depth not immediately visible—just as Christ's divinity was veiled in humanity.
- **Augustine:** 'The truth dwells within . . .' — this line calls us to see beyond appearances.
- **Franciscan Vision:** The true worth of a soul is measured not by power, but by *compassion lived quietly*.

His kindness is freely given;
No coin will he accept
His currency is love
His only concern, that you are well.

- **Matthew 10:8 (NIV):** 'Freely you have received; freely give.'
- **Acts 8:20:** 'You thought you could buy the gift of God with money!'
- This stanza creates a sacred contrast: earthly currency vs. heavenly values.
- 'His currency is love' — a striking image that redefines value in spiritual terms.
- **Ignatian Insight:** The true disciple serves without calculation—his only desire is the good of the other.

He is a giant—
A mighty man of moral worth.

- **Echoes Psalm 112:6–9**: 'Surely the righteous will never be shaken . . . their hearts are secure; they will have no fear.'
- **Augustine:** The great soul is not the one who rules others, but who rules himself by love.

When paths do cross
Kindness greets, and his heart is made known.
Then it dawns, as his chesed shines forth
This is as it was with Christ.

- **Chesed** (חֶסֶד): A Hebrew word meaning steadfast love, mercy, covenant faithfulness. It is used throughout the Old Testament to describe God's unwavering love:
- **Psalm 136:** 'His chesed endures forever.'
- **Exodus 34:6:** 'Abounding in chesed and truth.'
- The saint's love isn't just kind—it is *covenantal*. It reflects God's own *chesed*, just as Christ did.
- **Augustinian Theology:** Christ is the embodiment of divine mercy; the saint mirrors that reality quietly.

The saint is not the lofty;
He is the man who loves softly.

- **1 Corinthians 13 (NIV):** 'Love is patient, love is kind . . . it is not proud.'
- The use of *softly* evokes tender strength—love without noise, force, or pride.
- **Franciscan Humility:** Strength is not measured in volume, but in gentle endurance.

He is not a man who relishes wealth—
His only concern: your health.

- **Matthew 6:19–21 (NIV):** 'Where your treasure is, there your heart will be also.'
- The contrast between material gain and human well-being emphasizes the saint's simplicity and selflessness.
- **Ignatian Discernment:** What truly matters is not possessions, but the condition of one's soul and body.

His life is not bound by moral codes
Or by laws so vast and studied.
No dogma, creed, or scholar's clause
Can taint the sincerity of this gentle soul.

- **Romans 2:15 (NIV):** *'The requirements of the law are written on their hearts.'*
- The saint's holiness is not theoretical, but lived—beyond institutional systems, rooted in grace.
- **Augustine (On Christian Doctrine):** Doctrine without love is useless. This saint embodies the law of love.

He bears no title, no religious name—
The law of grace is written in his heart.'

- **Hebrews 8:10 (NIV):** *'I will write my laws on their hearts . . .'*
- **Franciscan Simplicity:** St. Francis resisted ecclesial titles. This saint is 'unknown' not because he lacks faith, but because he is not concerned with titles.

The Word in their Voices

He acts justly and he loves mercy
and walks humbly.

- **Micah 6:8 (NIV):** 'What does the Lord require of you? To act justly, love mercy, and walk humbly with your God.'
- The central ethical vision of Scripture is fully embodied in this man.
- **Ignatian Spirituality:** A life in Christ is one of action, compassion, and humility.

He carries forward love's gentle flame.

- **2 Timothy 1:6 (NIV):** 'Fan into flame the gift of God . . .'
- The flame symbolizes ongoing, quiet transmission of divine love.
- This is a deeply Franciscan image: carrying divine light not through dominance, but through presence.

When you meet this saint
Your heart will stir—your eyes gently opened.
You will be moved by joy inscrutable
For in the simplest acts
Come the greatest gifts.'

- **Luke 24:31 (NIV):** 'Then their eyes were opened and they recognized him . . .'
- **Philippians 4:7 (NIV):** 'The peace of God, which transcends all understanding . . .'
- 'Joy inscrutable' and 'eyes gently opened' echo the experience of spiritual awakening—a soft epiphany in the presence of grace.
- **Augustine (Confessions, Book I):** 'You have made us for Yourself, O Lord, and our hearts are restless until they rest in You.'
- **Ignatian Consolation:** A deep joy that reveals God in the ordinary—a hallmark of authentic spiritual encounter.

Final Reflection:

'The Unknown Saint', I try to portray as a theological portrait of incarnated grace. The saint depicted here may never be canonized or recognized, but in his silent fidelity, he becomes a mirror of Christ's hidden life.

By drawing from Scripture, Augustine's theology, Franciscan humility, and Ignatian discernment, I hope to awaken you, the reader, not to admiration alone—but to imitation. Something I am continually trying to do but fall miserably short.

With this poem, I invite the reader to see Christ again—not in fame, status, or noise, but in those who love with quiet fidelity.

RUTH

RUTH

INTRODUCTION

'Ruth (From Farewell to Fulfilment)' is a dramatic monologue, that reimagines the biblical story of Ruth from the heroine's perspective. Rooted in the themes of faith, loyalty, and redemption, the poem traces Ruth's journey from loss in Moab to fulfilment in Bethlehem.

The work is structured as a reflection on pivotal moments in Ruth's life: her decision to stay with Naomi, her labour as a gleaner, and the joy of motherhood with her son, Obed. The poem culminates in a powerful affirmation of God's faithfulness, drawing on the biblical concept of *chesed*—the steadfast love that weaves Ruth's story into the broader covenantal heritage of Israel.

The placing of Ruth in the Tanakh vs the Christian Bible is an important consideration when reflecting the message of Ruth. The Torah (the Law) and the Nehivim (prophets) are scriptures of God talking to us directly or indirectly. The Ketuvim (writings) are the collection of scripture showing humanity's response to his word. God is referenced indirectly. This is explained and developed in the in the discission following the poem and its annotations. This is the first part of my discussion on understanding the Hebrew language, culture, and traditions to appreciate the treasure that we have as scriptures.

Notes to Ruth:

The story of Ruth is a timeless testament to resilience and divine providence. In this poem, I sought to capture Ruth's inner voice, reflecting on her journey from exile to belonging. The title, 'From Farewell to Fulfilment,' encapsulates the movement from grief to grace, mirroring the transformation that unfolds within Ruth's life and heart.

By including the Aaronic Blessing and the epigraph from Ruth 1:16, I aimed to emphasize the sacred nature of Ruth's choice—a decision not only to embrace a new people but also to embrace a new faith. The final stanza serves as a benediction, acknowledging that the legacy of Ruth's faithfulness is not merely personal but transgenerational, woven into the scroll of divine mercy.

My hope is that this poem not only honours the spiritual richness of Ruth's story but also inspires reflection on how acts of loyalty and love ripple through generations, echoing the steadfast love of God.

Explanatory notes before you read:

1. Hashem—the Jewish name for God – (It literally means The Name).
2. Hesed—loving kindness, steadfast love.
3. B'rit Milah—covenant of circumcision.

Ruth (From Farewell to Fulfilment)

'Where you go, I will go . . . your people shall be my people, and your God, my God.'

It is time for his B'rit Milah
My blessed gift from Hashem
With clarity now I see His hand in my life
Oh, such joy when once was strife.

I lift my light and my love from his cradle
Obed's warmth against my chest
His father's arms around me
Boaz's love a shelter and a home
The three of us on Eagles' wings.

My mind strays, for a moment, to Moab—
To that grave where I buried Mahlon
And all before that was my life—
Orpah beside me, Naomi weeping.

All three of us widowed, hollowed, and lost.
The men we loved were gone.
In their place; a future, leaving a promise
Of a silent and empty void to come.

Only Naomi's voice pierced the darkness—
In her whispers, the name of Hashem.
She proclaimed Him by day and by night
Teaching His ways by table-light and on the road.
A graceful channel for His love and peace
In her grief, she bore Him still.
The secret cord that bound us as family.

And I—foreigner, widow, wanderer—
Found peace not in gods of my childhood
But in Hashem who steadied Naomi's sorrow.
So I clung to her
To her people, her land
And to her God who had become mine.
My restless heart stilled when I rested in him.

Three times she bade me turn back
To my home, to my people, and my gods.
Three times I chose the road ahead
Binding myself to her.

For where else could I go
But to the heart where *chesed* lived?
I had crossed the threshold
From Moabite to daughter of Hashem.

In Bethlehem I gleaned with aching limbs
Amid scents of warm and nutty ripe grains of barley
A promise of food for the day.
For her, for Him, I laboured.
My future still uncertain; lingering fear remained.

What would become of us?
Then he came—this man of kindness—
A gentle voice, a blessing uttered
From lips that did not yet know me
But blessed me all the same.

Boaz—our redeemer—
Saw me as more than a Moabite girl.
He saw a daughter of Hashem.
He knew my life and my all
And I, amidst the scorching sun
Kneeling and gathering in the dust
Stood in the light of love.

Naomi smiles, and she cries
Tears not of loss and goodbyes but of Joy.
Hashem's Peace is upon her
As she gazes upon her grandson, her husband's seed.

She who gave me a name
I now give back a legacy.
For in redeeming me
Boaz redeemed her and Elimelech.

Obed's cry brings me back to this moment
I hold him tightly in my arms—
A servant of God born of sorrow and grace.
I turn to Boaz, and I am now complete.

What lies ahead—
I do not know.
Yet this truth—
Rests upon my heart.

The God of Abraham, Isaac, and Jacob
Has written us into the scroll of his mercy.
And His *chesed* will chase us for generations to come.

Annotations and Explanations for the Poem

1. *Obed's Warmth Against My Chest*

   - **Reference—Ruth 4:17:** This line symbolizes hope and new beginnings, as Obed represents the continuing lineage of David, emphasizing the importance of family and legacy resulting from Ruth's journey.

2. *To That Grave Where I Buried Mahlon*

   - **Reference—Ruth 1:5:** This directly addresses Ruth's personal grief over her husband's death, underscoring the emotional weight of loss that drives her journey.

3. *Orpah Beside Me, Naomi Weeping*

   - **Reference—Ruth 1:14:** This mentions the collective sorrow of three widows, emphasizing the theme of loyalty and choice. It highlights Orpah's decision to return home versus Ruth's steadfast commitment to Naomi.

4. *In Her Whispers, the Name of Hashem*

   - **Reference to the Shema (Deuteronomy 6:4–5):** Naomi's mention of the name of Hashem emphasizes her role as a spiritual guide, instilling faith in Ruth. The Shema's command to love God and keep his words in daily life is reflected in how she teaches Ruth about their faith, reinforcing the act of proclaiming God's name both at home and during their journey.

5. *Proclaimed Him by Day and by Night*

   - This line echoes the Shema's teaching to integrate God's commandments into everyday life, emphasizing the continuous nature of their faith. Naomi's efforts to instil this belief in Ruth elevate her role as a mentor.

6. *Teaching His Ways by Table Light and on the Road*

    - **Connections to: Isaiah 26:3:** This conveys the importance of learning and discussing faith throughout daily experiences, stressing how familial bonds help nurture one's spiritual life.

7. *Three Times She Bade Me Turn Back*

    - **Reference—Ruth 1:11:** This line symbolizes Ruth's unwavering commitment and loyalty to Naomi. Her repeated choice to stay illustrates the depth of her love and determination amidst hardship.

8. *Heart Where Chesed Lived*

    - **Reference—Micah 6:8:** The term *hesed* signifies loving kindness, which is central to Jewish ethics. This line evokes the nurturing essence of God's love, which Ruth embodies as she chooses to remain with Naomi.

9. *In Bethlehem I Gleaned with Aching Limbs*

    - **Reference—Leviticus 19:9–10:** This acknowledges the practice of gleaning, which provided sustenance for the poor, highlighting Ruth's hard work and commitment to care for Naomi.

10. *My Future Was Still Uncertain; Lingering Fear Remained*

    - This conveys Ruth's vulnerability and anxiety about her new life, portraying her realistic emotional state as she navigates the unknown.

11. *Then He Came—This Man of Kindness*

    - **Reference—Ruth 2:20:** This is an acknowledgment of Boaz's role as a kinsman-redeemer, indicating his kindness and benevolence, which significantly impacts Ruth's journey toward hope.

12. *Boaz—Our Redeemer*

    - **Reference—Ruth 4:1–10:** Boaz's role as a redeemer is central to the narrative, showcasing themes of redemption and the importance of community support.

13. *Saw Me as More than a Moabite Girl*

    - **Reference—Ruth 2:10:** This line emphasizes Boaz's recognition of Ruth's worth and potential, connecting it to her acceptance and identity within the Israelite community.

14. *Stood in the Light of Love*

    - **Reference—John 8:12:** Light symbolizes hope and divine presence. This moment marks Ruth's transition into a new life filled with love and **acceptance.**

15. *Hashem's peace upon her*

    - **Reference—Numbers 6:24–26:** This invokes the Aaronic Blessing

16. *Her husband's seed*

    - **Reference—Deuteronomy 25:5–10:** This is theologically significant because it reflects the concept of Levirate marriage and redemption of marriage in ancient Israel.

17. *The God of Abraham, Isaac, and Jacob*

- **Reference—Exodus 3:6:** By invoking the patriarchs, Ruth establishes her new identity within the Israelite tradition and emphasizes the covenantal relationship with God.

18. *Has Written Us into the Scroll of His Mercy*

- **Reference—Psalm 69:28:** This reflects God's promise of mercy, emphasizing the theme of inclusion and compassion within the familial and spiritual lineage.

19. *His chesed Will Chase Us for Generations to Come*

- **Reference—Psalm 23:6:** This echoes the idea of God's unfailing love following His people, underscoring the continuity of divine mercy through Ruth's lineage.

RUTH

The Book of Ruth reveals that God's choice of leaders is neither random nor based on earthly standards. His hand moves with grace, but also with discernment, weaving together lives marked by covenant loyalty, faith, and righteousness. Ruth, a Moabite widow, was not chosen because of her pedigree, but because of her steadfast devotion to the God of Israel. Her story shows us that in God's kingdom, covenant loyalty trumps bloodline and worldly status.

Through Ruth's quiet faithfulness, God was already preparing the way for the Messiah. Her inclusion into the lineage of King David—and ultimately of Christ—teaches us that God's great plan of salvation has always been built upon hearts that cling to him. Ruth's life is a testimony that faithfulness to the covenant brings a person into God's saving purposes, regardless of their past or heritage.

In the same way, when Christ came, he opened the way for all of us—Jew and Gentile alike—to become adopted sons and daughters of God, not by natural descent but by covenant faithfulness through grace. Ruth's story whispers the greater story to come that those who cling to God in loyalty and love will find a home in his family and a place in his unfolding plan of redemption.

Devotional Reflection: *'Covenant Loyalty Over Pedigree: The Heart of God's Redemption'*

In the quiet pages of the Book of Ruth, we glimpse the timeless way God works not through grand displays of power, but through simple acts of loyalty, love, and faith.

When Ruth clung to Naomi with the words, 'Your people shall be my people, and your God my God' (Ruth 1:16), she crossed a threshold. In that moment of simple, sincere devotion, covenant loyalty trumped pedigree. She was no longer a Moabite by identity, but a child of the living God by faith. God saw her heart, not her bloodline.

Later, Boaz blesses Ruth, declaring, 'May the Lord repay your work . . . under whose wings you have come to seek refuge' (Ruth 2:12).

Ruth had taken shelter not in human strength, but under the wings of God himself. Her trust in the covenant brought her under divine protection, showing that true belonging is determined by faith and trust, not by the accidents of birth.

At the story's end, the women of Bethlehem bless Naomi, praising the Lord who 'has not left you without a redeemer' (Ruth 4:14). Behind every sorrow and every small act of faithfulness, God had been weaving a tapestry of redemption. The child born would become the ancestor of David—and through David, the ancestor of the Messiah. Ruth's story is not only about personal redemption but about the preparation of salvation for the whole world.

In Ruth, we see that God's hand moves through covenant faithfulness. Her life prefigures our own adoption into the family of God—not by natural descent, but by grace through faith. As Christians, we are sons and daughters of God because we, too, have chosen to cling to His covenant through Christ.

God's heart remains the same: he does not choose leaders or heirs randomly. He prepares hearts marked by faith, devotion, and loyalty to him. And through such hearts, he brings about his great work of redemption.

Application Today:

God Chooses the *faithful*, not the *flashy*.

Main Scripture Anchor: Ruth 1:16–17, Ruth 4:14–17

Your people shall be my people, and your God my God.
Blessed be the LORD, who has not left you this day without a redeemer . . .

I. God's Pattern of Preparation
- God's choice of Ruth was not accidental—she was chosen for her covenant loyalty and steadfast faith.

- Her loyalty led to David, Israel's greatest king, and ultimately to Christ.
- This was a pattern repeated in Mary: humble, obedient, faithful—chosen to bear the Son of God.
- Key idea: God doesn't randomly use 'anyone'—he carefully prepares 'someone' with the right heart.

II. Covenant Loyalty Trumps Pedigree

- Ruth was a Moabite—a Gentile, technically an outsider.
- Yet her heart aligned with God's covenant, showing that faith defines belonging, not bloodline.
- God elevates those with a faithful spirit, not necessarily a noble background.
- Application: Our faithfulness in small, hidden places matters deeply to God.

III. Contrast with Modern Leadership Discernment

- Today we often choose leaders based on soundbites, charisma, or political positions, not inner character.
- Many Christians, overlook deep ethical failings and harmful policies (e.g. cuts to Catholic social services) and divisive rhetoric while accepting specific soundbites from cunning individuals like 'abortion'
- Biblical warning:
  o Ecclesiastes 7:5: 'Better is the rebuke of the wise than the song of fools.'
  o Proverbs 16:2: 'The Lord weighs the motives of the heart.'

IV. God Looks at the Heart

- The Lord chose Ruth and Mary because of their faithfulness, not their fame. This was continued in David in Ruth's case.

- God's pattern: He prepares in obscurity those he intends to use publicly.
- We must not confuse public statements with private conviction.
- Discernment is a spiritual responsibility—especially in leadership and ministry.

V. Application: Discipleship and Discernment Today

- Are we cultivating the kind of covenant faithfulness God honours?
- Are we quick to elevate leaders who say the right things, but lack God-honouring character?
- Call to action: Be like Ruth and Mary—faithful, humble, devoted.
- Call to discernment: Test the spirits. Examine fruit, not fanfare.

Conclusion:

God's kingdom advances not through the loud, but through the loyal.

He chooses not based on power or pedigree, but on covenant love and inward truth.

Ruth, the Moabite, and Mary, the handmaid of the Lord, show us that when God chooses, He chooses hearts that are wholly his.

Biblical Scholarship Assessment

- **Date and Authorship:** The argument aligns with scholarly views that the Book of Ruth was composed after David's rise to prominence. The narrative itself mentions David by name (Ruth 4:17–22), which implies it was written when David was already known as king. Many scholars date Ruth to the post-exilic period (e.g. 5th–4th century BCE during the Persian era) based on its language and themes. Others, noting the story's positive tone toward Moab and the need to explain old customs, suggest an early monarchy date (soon after David's accession). In all cases, it's later than David's time, so the idea that Ruth was written after David became king is consistent with academic opinion. The author of Ruth is unknown—the text itself gives no name. (Jewish tradition once ascribed it to Samuel, but since David's kingship post-dates Samuel's life, Samuel is unlikely to have written the final form.) Modern scholars simply regard the author as an educated Israelite storyteller, possibly writing to address issues of the author's own time.

- **Divine Choice of a Leader:** Academically, the book's conclusion (the genealogy leading to David) is seen as theologically purposeful. It's not a random epilogue; it highlights how David's ancestors were people of exemplary faith and character. Scholars note that this ending 'elevates both the story and David' by reflecting 'David's worth through the quality of life of his forbears'. In other words, the virtuous lives of Ruth and Boaz cast a positive light on God's choice of David as king. This supports the argument's point that the message of Ruth emphasizes God's deliberate preparation of leaders. Rather than portraying David's rise as a happy accident or purely by human will, the book subtly shows God at work behind the scenes (through 'providential involvement in the lives of individuals') to bring about a worthy leader for Israel. Ruth's place in the lineage underlines that God's selection of David was both gracious and discerning—gracious in that he incorporated a Moabite convert into the royal line, yet discerning in that this convert (Ruth) was exceptionally faithful.

- **Covenant Loyalty over Ancestry:** Ruth's character strongly supports the idea that character and covenant loyalty matter more than bloodline. In the story, Ruth is a foreigner by birth, a Moabite—a people traditionally excluded from Israel (cf. Deuteronomy 23:3). Yet the narrative emphasizes her extraordinary commitment to Israel's God and family. One scholar observes that 'Ruth has demonstrated covenant fidelity and illustrated loyalty to YHWH and Israel', serving as a model of faithfulness. She 'made a clean break with her own people and was completely loyal to the nation and religion of her adopted family', showing that true Israelite identity is defined by faith and loyalty rather than ancestry alone. This theme fits into Covenant theology: Ruth's actions exemplify *ḥesed* (loyal love and kindness), a key covenant value. Boaz likewise shows *ḥesed* in how he protects and redeems Ruth. Theologically, the book suggests that God's covenant blessings extend to anyone who clings to him and his people with genuine loyalty. Thus far from promoting a simplistic 'God can use anyone (even a crook)' idea, Ruth teaches that God's grace welcomes outsiders but expects sincere faithfulness. God's choice to include Ruth in the messianic lineage demonstrates an 'overruling Providence and the all-embracing love of God' toward the faithful, without endorsing ungodly behaviour. In sum, the academic consensus affirms the argument's thrust: Ruth's message is that God sovereignly orchestrates his plan through people of noble character, valuing covenant faith over pure lineage.

Most scholarly arguments about the dating and purpose of Ruth rely on literary, linguistic, and socio-historical analysis—These methods make inferences based on patterns, themes, and cultural context, and they do often assume the book is responding to its own immediate human context (e.g., post-exilic debates about intermarriage).

There is an important theological dimension:

- *From a faith perspective,* the story's inclusion of a Moabite woman, and her prominent place in the line of David (and, in Christian tradition, Jesus), can be seen as divinely inspired preparation for the later inclusion of Gentiles in salvation history.
- *Christian interpretation,* especially, reads Ruth not just as a response to Ezra-Nehemiah but as part of God's broader plan, culminating in Christ. This view sees the book's themes as intentional and providential, transcending their immediate cultural context.

1. Human and Divine Authorship

Traditional Christian theology (and much Jewish thought as well) affirms both the human and divine authorship of Scripture:

- The text has real historical and literary context (human side).
- Yet the Holy Spirit inspires its deeper meaning and ensures it serves God's ultimate redemptive purpose (divine side).
- Thus, Ruth's message of inclusion may have immediate human relevance (e.g. a corrective to exclusivism), but also a timeless, prophetic significance pointing to God's universal plan.

2. Ruth as Divine Preparation for Gentile Inclusion

Biblical Pattern:

- Outsiders like Ruth, Rahab, and Tamar are placed in the genealogy of David and Jesus (Matthew 1).
- This foreshadows the Gospel's opening to the Gentiles.

Prophetic Typology:

- Early church fathers and many Christian theologians saw Ruth as a *type* (symbolic forerunner) of the church—an outsider brought in, redeemed, and made part of God's people.

3. Limits of Human Scholarship

- Scholarship is valuable for understanding historical context, but it can miss the *divine narrative* unless it is open to theological meaning.
- Inspiration means the book can speak to more than just its own time—it becomes a vessel for God's ongoing revelation.

4. Both-And, Not Either-Or

The book of Ruth can be both:
- A response to contemporary issues (such as Ezra-Nehemiah's debates).
- And, more profoundly, an inspired, providential work, anticipating the full inclusion of all nations in God's plan—a theme Jesus himself fulfils and the early church proclaims (e.g., Acts 10–11, Ephesians 2:11–22).

In Summary:

- *Human literary arguments* are helpful, but not exhaustive; they do not preclude deeper, divinely intended meaning.
- *Divine inspiration* means Ruth can both address Israel's immediate concerns and prophetically point to the inclusion of Gentiles in salvation—something only fully revealed in Christ.

Textual Criticisms

1. Layered Use and Reception

- Original Composition:

    Ruth could have been written earlier—perhaps simply to preserve a beloved family story, to explain David's Moabite ancestry, or to illustrate faithfulness and *hesed* (loving kindness).

- Secondary Use:

    Later, as Israel struggled with issues like intermarriage (Ezra-Nehemiah), the story of Ruth was brought forward or emphasized as a counterpoint—either cited directly, reinterpreted, or simply resonating in a time when such debates were active.

- Continued Relevance:

    As time went on, Ruth's message was seen as *timely* for new generations, whether as a challenge to exclusivism, a call to kindness, or (in Christian tradition) a prophetic signal toward the inclusion of Gentiles.

2. How This Works in Biblical Tradition

- 'Pulled up to form an argument':

This is precisely how many biblical books or passages gain new force:

- Earlier story → later argument:
  E.g. The story of Jonah is later read as a call for repentance (and even as a symbol of resurrection in Christian tradition); Isaiah's servant songs are given messianic meaning; Ruth is leveraged in debates about inclusion.

- Scripture as Living Word:
  This process shows Scripture's dynamic nature: texts are *re-read*, *re-applied*, and *re-understood* as communities face new challenges.

3. Divine Providence in Human Reception

- Providential Use:
  Even if Ruth wasn't originally written to 'combat' Ezra-Nehemiah, its *preservation and re-application* may itself be seen as God's providence—using an old story to speak anew in later crises.

- Canonical Context:
  Over time, the Spirit guides how Scripture is heard, ensuring God's purposes are continually revealed—sometimes in ways the original human author couldn't have foreseen.

4. Example: Ruth's Re-application

- Ezra-Nehemiah bans foreign wives:
  Ruth, as a Moabite woman who becomes the ancestor of David, challenges a simplistic reading of that ban.
- The text may not have originated as a 'polemic', but becomes an important voice in the debate.

5. Modern Application

- This layered, evolving use of Scripture is not just an ancient phenomenon. It's how the Bible continues to speak to new situations today—texts 'rise up' to meet the moment, sometimes in fresh and surprising ways.

Conclusion

- Ruth's original purpose may not have been polemical, but its later use—to combat exclusivism, to argue for inclusion, or to model kindness—is a testimony to how Scripture 'lives' in the community of faith.
- This layered approach honours both human and divine elements in the formation and use of Scripture.

This the heart of biblical interpretation:

God works not only in the writing, but also in the preservation, selection, and re-reading of sacred texts throughout history.

Exegesis vs Eisegesis

The tension in interpreting Ruth: Most scholarly arguments are *eisegetic* in that they try to say, 'Because Ruth was written about foreign women marrying in, it must be written to counter Ezra and Nehemiah's ban on marrying foreign women'. This is a human interpretation assuming the author is human and therefore can be subject to human literary scrutiny and analysis using our current literary devices. However, *the writer may be human*, but the *inspiration is divine in the form* of the Holy Spirit. Because God is preparing for Gentiles to be included in salvation through Jesus.

Many scholarly arguments about Ruth's purpose and dating are eisegetic—that is, they tend to project later concerns (like the Ezra-Nehemiah intermarriage ban) *back on to* the text, reading Ruth as a deliberate polemic against those policies. This approach, by definition, interprets the text through the lens of the interpreter's context or assumptions, sometimes at the expense of the text's own original voice or the possibility of divine intention.

From a faith perspective:

o   Ruth's story—especially her status as a Moabite and her place in David's and Jesus' lineage—can be seen as part of God's providential and prophetic plan, anticipating the inclusion of Gentiles in salvation.

o   The divine inspiration of Scripture means its meaning is not exhausted by human concerns or historical debates; it has a surplus of meaning, often revealed across the ages. It transcends the original time in which it was written and has a meaning for future generations.

   • While it's valuable to understand how Ruth might have functioned in the debates of its time (exegesis), we must be

careful not to reduce its meaning to just a human agenda (eisegesis).
- The deepest reading recognizes both the human and divine authorship of Scripture—and is open to the possibility that God intended Ruth to foreshadow the Gospel's universal scope, regardless of when or why it was first written.

In summary:

Scholarly readings sometimes fall into eisegesis, seeing Ruth only as a human argument against Ezra-Nehemiah, when in fact the text may carry a deeper, divinely inspired message that transcends its immediate historical context. A faithful reading of Ruth involves both sound exegesis and openness to the Holy Spirit's deeper meaning.

Ruth is not just a cultural story; it's a theological testimony. A Moabite woman brought into Israel's story, becomes the ancestor of Dvid and Jesus. That's not just literary; its salvation history.

Side-by-side comparison of how Ezra–Nehemiah and Ruth treat the topic of foreign women, followed by how Ruth anticipates Paul's theology of Gentile inclusion in the New Testament.

Part 1: Ruth vs. Ezra–Nehemiah on Foreign Women

Background Context

- After the Babylonian exile, Jewish leaders sought to preserve national identity.
- Ezra and Nehemiah were deeply concerned about intermarriage with foreigners, fearing religious corruption and loss of covenantal distinctiveness.
- Ruth, in contrast, tells the story of a foreign woman (Moabite) who becomes part of Israel and the ancestor of David.

Table: Ruth vs. Ezra–Nehemiah

Category	Ruth	Ezra–Nehemiah
Time Period	Set in Judges; likely written post-exile	Post-exilic (5th c. BCE)
Foreign Woman	Ruth, a Moabite (explicitly mentioned 7+ times)	Numerous unnamed foreign wives
Marriage Outcome	Ruth marries Boaz, a respected Judahite	Foreign marriages are dissolved (Ezra 9–10; Neh. 13)
Moral Judgment	Ruth is portrayed as virtuous, loyal, and faithful	Foreign wives are seen as a threat to purity and law
Religious Status	Ruth says, 'Your God shall be my God' (Ruth 1:16)	No mention of faith or conversion among the foreign wives
Lineage Result	Ruth becomes great-grandmother of David	Intermarriage seen as jeopardizing Israel's future
Divine View Implied	Inclusion of foreigner blessed by God	Intermarriage provokes national repentance

Interpretive Tension

- Ezra–Nehemiah reflects a nationalistic-protective posture during a vulnerable time.
- Ruth presents a personal narrative of faith and inclusion, highlighting covenant loyalty over ethnicity.

Theological synthesis: While national identity mattered post-exile, faith and covenantal loyalty transcended ethnicity—a theme which reaches its fullness in the New Testament.

Part 2: Ruth and Paul's Theology of Gentile Inclusion

Paul develops a theology where Gentiles are full heirs in the covenant through faith in Christ—not through ethnicity, law, or descent.

Ruth's Themes That Anticipate Paul

Theme in Ruth	Pauline Parallel
Ruth, a Gentile, is accepted into Israel	Gentiles are grafted into Israel (Romans 11:17–24)
Acceptance based on faith and loyalty	Inclusion based on faith, not the law (Gal. 3:28–29)
Ruth becomes part of the Messianic line	Gentiles become co-heirs with Jews in Christ (Eph. 2:11–22)
Ruth says: 'Your God . . . your people . . .'	Gentiles once far off are now citizens of God's people (Eph. 2:12–19)
Redemption through Boaz the redeemer	Redemption through Christ the Redeemer (Titus 2:14)

Key New Testament Passages

- Romans 9–11: Gentiles are grafted into the olive tree of Israel.
- Galatians 3:28–29: In Christ, there is neither Jew nor Gentile; all are Abraham's offspring.
- Ephesians 2:11–22: Christ has broken down the dividing wall, making one new humanity.
- Matthew 1:5: Ruth is named in Jesus' genealogy, as part of the divine plan for Gentile inclusion.

Summary

Viewpoint	Ezra–Nehemiah	Ruth	Paul
Foreign women	Problematic; threaten holiness	Exemplary; loyal, faithful, blessed	Equal heirs through Christ
Inclusion based on	Ethnic/legal separation	Personal loyalty and faith	Faith in Christ, not ethnicity or Torah
Covenant identity	Ethnic Israel	Expanded to include outsiders like Ruth	Jew and Gentile united in one body
Salvation history	Focus on purity and survival	Lineage of David prefigures Messiah	Fulfilment in Jesus as redeemer of all

Conclusion:

1. Ruth serves as a theological bridge: she challenges narrow interpretations of covenant identity based on ethnicity and anticipates the full Gentile inclusion that is central to Paul's gospel.
2. The Story of ruth is a whisper to Christ's plan to include Gentiles into salvation
3. While Ezra–Nehemiah addresses specific post-exilic crises, Ruth reflects God's broader purpose—faithful outsiders are not just welcomed, they become central to redemption.
4. Paul's theology builds on that foundation: salvation is open to all through Christ, regardless of origin, by faith.

Ruth in Hebrew and Christian Bibles

In Ruth, it is important to appreciate where Ruth resides in the Christian Bible compared to the Tanakh. The reasons for these differences and why we need to know them is important in understanding the text.

In the *Tanakh (תנ״ך), the Hebrew Bible, the three divisions—Torah, Nevi'im, and Ketuvim*—each play distinct and deeply interconnected roles in shaping Jewish theology, history, and identity.

1. Torah (תּוֹרָה)

'Instruction' or 'Law'

- Books: Genesis, Exodus, Leviticus, Numbers, Deuteronomy.
- Role:
  o The foundation of Jewish life, theology, and law.
  o Contains narratives of creation, the patriarchs, the Exodus, and the Sinai covenant.
  o Central focus is on God's covenant with Israel and the mitzvot (commandments) given through Moses.
- Function: Prescriptive and narrative; it defines identity, morality, and legal obligations.

2. Nevi'im (נְבִיאִים)
'Prophets'

- Books: Divided into Former Prophets (e.g., Joshua, Judges, Samuel, Kings) and Latter Prophets (e.g., Isaiah, Jeremiah, Ezekiel, and the Twelve Minor Prophets).
- Role:
  o Continues the historical narrative from the Torah.
  o Features prophetic voices who interpret Israel's history through the lens of covenant faithfulness, divine judgment, and hope for restoration.

- Function: Theological commentary on Israel's behavior in light of the Torah; calls for repentance and faithfulness to God.

3. Ketuvim

'Writings' (כְּתוּבִים) –

- Books: A diverse collection including Psalms, Proverbs, Job, Song of Songs, Ruth, Lamentations, Ecclesiastes, Esther, Daniel, Ezra–Nehemiah, and Chronicles.

What Did the Ketuvim Represent Collectively?

- **Spiritual Response and Wisdom**:
  - Unlike Torah (law) and Nevi'im (prophecy), Ketuvim often represents the response of humanity to God rather than direct divine speech.
  - Psalms is a key example—prayers, praises, and laments directed from people to God.
  - Proverbs and Ecclesiastes reflect wisdom traditions, offering guidance on living well in a complex world.

- **Liturgical and Devotional Use**:
  - Many texts in Ketuvim were used in temple liturgy, personal worship, or synagogue readings, especially during festivals (e.g., Ruth on Shavuot, Lamentations on Tisha B'Av).

- **Diaspora and Post-Exilic Reflection**:
  - Books like Esther and Daniel reflect Jewish life under foreign rule, emphasizing God's providence, faithfulness in exile, and the challenge of maintaining identity.

- **Historical Retrospection and Theology:**
  - Chronicles retells the history from Genesis to the Babylonian exile, reinterpreting it with temple-centred theology, showing a priestly, retrospective viewpoint.
  - Ezra–Nehemiah highlight restoration and community reform, particularly focusing on Torah obedience in the post-exilic community.

Ancient Evidence for the Shape of the TaNaKh

When Jesus alludes to the order of the Hebrew Bible, he assumed a three part design, which agrees with other contemporary Jewish authors who allude to the ordered sections.

- **Luke 24:44:** 'This is what I told you while I was still with you: Everything must be fulfilled that is written about me in the Torah of Moses, the Prophets and the Psalms.'
- **Luke 11:51:** 'Therefore this generation will be held responsible for the blood of all the prophets that has been shed since the beginning of the world, from the *blood of Abel to the blood of Zechariah*, who was killed between the altar and the sanctuary' (Matthew 23:35).
- Abel was murdered by Cain *in Genesis 4*, and Zechariah son of Jehoiadah was murdered by Joab in 2 Chronicles 24, which corresponds to the TaNaKh order.
- **Prologue to the Wisdom of Ben Sirah**: 'Many great teachings have been given to us through the Law [Torah], and the Prophets [Nevi'im], and the others that follow them Kethuvim]... So my grandfather Yeshua devoted himself especially to the reading of the Law and the Prophets and the other scrolls of our Ancestors.'
- **Dead Sea Scrolls (4QMMT):** 'The scrolls of Moses, the words of the prophets, and of David.' Some precepts of the Law (מקצת מעשי חתורה)

- **Philo of Alexandria (De Vita Contemplativa, 25):** 'The laws and the oracles given by inspiration through the prophets and the Psalms, and the other scrolls whereby knowledge and piety are increased and completed.'

HEBREW BIBLE (aka Mikra or TaNaK/ Tanakh)	ORTHODOX BIBLES (based on larger versions of LXX; exact contents & editions vary)	CATHOLIC BIBLE (based on Alexandrian canon of LXX; with seven Deuterocanonical books)	PROTESTANT BIBLE (retains Catholic order, but seven Apocrypha removed)
Torah / Books of Moses 1) *Bereshit* / Genesis 2) *Shemot* / Exodus 3) *VaYikra* / Leviticus 4) *BaMidbar* / Numbers 5) *Devarim* / Deuteronomy	Pentateuch 1) Genesis 2) Exodus 3) Leviticus 4) Numbers 5) Deuteronomy	Pentateuch (Law) 1) Genesis 2) Exodus 3) Leviticus 4) Numbers 5) Deuteronomy	Law (Pentateuch) 1) Genesis 2) Exodus 3) Leviticus 4) Numbers 5) Deuteronomy
Nevi'im / Former Prophets 6) Joshua 7) Judges 8) Samuel (1&2) 9) Kings (1&2) Ketuvim 1) Psalms 2) Proverbs 3) Job 4) *Song of Songs* 5) *Ruth* 6) *Lamentations* 7) *Ecclesiastes* 8) *Esther* 9) Daniel 10) Ezra-Nehemiah 11) Chronicles	Historical Books 6) Joshua 7) Judges 8) Ruth 9) 1 Kingdoms (= 1 Sam) 10) 2 Kingdoms (= 2 Sam) 11) 3 Kingdoms (= 1 Kings) 12) 4 Kingdoms (= 2 Kings) 13) 1 Chronicles 14) 2 Chronicles 15) 1 Esdras 16) 2 Esdras (=Ezra + Nehemiah) 17) Esther (longer version) 18) JUDITH 19) TOBIT 20) 1 MACCABEES 21) 2 MACCABEES 22) *3 Maccabees* 23) *4 Maccabees*	Historical Books 6) Jhua 7) Judges 8) Ruth 9) 1 Samuel 10) 2 Samuel 11) 1 Kings 12) 2 Kings 13) 1 Chronicles 14) 2 Chronicles 15) Ezra 16) Nehemiah 17) TOBIT 18) JUDITH 19) Esther (longer version) 20) 1 MACCABEES 21) 2 MACCABEES	Historical Books 6) Joshua 7) Judges 8) Ruth 9) 1 Samuel 10) 2 Samuel 11) 1 Kings 12) 2 Kings 13) 1 Chronicles 14) 2 Chronicles 15) Ezra 16) Nehemiah 17) Esther (shorter version)

The Tanakh

Section	Category	Books
Torah	Law	Genesis, Exodus, Leviticus, Numbers, Deuteronomy
Nevi'im	Former Prophets	Joshua, Judges, Samuel, Kings (1st and 2nd Combined)
	Latter Prophets	Isaiah, Jeremiah, Ezekiel, The Twelve
		The Twelve: Hosea, Joel, Amos, Obadiah, Jonah, Micah, Nahum, Habakkuk, Zephaniah, Haggai, Zechariah, Malachi
Ketuvim	Emet (Truth)	Psalms, Proverbs, Job
	Megillot (5 Scrolls)	Song of Songs, Ruth, Lamentations, Ecclesiastes, Esther
	Other Writings	Daniel, Ezra-Nehemiah, Chronicles (1st and 2nd Combined)

HEBREW

Why We Need to Appreciate It

Why We Need to Appreciate Hebrew

Introduction: On the Beauty and Necessity of Understanding Hebrew

This section of my book begins with a reflection on the importance of understanding Hebrew in appreciating the Bible's full depth. Let me be clear from the outset: it is not necessary for everyone to study Hebrew as a language or to master its grammar. But it is, I believe, essential for those who seek to engage seriously with Scripture to recognize and appreciate the power of Hebrew words and to understand how they shape the meaning of the biblical text.

The original Hebrew Bible—the Tanakh—was written in Hebrew (and parts in Aramaic), and much of the Christian Old Testament is a translation of this text. From the fifteenth to the twentieth century, translators brought the Bible into English through their own cultural and theological lenses. Their work, while often faithful and devout, reflects the interpretive decisions they had to make based on their understanding of Hebrew at the time.

However, in the past century, new discoveries—especially the Ugaritic texts uncovered in the 1920s—have shed important light on Hebrew vocabulary, idioms, and verb systems. These discoveries have clarified meanings and revealed nuances that were previously hidden or misunderstood. As a result, when we read the Bible in English, we are not necessarily reading the 'wrong' text—but we are reading a version filtered through interpretation.

This is especially important when we come to passages that are theologically rich or textually complex. In such cases, returning to the source—the Hebrew—can reveal insights and layers of meaning that might otherwise be obscured.

In the New Testament, though written in Greek, we must remember that Jesus and his disciples spoke Aramaic or Hebrew. To fully grasp the connotations of their words, we should try to understand how a Hebrew-speaking mind would have understood concepts like mercy, righteousness, and law. This mindset can dramatically shift our reading and deepen our understanding.

I begin this section with the story of Jesus and the woman caught in adultery—a passage both enigmatic and powerful. The moment where Jesus writes in the sand has fascinated generations of readers and theologians. Many theories have been proposed about what he might have written, but most have been shaped by English or Western interpretive frameworks.

Yet Jesus was a Jew. He would have spoken in Hebrew or Aramaic and been thoroughly versed in the Torah, the Prophets (Nevi'im), the Writings (Ketuvim), and the interpretive traditions of the Midrash. This inspired me to present my own theory—grounded in the structure, spirit, and sacred rhythm of the Hebrew Scriptures—about what he might have been writing.

I do not present this theory as dogma. It is not *the* answer. Rather, I hope it serves as an invitation—an opening of the door for you to begin reading and meditating on the Bible in a deeper and more layered way. Because to read the Bible only in English is, in many ways, like looking at the reverse side of a finely woven tapestry—you see the form, but not the full beauty.

When you begin to encounter the Scriptures in Hebrew—even through basic appreciation rather than technical mastery—you begin to see the pattern from the front, in all its texture, colour, and meaning.

I pray that this section will stir your heart to study, to reflect, and to approach the Word of God with new eyes—and a renewed awe.

JESUS FORGIVES THE ADULTERESS
(Writing in the Sand)

Jesus

Here come the indignant crowd with raised voices,
Parading their idea of righteous faith.
Feigning to hate sin while sinning in this very act—
They come to challenge, to trap
As if faith were a spectacle for entertainment.
They cannot accept the Torah I gave
Meant not to bind but to bring life.

Pharisees and Sanhedrin
Learned in the letter, blind to the Spirit—
Dripping with arrogance and pride.
They place a woman at my feet
And invoke the law of adultery
As though stoning is its only end.

They know I speak of mercy—
Divine mercy, a treasury inexhaustible.
They set a snare, like hunters seeking prey.
They wait for me to fall.
But I am the Shepherd, not the prey.

I look down at her.
Then I look at them.
I brought them out of Egypt
Parted the Red Sea, gave them a nation
Walked with them in the Tabernacle.
I sent prophets to teach justice and compassion.
Jeremiah spoke for me:
'I will remember their iniquities no more.'

Yet here they stand, forgetting my mercy
Remembering each other's sins.
Condemning when I desire love
Sacrificing when I ask for a contrite heart.

I look again at the woman—shivering, afraid.
They know not what they've done.
They cast her before me, unknowing
They've thrown her into the presence of Hashem—
To their and her Savior.
To the Author and Perfecter of their faith.

The Woman

I am a lowly woman, ashamed and beaten
I look up to him—they call him Yeshua.
I've heard him speak of a new world
A kingdom built on love and hope.
I longed to meet him
But not like this.
I bow down in awe of him.

He looks down—and I tremble.
I am cold.
Shaking.
Ashamed.
His words are beautiful
Full of mercy and kindness.
But I do not deserve his presence.
To be near him is to stand on holy ground.

I whisper the Shema
For surely I will die.
How could Adonai forgive one such as me?
Even though I was taken by force
I blamed myself—I did not fight.
Now, as death draws near
I find strange comfort when beside him.
To see him. To hear him.

Jesus

As I face the crowds in front of her
She looks away, ashamed and bereft of hope—
But I know her.
She is one of mine, my lost sheep.
What fools these crowds are
Twisting the beautiful Law I gave—

Weaponizing the Law to kill
when it was meant to fulfil the human heart
Usurped now for power and pride
They dare try to trap the One who wrote it.
Even now, the Father and Spirit and I smile—not with mirth, but with mercy.

We gave them free will.
And so—I stoop and teach.

I write in the sand.
Once, I wrote with fire on stone for Moses.
Now, I write with my finger in dust.
A footnote to the Law.
'Gam shneihem'—Both shall be punished.
Where is the man?

The Woman

Behind him, I peek through trembling fingers.
He writes in the sand.
And somehow
I feel peace.
His presence is a shield.

They scream and demand judgment.
But he stands.
And says
'Let the one without sin cast the first stone.'

Then he stoops again.
And writes:
'You shall not bear false witness. You shall not kill.'

Jesus

I stand.
And they fall away.
Shame overwhelms rage.
Their trap is undone.
They see now—
This was never about justice.
Only death.
But there will be no spectacle today.

The Woman

I still kneel.
But I see him clearly now.
He is my shepherd
I am the lost sheep, and he has come for me.
He is my Lord and my God.

The crowds dissipate.
Life is restored.
When I thought death would be my final gift
I received mercy instead.

I rise slowly, unafraid.
His eyes are full of peace—
Peace I've never known.
Peace I never want to lose.

Jesus

I turn to her.
Her fear is now gratitude.
She has hope where there was none.
In her sin, she knew she needed healing.
She knocked. She asked.
And she received.

If only all my sheep knew this simple truth.
I look upon her and place my peace on her.
'Go. Sin no more.'
Soon, I will release all who ask
From every burden of sin.

The Woman

I hear his forgiveness—
And my heart leaps.
As Jeremiah promised
He remembers my sin no more.

I am his sheep, and I know his voice
I go back to my family
But I will follow him all the days of my life.
I love—because he loved me first.
I serve—because he saved me.

And I await the day
For final rest in him.
The source of true and everlasting peace.

Annotation: 'Jesus Forgives the Adulteress'

Jesus

Here come the indignant crowd with raised voices
Parading their faith with righteous anger.

- **John 8:3–6:** The scribes and Pharisees bring the woman as a test.
- **Matthew 23:27–28:** Jesus critiques hypocrisy—outward righteousness masking inner sin.
- **Isaiah 29:13:** 'These people. Draw near with their mouth . . . but their hearts are far from me.'
- 'Righteous anger' underscores their self-justified rage—an anger that masquerades as zeal for God.

Feigning to hate sin while sinning in this very act—
They come to challenge, to trap
As if faith were a spectacle for entertainment.

- Their act is a public shaming; it is performative, not redemptive.
- **St. Augustine (Tractate 33 on John):** 'They brought her to the Teacher not to learn, but to accuse both her and Him.'
- **St Augustine** further notes with irony: 'They sought to punish adultery with blood, while themselves committing spiritual adultery by forsaking mercy.'

They cannot accept the Torah I gave
Meant not to bind but to bring life.

- **Deuteronomy 30:19:** The Law offers life and blessing.
- **2 Corinthians 3:6:** *'The letter kills, but the Spirit gives life.'*
- **Romans 7:10:** Paul, 'The commandment that was intended to bring life actually brought death.'

The Word in their Voices | 285

Pharisees and Sanhedrin
Learned in the letter, blind to the Spirit—
Dripping with arrogance and pride.

- **Echoes Romans 2:17–24:** Those who boast in the Law but dishonour God by misusing it.
- **St. Francis (Admonition 26):** Warns against religious pride disguised as piety.

They place a woman at my feet
And invoke the law of adultery
As though stoning is its only end.

- **Leviticus 20:10 and Deuteronomy 22:22:** Both parties to adultery are to be punished.
- The absence of the man is a revelation of injustice.

They know I speak of mercy—
Divine mercy, a treasury inexhaustible.

- **Luke 6:36:** 'Be merciful, just as your Father is merciful.'
- Reflects the teaching of Hosea 6:6: 'I desire mercy, not sacrifice.'

They set a snare, like hunters seeking prey.
They wait for me to fall.
But I am the Shepherd, not the prey.

- **Psalm 23/John 10:11:** The Good Shepherd lays down his life, not the accused.
- Also reflects Isaiah 53:7, where the Suffering Servant is silent before accusers.

Salvation History Recalled

I look down at her.
Then I look at them.
I brought them out of Egypt
Parted the Red Sea, gave them a nation
Walked with them in the Tabernacle.
I sent prophets to teach justice and compassion.
Jeremiah spoke for me:
'I will remember their iniquities no more.'

- **Exodus 14, Leviticus 26, Jeremiah 31:34:** Allusions to God's covenantal faithfulness.
- **Jesus speaks with the voice of YHWH**—He is not only interpreting Scripture; He is its author and fulfilment.
- **Augustine:** 'They used the woman as bait. But they cast her before the net of mercy.'

Yet here they stand, forgetting my mercy
Remembering each other's sins.

- **Matthew 18:33:** Parable of the unmerciful servant.
- **Psalm 103:12:** God casts sins as far as the east is from the west.
- They cast her before me, unknowing,

They've thrown her into the presence of Hashem—
To their and her Savior.
To the Author and Perfecter of their faith.

- **'Hashem' (Hebrew:** *The Name***)** shows reverence for God's holiness.
- **Hebrews 12:2:** 'Looking to Jesus, the author and perfecter of our faith.'

The Woman

I am a lowly woman, ashamed and beaten.
I look up to him—they call him Yeshua.

- **Psalm 34:18:** 'The Lord is close to the broken-hearted.'
- **Psalm 51:17:** 'A broken and contrite heart, O God you will not despise.'
- 'Yeshua' means *salvation*—his very name points to her hope.

I've heard him speak of a new world
A kingdom built on love and hope.
I longed to meet him
But not like this.
I bow down in awe of him.

- This moment evokes the reverence of Exodus 3:5—Moses before the burning bush.

I whisper the Shema
For surely, I will die.

- **Deuteronomy 6:4–5:** 'Hear, O Israel . . .'
- The Shema is traditionally recited at the hour of death or danger.

Even though I was taken by force
I blamed myself—I did not fight.
Now, as death draws near
I find strange comfort when beside him.
To see him. To hear him.

- This reframes the woman not only as an accused sinner but potentially a victim of exploitation—adding real-world realism.

- **St. Francis** would say this woman is Christ's 'least and lowest', the one he most desires to embrace. His famous saying 'We are what we are before God, and no more'.

Jesus (Writing in the Sand)

She is one of mine, my lost sheep.

- **Luke 15:4–7:** Parable of the Lost Sheep.

Weaponizing the Law to kill
when it was meant to fulfil the human heart
Usurped now for power and pride

- **Matthew 12:7:** 'If you had known what this means, 'I desire mercy, not sacrifice,' you would not have condemned the innocent.'
- **Augustine:** 'The law was given, not to condemn, but to lead to grace.'
- Even now, the Father and Spirit and I smile—not with mirth, but with mercy.
- A rare Trinitarian moment of shared compassion, not condemnation.
- Reflects the unity of divine action in John 5:19 and the love of John 3:17.

Once, I wrote with fire on stone for Moses.
Now, I write with my finger in dust.
A footnote to the Law.
'Gam Shneihem'—Both shall be punished.
Where is the man?

- **Exodus 31:18:** God writing the Law on tablets.
- **Leviticus 20:10:** Both the man and woman must be judged.
- Jesus exposes hypocrisy and injustice by citing the Law itself.

The Word in their Voices | 289

- **St. Augustine:** The same finger that wrote the law now writes with Grace

The Woman

His presence is a shield.

- **Psalm 28:7:** 'The Lord is my strength and my shield.'

They scream and demand judgment.
But he stands.
And says
'Let the one without sin cast the first stone.'

- **John 8:7:** Jesus' words pierce to the conscience.
- **Augustine:** 'The two were left alone: misery and mercy.'

Then he stoops again.
And writes:
'You shall not bear false witness. You shall not kill.'

- **Exodus 20:13–16:** Jesus reminds them of the *higher demands* of the Law they misuse.

Jesus

There will be no spectacle today.

- Quiet power. Jesus refuses the public bloodlust, choosing mercy over theatre.
- **Isaiah 42:2:** 'He will not shout or cry out or raise his voice in the streets.'

The Woman (Transformed)

I still kneel.
But I see him clearly now.
He is my shepherd.
I am the lost sheep, and he has come for me.
He is my Lord and my God.

- **John 20:28:** Thomas' confession becomes hers.
- Her kneeling recalls the reverence due to the True Shepherd of Psalm 23.
- Peace I never want to lose.
- **John 14:27:** 'My peace I give to you . . .'

Jesus

She knocked. She asked.
And she received.

- **Matthew 7:7:** The structure mirrors the invitation to seek and find.

'Go. Sin no more.'
Soon, I will release all who ask
From every burden of sin.

- **John 8:11:** The original line.
- Prefigures the Cross—the moment of ultimate release.

The Woman (Conclusion)

I hear his forgiveness—
And my heart leaps.
As Jeremiah promised
He remembers my sin no more.
I am his sheep, and I know his voice.

- **Jeremiah 31:34, John 10:27:** She affirms belonging, identity, and security in Christ.
- **Augustine:** 'To be known by God is to be healed.'

I go back to my family
But I will follow him all the days of my life.
I love—because he loved me first.
I serve—because he saved me.
And I await the day
For final rest in him, the source of true and everlasting peace.

- **Psalm 23:6, Revelation 14:13, and Augustine's Confessions I.1**
  'Our hearts are restless until they rest in You.'
- **Matthew 11:28:** 'Come to me, all who are weary and burdened, and I will give you rest.'
- **Hebrews 4:13:** 'There remains a Sabbath rest for the people of God.'
- **Revelation 14:13:** 'Blessed are the dead who die in the Lord . . . they will rest from their labour.'

What Did Jesus Write in the Sand?

A simple but deep look at John 8:1-11:

In John 8, religious leaders bring a woman caught in adultery to Jesus. They say the Law of Moses commands that she be stoned. They are trying to trap Jesus—if he agrees, he might seem harsh or break Roman law; if he disagrees, they can accuse him of opposing Scripture.

But instead of answering them, Jesus bends down and writes with his finger on the ground. He then stands and says,

'Let the one without sin among you cast the first stone.'

One by one, the accusers walk away. Finally, Jesus turns to the woman and says,

'Neither do I condemn you. Go, and sin no more.'

The question remains: What did Jesus write?

The Bible doesn't say. But based on the language and Jewish traditions of the time, here are some compelling insights:

1. Hebrew was written without vowels or punctuation.

In Jesus' time, Hebrew was written with only consonants. That means a group of letters could be read more than one way depending on:

- how it was pronounced,
- where the word breaks were placed,
- or how it was understood in context.

Example:

- The letters רע could mean either 'evil' (ra) or 'friend/neighbor' (re'a).

Jesus may have written a word from the law that looked like it condemned the woman—but could just as easily point back at the accusers themselves.

This type of wordplay was common in Jewish teaching.

2. One letter could change the whole meaning.

Some Hebrew letters look or sound very similar—especially when written quickly, like with a finger in the sand. Mistaking one for another could completely change a word.

Examples:

- ד (dalet) and ר (resh) are nearly identical.
- ב (bet) and כ (kaf) are easy to confuse.
- A small shift could turn 'judgment' into 'nonsense,' or 'man' (אדם) into 'nation' (ארם).

Jesus might have written a key word from the Law but subtly changed one letter to allow for multiple meanings—perhaps turning a judgment on the woman into a reflection of the crowd's own guilt.

3. The Law demanded both man and woman be punished.

The law they were quoting (Deuteronomy 22:22–24) said that *both* the man and the woman caught in adultery must be stoned.

But the accusers only brought the woman.

Jesus may have written the Hebrew words שניהם (*sheneihem*, 'both of them') to silently ask, *'Where is the man?'*

This would have revealed the partial and unjust application of the Law—and their real motives.

4. The word *stone* had hidden meanings in Hebrew.

In Hebrew, the word for *stone* is אבן (even).

This word can be split into two smaller words: בן + אב = father + son.

Some Jewish teachers taught that this hints at relationships or family legacies. So by writing *stone*, Jesus might also have been reminding the crowd of the deeper, human bonds involved—or even hinting at his own identity as the Son of the Father.

Also, 'אבן' (stone) is one letter away from און (aven), which means 'sin' or 'iniquity'. The difference is just one letter.

In Jesus' writing, the word might have been ambiguous on purpose—was it a *stone* or *sin*? That subtle uncertainty would cause the crowd to stop and reflect: *Are we right to cast this stone? Or are we guilty too?*

5. He might have quoted a phrase that had two possible meanings.

The phrase 'You shall purge the evil from among you' appears in both

- the law on adultery (Deut. 22),
- and the law about false witnesses (Deut. 19).

If Jesus wrote only that phrase—ובערת הרע מקרבך—the people may have assumed he was agreeing with the punishment.

But the same line also applies to false witnesses.

Was Jesus actually pointing the finger at the accusers?

This is a brilliant example of double meaning—letting them reflect and judge themselves.

6. Like the 'writing on the wall' in Daniel, the message required interpretation.

In Daniel 5, a mysterious message is written on a wall—just a few consonants—that only Daniel can interpret.

Jesus may have done something similar: writing a message with hidden meaning that required careful reading.

This could explain why the accusers left 'one by one'. Each person may have understood the writing differently, depending on what it revealed about their own heart.

7. Writing in dust had symbolic power.

In Jeremiah 17:13, the prophet says,
'Those who turn away from the Lord shall be written in the earth'.
Some early Christians believed Jesus was fulfilling this verse.

By writing in the dust, he was showing that the accusers, not the woman, had forsaken God's mercy—and their names were now 'written in the earth' as a sign of judgment.

8. Jesus may have evoked the law about the adulteress ritual.

In Numbers 5, if a woman was suspected of adultery without proof, the priest would write curses on a scroll then wash the ink into a bowl of dusty water, which she would drink.

Jesus, writing in the dust, may have been reversing that ritual

- not to curse the woman
- but to cancel the accusation.

Instead of proving her guilt, he allowed the dust to absorb and erase the judgment.

9. Jesus would have been fully trained in these interpretive techniques.

Jesus was not an outsider to Jewish tradition. He was a recognized teacher (Rabbi) in his time, often called Rabbi by others in the Gospels.

As a teacher of the Torah, Jesus would have been deeply familiar with

- how Hebrew was written and read,
- the use of consonant-only texts,
- scribal warnings about look-alike letters,
- midrashic interpretation (creative re-reading of Scripture),
- and oral traditions like 'al tiqrei . . . ela . . .' ('Don't read it this way, but that way').

These weren't secret codes—they were common tools among Jewish scholars, and Jesus would have known how to use them masterfully.

So when he bent down to write, he likely did so with full awareness of how each letter, word, and phrase could be understood in more than one way and how that would challenge and convict his audience.

This also explains why the older, more experienced men left first—they understood what he was doing.

Conclusion:

We don't know exactly what Jesus wrote. But based on the culture, language, and teaching styles of his time, we can reasonably guess that he used

- clever wordplay,
- visual symbolism,
- and legal precision

to turn a public trap into a private moment of conviction.

With just a few letters in the dust, Jesus upheld the Law, unmasked injustice, and offered grace.

His silent writing became a powerful sermon:

The same Law that condemns sin also demands integrity, compassion, and truth.

Those who wield judgment must be free from guilt themselves.

And above all, mercy triumphs over condemnation.

The Sacred Name of God: The Importance of Hebrew in Understanding Scripture

Now, I would like to reflect briefly on a deeper layer of meaning that emerges when we consider the Hebrew and how this connects to the sacred language of the Old Testament.

The original Scriptures were written *in Hebrew*, a language rich in nuance, symbolism, and reverence for the divine. One of the most profound examples of this is the divine name: *YHWH*, often referred to as the **Tetragrammaton.** This name, revealed to Moses in the burning bush (Exodus 3:14–15), is considered so sacred in Jewish tradition that it is never pronounced aloud. It is, in a sense, unpronounceable—not just out of reverence but because its very construction resists articulation. It points to God's mystery: 'I am who I am' or more accurately respecting the tense in which it was written 'I will be who I will be'—a being beyond human grasp, beyond speech beyond time and space.

To preserve this reverence, Jewish scribes developed a remarkable tradition known as *ketiv* and *qere*—'what is written' (*ketiv*) versus 'what is read' (*qere*)**.** In the Masoretic Text, the consonants YHWH were written, but the vowel markings were taken from substitute words like *Adonai* ('Lord') or *HaShem* ('The Name'). These markings served as a cue: when you see *YHWH*, you don't say it—you say *Adonai* or *HaShem* instead.

HaSh**e**m: vowels placed after consonants YHWH -Y**a**hw**e**h
Ad**o**n**a**i: vowels placed after consonants YHWH - Y**a**h**o**w**a**h (became Jehovah later in English)

Unfortunately, later translators, unfamiliar with this *qere/ketiv* convention, misread the combination of YHWH with the vowels of Adonai and coined names like 'Jehovah' or 'Yahweh'—which are *linguistic hybrids* that distort the sacred practice. Such misreadings, though unintentional, violate the very commandment they seek to uphold: 'You shall not take the name of the Lord your God in vain' (*Exodus 20:7*).

Understanding this helps us see the *humility and depth of Jewish reverence*. It also teaches us a critical lesson: that Scripture is not merely a text to be translated, but *a sacred inheritance to be interpreted—in light of its language, tradition, and cultural reverence.*

Jesus, a Jew immersed in these traditions, would have been fully conversant with this practice. His writing in the dust (John 8:6) is mysterious, but perhaps it hints at divine authorship—a silent echo of Sinai—reminding us that God's law is both written and unwritten, revealed and concealed.

As Christians and Catholics, we are heirs of this tradition. While we need not be fluent in Hebrew, we must develop a respectful awareness of the language's role in shaping sacred Scripture. *Without this, we risk flattening its meaning, mistranslating its truth, and misusing its holiness.*

Let us approach the text with both faith and reverence—seeking not just to read it, but to *listen* through it, for the **Voice of God still writing in the sand.**

John 21:9-11. The symbolism of 153 fish caught.

Now as an epilogue, perhaps as a teaser to my next book—God willing, I will be able to finish soon—I present to you *John 21:9–11*:

'When they got out on land, they saw a charcoal fire in place, with fish laid out on it, and bread. Jesus said to them, 'Bring some of the fish that you have just caught.' So Simon Peter went aboard and hauled the net ashore, full of large fish, 153 of them. And although there were so many, the net was not torn.'

This passage—and particularly, the number 153—has confounded biblical commentators and Church Fathers for centuries. The specific count of fish caught, along with the remarkable note that 'the net was not torn', is clearly meant to carry symbolic weight. However, many interpretations have struggled due to a crucial oversight: the tendency to view these numbers through the lens of Roman or modern Arabic numerals.

It's important to remember that when the disciples spoke with Jesus, they did so in Aramaic or Hebrew. The Gospel texts were later written in Greek, primarily for a Hellenistic audience. But the original meaning, especially of numbers and symbols, would have been rooted in Hebraic thought and language.

Thus to understand the number 153, we must approach it not through Greek or Roman mathematical systems, but through Hebrew gematria—the ancient Jewish tradition of assigning numerical value to letters. In this context, 153 is expressed by the Hebrew letters קנג (Kuf–Nun–Gimel), each rich with symbolic meaning. In what follows, I present what this number reveals when seen through its original Hebrew lens.

I will first present what the traditional interpretation is and then give you the interpretation when viewed through Jewish lenses. I leave it to you to make up your own mind.

The Word in their Voices

1. Literal and Historical View

Plain reading: The number 153 may simply reflect the exact count of fish caught—emphasizing the abundance of the miracle and the eyewitness realism of the Gospel.

It shows the net did not break, despite the large number, which may symbolize the unity and strength of the Church even as it gathers many people.

2. Symbolic and Theological Interpretations

a.) Universal Mission of the Church

St. Jerome (fourth century): Ancient zoologists believed there were 153 species of fish in the world. So, the catch symbolized the universal scope of the Gospel: Jesus calls the apostles to bring all nations—all 'types' of people—into the Church.

b) Triangular Number

Augustine saw 153 as a symbolic blend of grace (3) and law (10)—linked to the triangle of 17:

$$1 + 2 + 3 + \ldots + 17 = 153$$

Number 17 is symbolically seen as 10 (law/commandments) + 7 (spiritual perfection/grace). So, 153 may represent the fullness of divine order—law fulfilled by grace.

c) Link to Ezekiel's Temple River (Ezek. 47)

In Ezekiel 47:10, fishermen catch many kinds of fish in the healing river flowing from the new Temple. John may be echoing this prophecy, showing that Jesus is the true Temple, and his resurrection inaugurates the healing of the nations.

3. Spiritual/Mystical Interpretations

Church fathers saw the unbroken net as the unity of the Church, capable of embracing vast diversity without division—under Christ's command.

4. Narrative and Apostolic Authority

This scene in John 21 mirrors Luke 5, when Peter caught fish at Jesus' word and was called to be a fisher of men.
The post-resurrection repetition shows Peter's restoration, the ongoing mission, and the fruitfulness of obedience to Christ.

Conclusion: What Does 153 Mean?

The number 153 may carry multiple layers of meaning:

- A concrete miracle rooted in history
- A symbol of totality, representing all nations
- A nod to biblical numerology and gematria: 'Sons of God'
- A sign of the Church's mission, unity, and fruitfulness

Let's now view this through Hebrew lenses.

The number 153, when written in Hebrew gematria notation, is:
קנג **(Kuf–Nun–Gimel)**

(Arrows indicate direction of reading, on Hebrew its right to left and in English left to right.)

Letter Breakdown:

- ק (Kuf) = 100
- נ (Nun) = 50
- ג (Gimel) = 3

Possible Symbolic Significance:

1. Individual Letter Symbolism:

- ק **(Kuf):** Often associated with *holiness* (*kadosh*) or the line between holiness and the mundane, as it slightly 'descends' below the baseline in script—hinting at descent for the sake of elevation.
- נ **(Nun):** Stands for *nefila* (falling) or *nes* (miracle). In the Psalms, the missing Nun in the acrostic of Psalm 145 is traditionally explained as avoiding mention of downfall.
- ג **(Gimel):** Symbol of *giving* or *g'milut chasadim* (acts of kindness); associated with the 'rich man running to the poor man' (Gimel chasing Dalet in alphabet).

These three could be read together as a mystical progression:

- A divine descent (ק)
- Into the fallen world (נ)
- To bring kindness and redemption (ג)

2. Aramaic Implication:

In Aramaic script, the letters look different, but the values are the same. The concept of gematria applies across both Hebrew and Aramaic contexts, as both share the same alphabet and numerical assignments.

There's no commonly recorded use of 153) קנג) as a word or acronym in Tanakh or Talmudic Aramaic, but Kuf–Nun–Gimel could be interpreted midrashically or kabbalistically by scholars or mystics.

ק (Qof) – 100

- Symbolism: Often associated with holiness (קדושה) or that which stands at the boundary between holiness and impurity.
- Interesting note: The letter ק 'descends' below the baseline in Hebrew script—some rabbis see this as holiness reaching down

into the world, or sometimes as the fallen state yearning for redemption.

Possible association: righteousness or potential holiness.

נ (Nun) – 50

- Symbolism: Often associated with falling (נפילה), *humility, or hiddenness.*
- In Psalm 145, the verse for Nun is notably missing, traditionally because it refers to 'the fallen' (נופלים).
- Yet נ is also the first letter in נס (nes), meaning miracle or banner—a sign from above.

Possible association: fallen or in need of uplifting.

ג (Gimmel) – 3

- Symbolism: Grace, kindness, restoration
- ג means, 'the rich giving to the poor'.

Putting it Together: קנס (Qof–Nun–Samekh):
- ק — God's Holiness
- נ — Humanity's need
- ג — The gift of salvation

So קנג can be read spiritually as

'The holy one reaches into the realm of the fallen and redeems it through acts of kindness and grace'.

This aligns with the gospel theme:
'While we were yet sinners, Christ died for us' (Romans 5:8)—grace (gimmel) lifting the fallen (Nun) through a holy act (Qof))

Element	Symbol	Scriptural Link	Messianic Meaning
ק (100)	Holiness descending	Psalm 113:6: 'Who humbles Himself to behold the things in heaven and on the earth.'	The Messiah descends into the world to redeem it.
נ (50)	The fallen	Psalm 145:14: 'The Lord upholds all who fall.'	Messiah lifts the fallen, especially sinners and the outcast (cf. Luke 15).
ג (3)	Grace and giving	Isaiah 55:1: 'Come, buy without money . . .'	Messiah gives freely of the Kingdom—g'milut chasadim.

Here is a phrase that matches the gematria of 153 exactly:

בני האלהים *Bnei HaElohim* — 'Sons of God'

This directly aligns with the scene in John 21, where the 153 fish symbolize the gathering of all people into God.

CONCLUSION

And so, we come to the end of this book.

We began with reflections on the papacy—an introduction *by* the Popes and *to* the Popes. Through them, I sought to express what their voices, actions, and legacy mean for the Church today: the continuity of our faith, the resilience of our tradition, and the ongoing proclamation of the Gospel.

In this journey, I offered poems that serve not just as verses but as windows into Scripture. Each poem is a kind of Bible study in itself—woven with references to the sacred texts and shaped by the voices of those who lived within the biblical stories. Through them, I have tried to bring the Scriptures to life—to feel what they felt, to imagine the world they inhabited, to stand in their sandals and see Christ through their eyes.

This, for me, is a powerful form of meditation. It allows us to enter not only the minds and hearts of biblical figures but also their era—their customs, their languages, their hopes and fears. In doing so, we draw closer to Jesus—not just as an idea or a doctrine, but as a living person who walked among us.

As Catholics, I believe we are called to reflect our faith not only in what we believe, but in how we live. Our actions must be rooted in Scripture, guided by the teachings and traditions of the Church. Without this foundation, our faith risks being misunderstood, dismissed, or diluted.

Perhaps more than in any other Christian tradition, Catholicism is steeped in Scripture. Yet it is so deeply woven into our liturgy, our prayers, our rituals, that we sometimes take it for granted. We forget to pause and ask, *Why do we do what we do? What is the deeper meaning behind our customs?*

That is what I have hoped to explore through these poems—not only to stir the heart but to awaken the mind.

I have also tried to highlight the importance of the original languages of Scripture—Hebrew and Greek. While one need not be a scholar in ancient tongues, it is essential to remember that the disciples and early followers of Christ thought in deeply Hebraic ways. Their worldview, expressions, and understanding of God were shaped by centuries of Jewish tradition. To grasp their intent and meaning, we must approach Scripture with reverence for that mindset.

More than anything, I have learned the value of slowing down. Of reading Scripture not just to finish a passage, but to listen—word by word—for what God is saying.

My hope is that this book has opened a door for you. That it has deepened your appreciation of our Catholic faith and rekindled your love for the Church. This is my heartfelt invitation: to contemplate, to cherish, and to rediscover the beauty of the Gospel and the richness of our tradition.

Finally, I want to leave you with my most personal piece in this book—'Jesus, Do I Know You.' It was born out of a retreat, from a simple but piercing question: *Do you really know him?* Not know *about* him, but know him as the Living One, the Friend, the Crucified, the Risen, the Stranger at your door.

I have come to believe that Jesus is not someone to be studied as an idea or held in the mind as a theory of love. He is a life to be lived. A person to be followed. He is not distant—he is all around us. In the silence of prayer, in the face of the poor, in the breaking of the Bread.

And so, before I say thank you and goodbye, I leave you with this poem—not as a conclusion, but as a beginning. A final question to carry with you beyond these pages:

Do you know him? And even more—does he know you?

Let this be your prayer . . .

Jesus, Do I Know You

'Noverim me, noverim Te.'
—St. Augustine, Soliloquies I.1
(*Let me know myself, let me know You*)

I stand alone and bow my head
Before me lies the Holy Bread.
I lift my eyes—and there I see
The Lord who gave his life for me.

Jesus, do I know you?
You bore the cross, endured the pain
You suffered scorn, despised, and slain—
You paid our price with mercy's coin
That we might rest in you, anointed and joined.

Jesus, do I know you?
You taught, you healed, you stooped to serve
You chose the path we don't deserve.
You are the cornerstone of our faith,
And blessed Peter to be the Church's rock.

Jesus, do I know you?
The prophets spoke of law and light
Of majesty and holy might.
The apostles spoke of grace and love
Of mysteries revealed from above.

Jesus, do you know me?
Have I spoken heart to heart?
Were my prayers but hollow parts—
Petitions emptied, cold and brief,
Without revealing who I've become?

Jesus, do you know me?
Did I seek your guiding hand?

Did I praise the path your wisdom planned?
For every gift, both seen and veiled
For all the times when grace prevailed?

Jesus, do you know me?
Have I borne my soul to you?
Asked forgiveness, made paths new?
Begged you, Lord, to light my way,
And guide my steps through righteousness each day?

Jesus, I should have listened.
I should have answered joyfully—
With all my life and hope and breath,
Proclaimed you even unto death.

Jesus, I should have seen you
In the faces cast aside—
The weary, hungry, those who cried
The poor, the broken, and the bound—
Your image waits in all around.

I kept you captive in my mind
A thought, not lived, a love confined.
I opened my heart—and grace poured in;
I saw Your face where none had been.

With eyes unblinded, now set free
I'd tend the wounds of Calvary—
I'd love and feed and share and care
And meet you in the lowly there.

Once a prisoner of my mind
Now you live within my heart;
I—your vessel, poor yet blessed—
Bear forth your peace where sorrows part.

ANNOTATION: JESUS DO I KNOW YOU

Before me lies the Holy Bread
- **John 6:51 (NIV):** 'I am the living bread that came down from heaven. Whoever eats this bread will live forever.'
- **Augustine:** 'Recognize in the bread what hung on the cross' (Sermon 272).
- **Franciscan:** Francis saw the Eucharist as the 'humility of God', making Himself lowly to be received.
- **Ignatian:** Emphasis on Christ present in the sacrament invites *contemplation of the encounter*—Jesus as companion at the table.

You paid our price with mercy's coin
- **Mark 10:45 (NIV):** 'The Son of Man . . . gave his life as a ransom for many.'
- **Augustine:** Christ's death is the act of supreme grace—not merited but freely given.
- **Franciscan:** The Cross reveals perfect love in voluntary poverty and vulnerability.
- **Ignatian:** Meditating on Christ's Passion brings the retreatant into personal relationship with the suffering Jesus.

And blessed Peter to be the Church's Rock
- **Matthew 16:18 (NIV):** 'You are Peter, and on this rock I will build my church.'
- **Augustine:** Emphasizes the unity of the Church rooted in apostolic faith.
- **Franciscan:** Though wary of hierarchical power, Francis was radically obedient to the Church and the pope.
- **Ignatian:** Encourages discernment and obedience within the Body of Christ, founded on Peter.

Were my prayers but hollow parts—
Petitions emptied, cold and brief

- **Isaiah 29:13 (NIV):** 'These people come near to me with their mouth . . . but their hearts are far from me.'
- **Augustine:** 'Late have I loved you . . . you were within me, but I was outside' (Confessions).
- **Franciscan:** Prayer must arise from poverty of spirit, not rote form.
- **Ignatian:** Calls for the *Examen*—daily reflection to see whether prayer flows from sincerity and encounter.

Did I praise the path your wisdom traced?
- **Proverbs 3:5–6 (NIV):** 'Trust in the Lord . . . and he will make your paths straight.'
- **Augustine:** God's providence often unfolds in mystery, but the heart at rest in God follows trustingly.
- **Franciscan:** Acceptance of 'the lesser way' as Christ's chosen path.
- **Ignatian:** God's will is revealed not in ease, but in the alignment of path, peace, and purpose.

Begged you, Lord, to light my way
And guide my steps through righteousness each day?
- **Psalm 23:3 (NIV):** 'He guides me along the right paths for his name's sake.'
- **Augustine:** God's grace guides not just the goal, but every daily step.
- **Franciscan:** Christ walked the humble path—our righteousness is in walking with him.
- **Ignatian:** 'Discernment of spirits' helps us stay on the righteous path—day by day, choice by choice.

Your image waits in all around
- **Genesis 1:27 (NIV):** 'God created mankind in his own image . . .'
- **Matthew 25:40 (NIV):** 'Whatever you did for one of the least of these . . . you did for me.'
- **Augustine:** Every human is a mirror of God's presence.

- **Franciscan:** Central. Christ is found in the leper, the stranger, the poor.
- **Ignatian:** *Seeing God in all things*—especially in the overlooked and hidden.

I opened my heart—and grace poured in
- **Romans 5:5 (NIV):** 'God's love has been poured out into our hearts through the Holy Spirit.'
- **Augustine:** 'You called, You shouted, and You broke through my deafness.' (Confessions)
- **Franciscan:** Emphasizes God's initiative; grace meets us when we surrender.
- **Ignatian:** A moment of deep *consolation*—awakening to God's indwelling presence.

Once a prisoner of my mind, / Now You live within my heart
- **Galatians 2:20 (NIV):** 'It is no longer I who live, but Christ lives in me.'
- **Augustine:** From external searching to internal indwelling—'You were within.'
- **Franciscan:** Poverty of mind becomes the vessel of divine presence.
- **Ignatian:** True conversion leads to interior freedom and the abiding companionship of Christ.

Your peace flows through me and restless hearts are stilled
- **Philippians 4:7 (NIV):** 'The peace of God . . . will guard your hearts and minds in Christ Jesus.'
- **Augustine:** 'Our hearts are restless until they rest in You.'
- **Franciscan:** Instrument of peace—'Lord, make me a channel of Your peace.'
- **Ignatian:** Peace is the fruit of spiritual discernment and union with God's will.

Bibliography of Patristic and Theological Sources

St. Augustine of Hippo

- Augustine. *Confessions*. Translated by Henry Chadwick. Oxford: Oxford University Press, 2008.
- (For quotations such as "You have made us for yourself, O Lord, and our hearts are restless until they rest in you.")
- Augustine. *The City of God*. Translated by Henry Bettenson. London: Penguin Books, 2003.
- Augustine. *On Christian Doctrine*. Translated by D. W. Robertson Jr. Indianapolis: Bobbs-Merrill, 1958.
- Augustine. *Sermons*, various. In *The Works of Saint Augustine: A Translation for the 21st Century*. Edited by John E. Rotelle, O.S.A. Hyde Park, NY: New City Press, 1990–.
- (e.g., Sermon 358, "The victory of truth is love.")
- Augustine. *On the Trinity*. Translated by Edmund Hill. Brooklyn, NY: New City Press, 1991.

St. Thomas Aquinas

- Aquinas, Thomas. *Summa Theologiae*. Translated by Fathers of the English Dominican Province. New York: Benziger Bros., 1947.
- Available online via: https://www.newadvent.org/summa/
- (For theological references to ordo amoris, grace, and the nature of divine love.)
- Aquinas, Thomas. *Catena Aurea: Commentary on the Four Gospels*. Translated and edited by John Henry Newman. London: St. John Henry Newman Press, 1841.
- (Used for Gospel-based poetic and theological commentary.)

St. Francis of Assisi

- Francis of Assisi. *The Writings of Saint Francis of Assisi*. Translated by Paschal Robinson. Philadelphia: The Dolphin Press, 1906.
- (Includes the *Canticle of the Sun, Admonitions, Letters,* and *Rule of Life*.)
- Francis of Assisi. *The Earlier Rule (Regula non bullata)* and *The Later Rule (Regula bullata)*. In *Francis of Assisi: Early Documents*, Volume I: *The Saint*. Edited by Regis J. Armstrong, J.A. Wayne Hellmann, and William J. Short. New York: New City Press, 1999.
- Armstrong, Regis J., et al., eds. *Francis and Clare: The Complete Works*. New York: Paulist Press, 1982.

St. Bonaventure

The Soul's Journey into God (*Itinerarium Mentis et Deum*). Translated by Ewert Cousins. Mahwah, NJ: Paulist Press, 1978. Part of the Classics of western Spirituality.

Lewis, C.S

The abolition of Man. New York: HarperOne. Originally published 1943. London :Geoffrey Bles, 1943 HarperCollins.

a) Rabbi Akiva, Berakhot 61b

Epstein, Isidore, ed. *The Babylonian Talmud: Tractate Berakoth*. Translated by Maurice Simon. London: Soncino Press, 1938.

Steinsaltz, Adin. *The Koren Talmud Bavli: Berakhot, English Edition*. Translated by Rabbi Uri Kaploun. Jerusalem: Koren Publishers, 2012.

b) Ugaritic Texts

Pardee, Dennis. *The Ugaritic Texts and the Bible*. In *Ancient Israelite Religion: Essays in Honor of Frank Moore Cross*, edited by Patrick D. Miller, Paul D. Hanson, and S. Dean McBride, 137–154. Philadelphia: Fortress Press, 19

Patristic and Theological Quotations by Source

St. Augustine of Hippo

"You have made us for yourself, O Lord, and our heart is restless until it rests in you."

- *Confessions*, Book I, Chapter 1.
- Citation: Augustine. *Confessions*. Translated by Henry Chadwick. Oxford: Oxford University Press, 2008.

"Order is the arrangement of things equal and unequal, giving each its proper place."

- *City of God*, Book XIX, Chapter 13.
- Citation: Augustine. *The City of God*. Translated by Henry Bettenson. London: Penguin Books, 2003.

"My weight is my love; by it I am carried wherever I am carried."

- *Confessions*, Book XIII, Chapter 9
- Citation: Augustine. *Confessions*. Translated by Henry Chadwick. Oxford: Oxford University Press, 2008.

"The victory of truth is love."

- *Sermon 358,1*.
- Citation: Augustine. *Sermons*. In *The Works of Saint Augustine: A Translation for the 21st Century*. Edited by John E. Rotelle, O.S.A. Hyde Park, NY: New City Press, 1990–.

"Late have I loved you, beauty so old and so new, late have I loved you!"

- *Confessions*, Book X, Chapter 27.
- Citation: Augustine. *Confessions*. Translated by Henry Chadwick. Oxford: Oxford University Press, 2008.

"Take and read, take and read."

- *Confessions*, Book VIII, Chapter 12.
- Citation: Augustine. *Confessions*. Translated by Henry Chadwick. Oxford: Oxford University Press, 2008.

"Where your pleasure is, there is your treasure. Where your treasure is, there is your heart. Where your heart is, there is your happiness."

- *Sermon 311, 5.*
- Citation: Augustine. *Sermons*. In *The Works of Saint Augustine: A Translation for the 21st Century*. Edited by John E. Rotelle, O.S.A. Hyde Park, NY: New City Press, 1990–.

St. Thomas Aquinas

"The essence of virtue consists in the good ordering of love."

- *Summa Theologiae*, II–II, q. 23, a. 1.
- Citation: Aquinas, Thomas. *Summa Theologiae*. Translated by the Fathers of the English Dominican Province. New York: Benziger Bros., 1947.

"To love God is something greater than to know Him."

- *Summa Theologiae*, I–II, q. 27, a. 4, ad 2.
- Citation: Aquinas, Thomas. *Summa Theologiae*. Translated by the Fathers of the English Dominican Province. New York: Benziger Bros., 1947.

"Grace does not destroy nature but perfects it."

- *Summa Theologiae*, I, q. 1, a. 8, ad 2.
- Citation: Aquinas, Thomas. *Summa Theologiae*. Translated by the Fathers of the English Dominican Province. New York: Benziger Bros., 1947.

"God loves all things by willing them the good of their own being."

- *Summa Theologiae*, I, q. 20, a. 2.
- Citation: Aquinas, Thomas. *Summa Theologiae*. Translated by the Fathers of the English Dominican Province. New York: Benziger Bros., 1947.

St. Francis of Assisi

- "Lord, make me an instrument of your peace."
- Traditionally attributed to St. Francis; not found in his writings but widely associated with Franciscan spirituality.
- Citation: Anonymous. *Peace Prayer of Saint Francis*. Early 20th-century origin, but commonly included in Franciscan prayer books.

"What we are before God, that we are and no more."

- *Admonition 19, The Admonitions of St. Francis.*
- Citation: Francis of Assisi. *The Writings of Saint Francis of Assisi*. Translated by Paschal Robinson. Philadelphia: The Dolphin Press, 1906.

Unkown Saint : "His kindness is freely given;/No coin will he accept"

"Start by doing what is necessary, then what is possible, and suddenly you are doing the impossible."

- Attributed to Francis; not found in the earliest sources.
- Often cited in spiritual literature, included with caution.
- Citation: Traditional attribution, frequently included in Franciscan meditations.

Theological Quotations from St. Bonaventure by Poem/Theme

Poem: Holy Spirit

- Quotation: "Contemplation is the soul's loving return to the source from which it came."
  Source: *The Soul's Journey into God* (Itinerarium Mentis in Deum), VII.4.

Context in Poem: Referenced in annotations describing the Holy Spirit as the eternal bridge between the temporal and the eternal. The Spirit's presence draws the soul back to its source—God—in a movement of contemplative love, echoing Bonaventure's mystical theology.

Theme: Creation and the Ascent of the Soul

- Quotation: "The wise man will consider the greatness of the universe; the devout man will contemplate the mercy of God."
  Source: *The Soul's Journey into God*, Prologue, §1.

Context in Reflection: Used in the theological annotations to contrast mere intellectual observation of creation with the heart's deeper contemplation. This aligns with the emphasis on discernment—understanding not just with the intellect, but with faith and love.

Theme: Trinitarian Mystery and Hiddenness

- Quotation: "In this passing world, the footprints of God are seen, but not His face."
  Source: *Itinerarium Mentis in Deum*, VI.2.

Context in Reflection: Echoed in reflections about the Holy Spirit's veiled yet powerful work in salvation history—how God is perceptible through signs, but His full presence remains hidden until the final union.

Quotations or Thematic References to CS Lewis

Theme: Discernment, Conscience, and the Heart's Formation

- Referenced Idea: That moral judgment requires more than mere emotion ("gut feeling") or detached rationalism. Lewis argues for the cultivation of rightly ordered affections—what he calls *the chest*, the seat of magnanimity and moral discernment.
- This aligns closely with the central message of the poem *The Power of Sin Is the Law*, where it's emphasized that scripture and law must be received with discernment—not as abstract code nor emotional impulse, but through a heart aligned to covenantal love and grace.

Quotable Line Paraphrased or Alluded To:

- "Without the aid of trained emotions, the intellect is powerless against the animal organism." — *The Abolition of Man*, Lecture I.
- Lewis critiques modern education that divorces reason from feeling, resulting in "men without chests"—a world without virtue or the capacity to rightly discern.

Bibliography of Papal Encyclicals and Apostolic Documents

Pope Paul VI

- Paul VI. *Evangelii Nuntiandi* [Apostolic Exhortation on Evangelization in the Modern World]. Vatican Website, 8 December 1975. https://www.vatican.va.

Pope John Paul II

- John Paul II. *Redemptoris Missio* [Encyclical Letter on the Permanent Validity of the Church's Missionary Mandate]. Vatican Website, 7 December 1990. https://www.vatican.va.
- John Paul II. *Veritatis Splendor* [Encyclical Letter on Certain Fundamental Questions of the Church's Moral Teaching]. Vatican Website, 6 August 1993. https://www.vatican.va.

Pope Benedict XVI

- Benedict XVI. *Deus Caritas Est* [Encyclical Letter on Christian Love]. Vatican Website, 25 December 2005. https://www.vatican.va.
- Benedict XVI. *Spe Salvi* [Encyclical Letter on Christian Hope]. Vatican Website, 30 November 2007. https://www.vatican.va.
- Benedict XVI. *Caritas in Veritate* [Encyclical Letter on Integral Human Development in Charity and Truth]. Vatican Website, 29 June 2009. https://www.vatican.va.

Pope Francis

- Francis. *Evangelii Gaudium* [Apostolic Exhortation on the Proclamation of the Gospel in Today's World]. Vatican Website, 24 November 2013. https://www.vatican.va.
- Francis. *Laudato Si'* [Encyclical Letter on Care for Our Common Home]. Vatican Website, 24 May 2015. https://www.vatican.va.
- Francis. *Fratelli Tutti* [Encyclical Letter on Fraternity and Social Friendship]. Vatican Website, 3 October 2020. https://www.vatican.va.
- Francis. *Christus Vivit* [Post-Synodal Apostolic Exhortation to Young People and the Entire People of God]. Vatican Website, 25 March 2019. https://www.vatican.va.